CH00646554

"Too often, preaching is done with technical con[...]
and depth that come from meaningful time spent w[...]
Preaching, Kent Edwards reminds us why we prea[...]
about developing and preaching sermons that go far beyond the superficial. Edwards
offers preachers practical counsel for digging deeper as they proclaim God's Word and
reminds us that ultimately the power of a sermon depends on the work of the Holy
Spirit. Anyone who preaches will find much of value in this volume."

Michael Duduit
Editor, *Preaching* magazine
Dean, Graduate School of Ministry & Professor of Christian Ministry at
Anderson University in Anderson, SC.

"It is a joy to recommend *Deep Preaching: Creating Sermons That Go Beyond the
Superficial.* Dr. Edwards's emphasis on getting back to the original truth-intention of
the biblical authors in the biblical text and his urging that we do expository preaching
are two of my favorite encouragements for preachers and teachers today. Those who
practice the suggestions made in *Deep Preaching* will surely help end the enormous
famine of the Word of God in our day."

Walter C. Kaiser, Jr.
President Emeritus, Gordon-Conwell Theological Seminary, S. Hamilton, MA

"*Deep Preaching* is the most practical book on preaching that I have ever read. It
takes its readers on a journey that reveals the art of exegeting and creatively communicating the Scriptures. I know no other book on preaching that does this as well. It
stands out from the others."

Dan Kimball
Author, *They Like Jesus But Not the Church*

"This book is a powerful extension of homiletic theory beyond the seminary classroom and the study and into preachers' prayer closets and people's living rooms. It
explains how to connect the Big Ideas of God's Story both to my own story and the
stories of the people who sit in front of me each Sunday. This book will change how I
do sermon preparation, the ultimate test of any preaching book. It truly is a gift from
God."

Michael Krause
Teaching Pastor, Southridge Community Church, St. Catharines, ON Canada

"*Deep Preaching* speaks with strength both to the skills of preaching and the soul of
the preacher. Read this book with an open heart and mind, and you will grow significantly—as I did—in your ministry of the Word.

Brian Larsen
Editor, PreachingToday.com

"Anchored in Scripture and church history yet richly illustrated in today's idiom, *Deep Preaching* goes beyond the tasks of exegesis and homiletics to the core of effective preaching—the soul of the preacher. Dr. Edwards masterfully weaves the fundamentals of sermon preparation and delivery together with the preacher's "closet work" so that the text invades and reshapes not only the mind but also the soul. Congregations yearn for sermons that in their preparation have first changed the heart of the preacher. This book provides a dependable road map to that end."

Alice P. Matthews, Ph.D.
Academic Dean and Lois W. Bennett Distinguished Emerita Professor of Educational Ministries and Women's Ministries, Gordon-Conwell Theological Seminary

"Professor Kent Edwards's engaging book *Deep Preaching* masterfully takes the reader on a journey into both the philosophy and practice of effective preaching. As important as these aspects are, the unique contribution of the book is the specific, practical, thoughtful advice it proffers about how to bring the Holy Spirit into the process of understanding and preaching the biblical text. This alone is worth the price of the book."

J. P. Moreland,
Distinguished Professor of Philosophy, Talbot School of Theology
and author of *The God Question*

"*Deep Preaching* is not another book of homiletical gimmicks to entertain your people. This is about their transformation through deep preaching. But this kind of preaching comes only through a high cost to preachers, in what Kent Edwards insightfully describes as our "closet work." My exegesis students will all read this book, because it is an indispensable guide to the process of moving from a deep understanding of the biblical text, to a deep personal renewal by the Spirit of God, to a deep communication of the truths of Scripture, so that the Spirit produces deep transformation in the lives our people. This is a desperately needed book in an age of much shallow preaching."

Michael J. Wilkins (PhD)
Distinguished Professor of New Testament Language and Literature
Dean of the Faculty, Talbot School of Theology, Biola University

"In a time when sermons can be well prepared and polished but superficial, Kent Edwards calls us to 'Deep Preaching.' The section on closet work is an outstanding matrix for looking deep into God's Word and deep into the preacher's heart and mind to assure we are preaching our very best."

Dr. George O. Wood
General Superintendent, Assemblies of God

DEEP PREACHING

Creating Sermons That Go Beyond the Superficial

J. Kent Edwards

ACADEMIC

Nashville, Tennessee

ISBN: 978-0-8054-4695-1

Published by B&H Publishing Group
Nashville, Tennessee

Dewey Decimal Classification: 251
Subject Heading: PREACHING\SERMONS

Unless otherwise noted, Scripture quotes are taken from the *Holman Christian Standard Bible* ® Copyright © 1999, 2000, 2002, 2003 by Holman Bible Publishers. Used by permission.

Scripture quotations marked NASB are from the *New American Standard Bible.* © The Lockman Foundation, 1960, 1962, 1963, 1968, 1971, 1972, 1973, 1975, 1977. Used by permission.

Scripture quotations marked NIV are from the *Holy Bible, New International Version*, copyright © 1973, 1978, 1984 by International Bible Society. Used by permission of Zondervan Bible Publishers.

Photograph on page 94 used by permission of the El Paso County Historical Society.

Cartoon on page 125 is copyright ©2007 H. Schwadron. Used by permission.

Printed in the United States of America
3 4 5 6 7 8 9 10 11 12 • 17 16 15 14 13 12 11 10
VP

Contents

Dedication

To Haddon W. Robinson.
My friend, my mentor
and the deepest preacher I know.

Acknowledgments

Great thanks to my wife Nola and my sons Nathan and Jonathan, whose sacrifice allowed me to focus on writing this book.

Thanks to my deans, Dr. Dennis Dirks and Dr. Mike Wilkins at Talbot School of Theology for the sabbatical that made the writing of this book achievable. Thanks also to the elders and congregation at Woodland Hills Church for listening to parts of this book as sermons and giving me the space I needed to pour my heart into the pages of this book.

Many thanks also to Teri Wareing for going out of her way, on so many occasions, to read this manuscript in its entirety to make so many insightful suggestions. Thanks also to Jeremiah Ebeling, Daniel Eng and Kris Cash for all the assistance you gave to this project.

A 'tip of the hat' is owed to the folks at B&H Academic as well. I'm indebted to Jim Baird for believing in the value of this project (when no-one else did) and to Terry Wilder for seeing it through to the end!

Special appreciation to Mike Krause. I value your honesty, integrity and passion for communicating God's word. Your comments, questions and suggestions were greatly appreciated. And I'm proud of all that you have allowed God to do through you . . . so far!

May, 2009 Yorba Linda, California.

Introduction

Beyond an "A"

It was one of the worst experiences I have ever had in the classroom. I was standing at the back of the classroom, ensconced in a soundproof booth, listening on headphones to one of my students preaching a sermon to the class.

I have taught preaching for years and, in the process, listened to hundreds of beginning sermons. I can assure you that listening to a beginning preacher's first sermon is work. It's like screening a young Steven Spielberg's first attempt at filmmaking. You are pretty sure that his future films are going to get better, but what you are watching on the screen right now is not going to win an Academy Award.

This particular preacher, however, had my full attention. As I listened to the message I heard the student follow the "steps to preparing a sermon" that I had outlined earlier in the semester. This was a technically perfect message. He had based his message on a legitimate natural unit of Scripture. He had a clear "big idea" that arose legitimately from that unit of Scripture and was reflected in a clear homiletical outline. And my student was delivering the sermon with a level of polish seldom seen in an "Introduction to Preaching" course.

Given the performance of the student, you would expect that I, as a professor of preaching, would be beaming with pride. After all, my student had followed my rules. He had immersed himself in my template. I had to acknowledge that, according to the syllabus I had written, this sermon deserved the highest grade possible. I was going to give it an A. That realization made me want to weep. Why?

Because that sermon, despite being well organized and sporting only the soundest of exegesis, was trivial. Superficial. Emotionally vacuous. My student was handling one of the most profound truths in Scripture with the respect typically accorded to a trash container on its way to the curb. What my student was preaching was true but banal. He had gazed at the truth of Scripture without being overwhelmed by it. He had held the truth in his hands but, unlike Jeremiah, he had not eaten it. He knew God's Word externally but not internally. The sermon was shallow.

It reminded me of an incident that the late J. Vernon McGee told regarding a trip that he took to South Africa. As he was traveling through a small town he saw a group of boys clustered around a circle drawn in the dust at the side of the road. The famous preacher realized that the boys were playing a game that he had played as a boy—they were playing a game of marbles. As McGee came closer he noticed that the children had substituted small stones that were common in the area for the glass marbles so commonly used in North America. As McGee continued to examine the stones, however, he realized that these were not ordinary stones. They were diamonds. The children had no idea of what the true value of those stones was. They were treating the most precious stones in the world without regard for their true worth. They were playing marbles with diamonds. So was my student.

I don't think that every movie that comes out of Hollywood needs to be taken seriously but, when it comes to preaching, I cannot get the words spoken by Mr. Miyagi out of my mind. He was the one that said in *The Karate Kid*, "there are no bad students, only bad teachers." In this case I agree. My student was not to blame. He had only done what I had told him to do. The problem was mine. My best efforts at teaching preaching were producing superficial sermons. Something had to be done. I could not allow this to continue.

I have set out in this book to rethink preaching—to help preachers learn how to preach the powerful Word in ways that will powerfully change those who hear it. When a sermon is preached, the words of the preacher need not settle comfortably on the lives of the listeners like dust on a coffee table. Preachers can recreate the worlds of our listeners by respeaking the words that God used to create the universe.

I invite you to join me in casting off the lines that moor our ministry to the status quo and steer your preaching out of the comfortable shallows. Together we can move beyond the yawn-inspiring to the awe-inspiring—beyond the trite into the transforming. Let's refuse to settle for an "A" sermon. Let's embrace the challenge and learn the discipline of deep preaching.

The Challenges of Preaching Today

Preaching has never been easy. The Bible tells us and church history shows us that everyone who has stood to speak God's Word to God's people has faced enormous challenges. Preachers like Jeremiah, Amos, Stephen, Augustine, Martin Luther, and Jonathan Edwards did not stroll casually down the easy street of ministry. Everyone who has taken preaching seriously has faced serious challenges. But let's not underestimate the obstacles that you and I are facing.

Those who will dare to declare the Word of God this week will face unprecedented challenges. It may be tougher to preach today than ever before in history. Why?

The Information Challenge

Think of all you have to know in order to preach well.

- You have to be an expert in the ancient text. Since preaching is "the communication of a biblical concept,"[1] you and I cannot prep for Sunday the way that Oprah preps for her talk shows. Oprah tells people what she thinks as she reads magazines or surfs the net. We are called to tell people what God thinks as revealed in the biblical text. Karl Barth said that he preached with a newspaper in one hand—but not both! We must hold onto the Bible—and understand what it says.

---

[1] H. W. Robinson, *Biblical Preaching: The Development and Delivery of Expository Messages* (Grand Rapids: Baker Academic, 2001), 21.

- You have to be an expert of ancient culture. Understanding biblical texts is wonderful, but you also have to know the people for whom they were written. How, for example, did they select a spouse? Get married? Raise children? Prepare for old age? Bury their loved ones? And it is not enough to know just the details of ancient Hebrew and first-century Greek life. You also have to be able to compare and contrast the people of God with all of their pagan neighbors.
- Knowledge of church history is also helpful—for example, how was the text you are preaching and the idea it contains have been used and abused throughout the ages. Historical theology can be of enormous help to contemporary preachers. Remember the old adage: to fail to learn from the past is to doom yourself to repeat it!
- Knowledge of the present day is critical as well. In order to speak to people today you need to know the people of today. What concepts control their decision-making? Where did these ideas come from? A good grounding in developmental psychology, sociology, ethics, philosophy, and apologetics would not hurt. But don't forget that you have to read the local and regional newspapers (on line and in print) as well as the most influential journals. And don't forget movies, MTV and South Park. Mass communication is increasingly occurring in nonprint mediums. You not only have to read everything worth reading . . . now you also have to watch everything worth watching!
- Knowledge of tomorrow is also important. If you want to help people prepare for what is coming as well as what is, then it is important that you are familiar with what the trends are and where they are likely to take us. Who is your favorite futurist?

Preachers, like everyone else, have more information to deal with than ever before. According to Richard Wurman in his book *Information Anxiety*, a "weekday edition of *The New York Times* contains more information than the average person was likely to come across in a lifetime in seventeenth-century England."[2] We have a lot more reading to do than John Owen or John Bunyan ever did. And the backlog is growing. I am told that

> In every 24-hour period approximately 20,000,000 words of technical information are being recorded. A reader capable of reading 1,000 words per minute would require 1.5 months, reading 8 hours every day, to get through 1 day's technical output, and at the end of that period, he would have fallen 5.5 years behind in his reading![3]

---

[2] R. S. Wurman, *Information Anxiety* (New York: Doubleday, 1989), 20.

[3] H. Murray Jr., *Methods for Satisfying the Needs of the Scientist and the Engineer for Scientific and Technical Communication* in a press release, March 8, 1966, Washington, D.C. as quoted by M. R. Nelson in "We Have the Information You Want, But Getting It Will Cost You: Being Held Hostage by Information

You cannot preach well without knowledge. But knowledge alone will not make you a good preacher. In fact, it can hurt your preaching.

Knowledge can be a communication curse because the more you know about a subject the harder it is to present it in a simple, memorable fashion. As your knowledge grows, so does the temptation to dump all that knowledge on your listeners. If you don't beat this temptation into submission, your preaching will be either too long or too complicated. Or both.

The courses we have taken can take the zip out of our preaching. Loading 500 pounds of facts into your brain can have the same effect as hitching a 25-foot Airstream travel trailer to a NASCAR stock car. Knowledge can drag something inherently interesting into the slow lane. It can make you boring.

It takes enormous skill to be an interesting expert. But that is what the upturned faces are looking for every Sunday morning. They want you to know as much as a research scientist, to be as relevant as a syndicated talk-show host, and to be as entertaining as a stand-up comic.

Good preachers are like great chefs. They do not smother God's ideas under a bland sauce of data. They only use the garnishes that will set off their entrée to maximum effect. They keep the main idea of the text the main idea of their sermon.

The use and misuse of the enormous amount of knowledge available today is not the only significant challenge that preachers face today. Another is our multimedia environment.

The Media Challenge

We exist in a kaleidoscope of sensory bombardment. It is truly astonishing to see how technology has converged to allow the media to bombard us with sensate-rich messages.

Have you ever seen *Jurassic Park 3*? Not many people did—and for good reason. When my wife was away on a business trip a few years ago I rented the DVD and discovered that the story line was astonishingly bad. The only Jurassic Park movie not directed by Steven Spielberg, this installment—much like its predecessors—had humans running around an island being chased by dinosaurs. The plot was so predictable that I had trouble staying awake. In spite of the boredom, however, I not only watched the movie but the bonus disk as well! What I learned on the bonus disk was that the filmmakers had spent multimillions of dollars to create the most accurate and lifelike animatronics ever featured in any movie. This culminated in an incredibly realistic 44-foot hydraulic dinosaur made just for this flick!

How can a preacher compete against this? When even second-rate movies get millions of dollars of special effects spent on them, how can preachers vie

Overload," *Crossroads: The ACM Student Magazine*, http://www.acm.org/crossroads/xrds1–1/mnelson. html (accessed 11/5/2007).

for the attention of their audiences? And it's not just the movie industry that makes our job tougher.

Have you watched TV recently? The split screen concept pioneered by the hit show *24* is now being emulated across the industry. Not only do the prime-time cop shows have luscious sets, stunning costumes, and impossibly proportioned actresses, but now we also have up to four different scenes being shown simultaneously. And have you listened to the music playing in the background? Gone is the amorphous "muzac" of days gone by. Now we have hit songs playing at the climax of *CSI* that tie in perfectly to the theme of the episode. And all this is delivered in high definition to wide-screen plasma screens with theater sound systems. How do you plan to compete on Sunday morning? Some of us have trouble getting our Radio Shack lapel microphones working properly and the sound guy at the back of the room to turn us on.

I cringe when preachers tell me that they are "cutting-edge" because they use PowerPoint. If you think that a glorified overhead projector is cutting-edge then you are more lost than you realize. PowerPoint first came out in 1987! If you think you are going to "wow" people by twirling your clip art, you are not just behind the curve; you cannot even see today from where you are.

We should assume that every person who is coming to hear us preach has spent their week exposed to the finest in multimedia entertainment that our society has to offer. And that this has now become their benchmark for normal. Yet this makes it tough for us to compete. We preachers do not have access to the resources of George Lucas's Industrial Light & Magic. Nor can we ask the London Philharmonic to provide the sound track to next Sunday's sermon. So how can local pastors meet the impossibly high expectations of their parishioners?

And it gets worse. Not only do our media bombard the senses of our congregants—they also introduce them to our competition. It used to be that people who lived in a town could only listen to the preaching of those preachers who lived close by. Not anymore. While the introduction of cassette tapes may have broadened our exposure to other ministries, contemporary technology has unleashed an avalanche of exposure.

Your parishioners listen to other preachers on the radio, watch them on TV and on the Web, and download podcasts to their iPods. Like it or not, you are not the best preacher that your people have listened to this week. Your congregation has compared and contrasted you with the best-known preachers of the day. And, thanks to the power of editing, these electronic preachers they compare you with never stumble over their words, tell a joke that is not funny, or have a hair out of place. They come across as flawless communicators. And you do not. People in the pews want the electronic perfection projected by the religious superstars of our day. And we cannot give it to them. The electronic media have made it easier to compare preachers today than ever before.

Rodney Dangerfield used to complain that he got no respect. Thanks to the media, many local preachers can join his chorus.

The Truth Challenge

In addition to the challenges posed by the explosive growth of information and the enormous power and influence of the media, today's preachers must also deal with a strong cultural aversion to the very idea of religious truth. Many people today just don't think that religious truth is even possible.

You and I are ministering to one of the most intellectually schizophrenic cultures in history. Our culture enjoys receiving the "absolute truths" of the hard sciences. They want, for example, to know if there is a positive link between obesity and diabetes. Or, if drinking red wine and eating kidney beans will help them live to be 98. Or, how DNA tests can definitively establish whatever we want proved. People want scientific research to give them truth on which they can make accurate life choices. The only part of life that people think we cannot know with absolute certainty is our religious life.

In matters of religion people talk about "blind faith" and personal preference—not right or wrong. It is not politically correct to talk about another person's religious convictions as being false. We like being encouraged to choose our faith the same way that we select our Ben & Jerry's ice cream—based solely upon personal preference. "Willie Nelson's Peach Cobbler" ice cream is no better or worse a choice than "Cherry Garcia" or "Chunky Monkey." Likewise following Jesus is no better or worse a choice than following Mohammed or the feeling you get when you go for a hike in the mountains on Sunday morning. Whatever is true for you is fine. Whatever is true for me is equally fine.

It is increasingly difficult for preachers to make absolute statements about such topics as the reality of sin, the uniqueness of Jesus Christ, or the inerrancy of Scripture without raising howls of protest. People don't mind if you share your opinion—much like a radio talk-show host—as long as you don't claim to be speaking absolute truth.

What a terrible position for a preacher to be in! As representatives of the One who is the way, the truth, and the life, we have no choice but to speak truth. Truth is our business, our product. Biblical preaching—by definition—forces us to handle the absolute truth of God's word. Yet when we speak it we are called arrogant and insensitive. When we preachers fulfill our legitimate role as spokespeople of the Lord of the Universe we are labeled as intolerant fundamentalist extremists and get lumped together with Al-Qaeda. Not the kind of company any of us want to keep!

The Expectation Challenge

Preaching is even tougher when you cannot find the time you need to preach your best. If you are a pastor, especially a senior or solo pastor, you know first-hand about the crushing demands that ministry puts on you. And your family.

What does a church want?

- A high-powered visionary leader that sees the future and knows how to get there.
- A personal humility that makes you sensitive and responsive to the concerns of everyone in the church.
- A highly visible commitment to reproduce yourself in the next generation of leaders.
- You to play a prominent role in the community at large and lead by example in the area of one-on-one evangelism.
- A wonderful team player that befriends, motivates, and supervises the church staff.
- A paragon of hospitality who opens their home for youth group events whenever asked.
- An effective fund-raiser.
- A denominational leader of considerable influence to the wider church.
- A caring pastor who always tends to the needs of the local church (that pays their salary).
- The kind of counselor that James Dobson wishes he could be.
- A commitment to marriage that spurs you to spend six weeks of pre-marital counseling before performing the weddings of everyone who asks.
- A commitment to marriage that causes you to spend significant quantity and quality time with your wife and family.
- You to spend quality time in prayer seeking the face of God.
- Instantly answered e-mail.
- You to write the occasional best-selling book—on your vacation.

If this list frightens you, you are still probably way better off than many of my Asian students. Korean pastors, for example, have to preach every morning. Every morning! They also preach during midweek prayer meetings and twice on Sunday! The only thing harder on a preaching schedule than being senior pastor in a Korean church is to be a young associate in a Korean church. These junior pastors seem to have virtually no say in their schedule. And virtually no life. The expectations placed on them by their senior pastors make it almost impossible to preach well.

Churches of all ethnicities have expectations of their pastors. So do every one of the attendees. Together, those expectations can combine to squeeze so much time out of your schedule that you can't find the time you need to preach well. The pressure to be everywhere and everything to everyone has never been greater. Our consumer mentality demands top-flight service from its paid servants. And this is the enemy of good preaching. It has never been easy to preach, but it is especially tough today.

The Prestige Challenge

In days gone by the parson was considered to be the leading person in the community. Preachers were often the best educated and most respected members of their community. This is not true today. While a certain amount of respect may be accorded to the preacher within the Christian community, it is notably absent in society. Preaching is not a culturally prestigious occupation.

Fair or not, you and I are associated with every discredited preacher that hits the newswires. Remember Jimmy Swaggart and Jim Bakker? Our culture does. When the Reverend Ted Haggard—senior pastor of a high profile megachurch and president of the National Association of Evangelicals—announced amid accusations of drug use and liaisons with a male prostitute that "I am guilty of sexual immorality. . . . I am a deceiver and a liar. There is a part of my life that is so repulsive and dark that I have been warring about it for my entire life,"[4] he tarnished our reputation as well as his own.

As I write this chapter, the *New York Times* is featuring a story on how Senator Charles E. Grassley, the ranking Republican on the Senate Finance Committee, is investigating six prominent evangelistic ministries to determine whether they have illegally used donations to finance opulent lifestyles.[5] When high-profile preachers are publicly shamed, the luster of our office is stained.

When was the last time you watched a Hollywood movie that portrayed a preacher in a positive light? When have you seen a flick where the protagonist—paralyzed by an overwhelming problem—went to church and found in the words of God's spokesperson the eternal words they needed to solve their situation? The scriptwriters who pen Hollywood's hits could never imagine such a scenario. In times of crisis protagonists may turn to counselors, engineers, accountants, or personal trainers. Other professions get to be heroes but not preachers. Preachers are selected to portray dunces, charlatans, or predators of weak women and young boys. Not the kind of people you want to be when you grow up. Just ask your children.

In 2003, the Gallup organization surveyed 1,200 U.S. teens between the ages of 13 and 17 and asked them what they wanted to be when they grew up.[6] Our young people want to be doctors, nurses, teachers, and computer

---

[4] T. Olsen, *Christianity Today*, http://www.christianitytoday.com/ct/2006/novemberweb-only/144–58.0.html, (accessed 11/7/07).

[5] NY Times.com, http://www.nytimes.com/2007/11/07/us/07ministers.html, (accessed 11/7/07).

[6] J. Mazzuca, "Teen Career Picks," May 13, 2003, http://www.gallup.com/poll/8371/Teen-Career-Picks-More-Things-Change.aspx, (accessed 11/7/07).

techs, almost anything but a preacher. Clergy did not even make it onto the top 10. We rated even lower than lawyers.

TOP CAREER CHOICES FOR TEENS (AGED 13–17) 2003	
As of right now, what kind of work do you think you will do for a career?	
Doctor/Nurse/Medical	10%
Teacher	8%
Computer field	6%
Athlete	5%
Lawyer and Veterinarian	4%
Engineer	3%
Chef	3%
Musician	3%
Military	3%
Mechanic	2%

If you want to see how highly most people view preachers, tell the person sitting next to you on the airplane that you are a preacher. Chances are good that you will have lots of uninterrupted flight time to read your book. Or work on next week's sermon. There is precious little prestige in preaching.

The Challenge of Deep Preaching

Every preacher faces the challenges we've just discussed, but I am making your job more difficult. I am not asking you to preach with the pack. I'm asking for more. I am asking you to preach deeply.

I will ask you to set aside the primary place in your schedule for preaching. To devote your *best* time and energy to fully understand and creatively communicate God's Word to your people. And I am going to tell you that it is not enough to share your mind with your listeners. You have to share your heart as well as your mind.

Deep sermons arise from your soul as well as your mind. Biblical content is not enough. These sermons are not "whipped off" or available on a Web site. MasterCard is right. Deep sermons are priceless. And immensely challenging.

So why preach? Knowing the enormous challenges that await you this week, why bother preaching at all? Why should you give your primary energy to biblical proclamation? Why give your life to it? Why not go into counseling? Or life insurance? Why preach?

Chapter 2

The Reasons for Preaching Today

In preaching, the question "Why?" is far more important than "How?" Why? Because there is no reason to learn *how* to preach if you don't know *why* you should preach. If you think that preaching is the critical component of God's call on your life, then you will figure out a way to master it. If you are not convinced of the priority of preaching, then you will not become as effective in the pulpit as you could have. This is one of the reasons I am such a bad golfer.

The main reason I am not a good golfer is because I don't think golf is very important. In my opinion, spending six hours to play 18 holes—three times a week away from other activities (as well as my family) is a colossal waste of time. My priorities explain why I am such a lousy golfer. I golf poorly because I don't think it is worth my time to learn how to golf well. If you disagree with my opinion about golf you probably are a better golfer than I am. We make our priorities and then our priorities make us.

So how important is preaching to you? Is preaching optional? Is it merely an option on the menu of ministry? Is it a garnish that we can push to the side of the busy plate of pastoral responsibility? Or is it more? Is it the "main course" of what you do?

The priority you place on your preaching will determine, more than any other factor, how deep you preach. If you cruise Web sites and check out software products in the hope of finding something that will enable you to invest 23 minutes on a 20-minute sermon, then your priorities are clear. And they will preclude you from becoming a deep preacher.

You will not embrace the disciplines necessary and make the schedule changes required to become a deep preacher unless you are convinced to the core of your being that preaching is your primary calling. Preaching demands your best hours and energy.

If you rank preaching like I rank golf, you will preach as well as I play golf. The cornerstone of deep preaching is wanting to be a deep preacher even more than you want to be the next Tiger Woods. The first step to become a deep preacher is to place preaching as your top pastoral priority.

Why should you place preaching at the top of your ministerial priority list? Let me suggest three reasons why you should primarily invest your ministry in preaching. I preach for theological reasons, historical reasons, and pragmatic reasons.

This is why I continue to preach every week and why I am convinced that every church in every culture in every corner of the earth needs to have a vibrant preaching ministry.

Theological Reasons for Preaching

One of the greatest preachers of our day, John R. W. Stott, spoke with tremendous pastoral insight when he said:

> How can we be persuaded to go on preaching, and learn to do so effectively? The essential secret is not mastering certain techniques but being mastered by certain convictions. In other words, theology is more important than methodology.[1]

Theology *is* more important than methodology. There will be times in your ministry when you will be tempted to give up on preaching. Seasons of blessing come and go and are often as unpredictable as the weather. The one predictable thing is that sooner or later you will experience times of drought in your preaching. For weeks or months you will open the Scriptures and preach with passion and fidelity, and yet, little or nothing will seem to happen in the lives of your listeners. There will be no rain of blessing. No spiritual fruit bursting forth in the lives of your listeners. No observable results. During these times you will, as I have done, begin to think about investing your energy in other things. "If this is not working," we say to ourselves, "I am better off to do something else." But what?

The secret to preaching perseverance—and eventual excellence in preaching—lies in knowing *why* you preach. You will continue preaching in season and out of season if you understand the theological imperative of biblical proclamation. The techniques of rhetorical flourish will not sustain you through your ministerial dry spells. Gimmicks won't work. Theology will.

There are at least seven theological reasons why I am convinced that preaching is an indispensable element of Christian ministry.

---

[1] J. R. W. Stott, *Between Two Worlds* (Grand Rapids: Eerdmans, 1982), 92.

1. Because God Exists

"In the beginning God created the heavens and the earth."[2] The fundamental assumption of Scripture is that God *is*. The Bible does not try and prove God's existence; it simply presents God as a reality—like dirt and air—and moves on. God is not presented as a debatable item; He just is. He looms over the lives of all humankind in the same way that Mount Everest towers over the Himalayan Mountains, and you cannot successfully navigate through the Bible—or life—without recognizing God's presence. Our lives depend upon an awareness of God's existence. When people live as if only the physical is real, they doom their lives to total failure.

To be ignorant of God's existence is like residents of Vancouver Island being ignorant that they live surrounded by water. It is impossible to live successfully on an island without a conscious awareness that you are bounded by water. Ignorance is not bliss. It is the precursor to catastrophe. Without a knowledge of the water that surrounds them, it's only a matter of time until an unknowing resident will blissfully drive their car into the Pacific Ocean and drown. The undeniable existence of the ocean demands that the island residents modify their lives.

The existence of God demands similar life-modifying decisions. But you cannot adjust for what you do not know. Successful living begins with a knowledge of the God who surrounds and permeates every element of our lives.

God exists. He is the elephant in everyone's room. And those who try to ignore Him will be crushed by His enormous reality. Without a knowledge of God, you will make monumentally stupid and fatal decisions. Like driving your life into the ocean. Or opening your soul to massive moral infections. It is impossible to live successfully without understanding that He exists. All those who try, fail.

I preach because knowledge of God is the most important knowledge a person can have. People cannot live without it. They *must* learn about God.

2. Because God Is Not Silent

God did not have to reveal Himself to us. He could have easily kept Himself hidden behind a curtain of ignorance and, if He had, we would have been lost. Our destiny would have been beyond remedy. As theologian Carl F. H. Henry said so well,

> Had God insisted on remaining incommunicado we would know nothing whatever about him. . . . Under no circumstances whatever can God's secrets be wrested from him by intrusive human curiosity. . . . Apart from divine initiative man could not perceive even God's existence let alone his perfections and purposes. . . . Not even modern theologians armed with sophisticated technological gadgetry

---

[2] Gen 1:1. Unless otherwise noted, all Scripture quotations are from the Holman Christian Standard Bible (HCSB).

could spy on a reticent deity and program data about him. . . . The only confident basis for God-talk is God's revelation of himself.[3]

God realizes that our need to know Him is literally a matter of life and death. That's why He has gone to such enormous lengths to tell us about Himself. God knows that our lives depend on this information. And He has responded to our desperate need with overwhelming grace. He has communicated to us through what theologians have referred to as "general" and "special" revelation.

General Revelation. What is general revelation? It is information that God makes available about Himself to all people, in all places, and at all times. It is universally available God knowledge. God has used a variety of media to get this information out to us. He has, for example, used creation to reveal Himself to us.

> What can be known about God is evident among them, because God has shown it to them. From the creation of the world His invisible attributes, that is, His eternal power and divine nature, have been clearly seen, being understood through what He has made. As a result, people are without excuse.[4]

> The heavens declare the glory of God;
> the skies proclaim the work of his hands.
> Day after day they pour forth speech;
> night after night they display knowledge.
> There is no speech or language
> where their voice is not heard.[5]

Everyone who has admired the stunning beauty of a rose in bloom or the majesty of the Rocky Mountains has—at the same moment—glimpsed its divine designer. But to reinforce this communication God also speaks to people through their conscience. Our sense of right and wrong, however flawed it may be, is an echo of the universal moral standards that originate from the all-sovereign Lord.

> So, when Gentiles, who do not have the law, instinctively do what the law demands, they are a law to themselves even though they do not have the law. They show that the work of the law is written on their hearts. Their consciences testify in support of this, and their competing thoughts either accuse or excuse them.[6]

Some theologians see history as also being a form of general revelation—particularly the history of Israel. As we see God working His eternal purposes

---

[3] C. F. H. Henry, *God, Revelation and Authority*, vol. 2 (Waco: Word Books, 1983), 18.
[4] Rom 1:19–20.
[5] Ps 19:1–3, NIV.
[6] Rom 2:14–15.

in and through this small and seemingly unimportant nation, we glimpse God's hand on the tiller of history. History truly is God's story. As we watch the 6:00 p.m. news, we can catch yet another glimpse of God. He reveals Himself to us.

Why am I reminding you of such basic theology? Because we need to be reminded how seriously God takes self-communication. God is so concerned that people learn about Him that He does everything possible to get the word out.

God is obsessed with theological communication. Twenty-four hours a day, seven days a week, God uses every communication vehicle available to tell every person who has ever lived about Himself. God goes to greater lengths to tell people about Himself than a presidential candidate trying to win the primaries.

But don't think that we can ease off our preaching responsibilities because general revelation is good enough. It isn't.

Special Revelation. What is special revelation? It is additional information—not generally available—that God makes available about Himself to specific people at specific places and times in history. Some examples of special revelation are:

- *Miracles.* While none of us witnessed the parting of the Red Sea, those who did saw the power, grace, and judgment of God in an unforgettable way. Those who have experienced miracles learned about God through their experience.
- *Angelic visitations.* When Gabriel appeared and spoke to Daniel, Zechariah, and Mary, they learned about God and His work in the world.
- *Jesus.* Those people who encountered Jesus during His time on earth also learned about God. Jesus said so directly: "The one who has seen Me has seen the Father."[7] And the writer of the book of Hebrews is clear that Jesus was a living, breathing source of information about God.

  > Long ago God spoke to the fathers by the prophets at different times and in different ways. In these last days, He has spoken to us by His Son, whom He has appointed heir of all things and through whom He made the universe.[8]

- *Scripture.* The Bible is the clearest and most comprehensive source of information that God has provided us. Not every person who ever lived has owned or even seen a copy of the Scriptures, but those who

---

[7] John 14:9.
[8] Heb 1:1–2.

have had a Bible were given a wonderfully rich opportunity to learn about God.

The best way to get to know anyone is to listen to them. In the Bible God speaks, and invites us to pull up a chair and listen to His heart. As theologian Millard J. Erickson points out, "God does not merely demonstrate through his actions what he is like; he also speaks, telling us about Himself, his plans, his will."[9] God speaks his mind to us—person to person—in His word.

Why wasn't God satisfied with just general revelation? Why did God go having us look around at His creation? Was there anything wrong with general revelation? Famed theologian B. B. Warfield addressed this issue when he pointed out that

> The purpose of special revelation is not to correct, much less to set aside general revelation. General revelation needs no correction—God has not revealed himself falsely or misleadingly in it. . . . God does all things well. The occasion of special revelation is extraneous to the organism of revelation itself, and lies in the necessity of meeting altered circumstances.[10]

There is nothing inherently wrong with general revelation. But general revelation is unable to address what Warfield referred to as "altered circumstances," the altered circumstances created by sin. The fall of humanity changed everything, including the kind of information God needed to tell us. Now God has to tell us how to be saved from our sins. And this is a message that general revelation cannot deliver.

Having your breath taken away by the sheer beauty of a sunset on the North Shore of Oahu cannot save you. Neither can the magnificence of the Grand Canyon. On its own, general revelation has never saved anyone. By staring at a flower you will never understand that Jesus Christ, the God-man, died on the cross as a propitiation for our sins. General revelation just does not have the bandwidth required to communicate the amount of information necessary to save us from our sin. This is why He gave us special revelation. This is why He has performed miracles, sent His son, and has given us Scripture.

Why has God gone beyond general revelation and communicated through special revelation? Love. God knows that unless we learn more about Him we will perish. Without divine knowledge we will die in our sin-soaked ignorance. Nothing less than eternity hangs in the balance.

We preachers share God's communication priorities. When we preach we work in harmony with God's enduring passion and share His main concern to

---

[9] M. J. Erickson, *Christian Theology*, vol 1 (Grand Rapids: Baker, 1983), 187.

[10] J. E. Meeter, ed., *Selected Shorter Writings of Benjamin B. Warfield*, vol. 1 (Nutley: Presbyterian and Reformed, 1970), 27.

tell people about Himself. As you rise to speak God's Word this Sunday you will be joining an immense and eternal choir that sings unceasing songs with inspired lyrics—lyrics that warn and warm people about the God who loves them.

I have given my life to preaching because the priority that God places on self-communication demonstrates how desperately people need to hear what He has to tell them. Unless people hear from God's special revelation they will die in their sins. I preach because I want to share God's passion.

3. Because of the Nature of God's Written Word

The Bible is deceptive. Because it looks like a regular book, it can easily be mistaken for one. *But it isn't.* The Bible stands apart from all other books, not just because of its Amazon rankings—it is the #1 best-seller of all time—but because it is not an ordinary book. It is a supernatural book.

The Bible is unique because of its authorship. God Himself wrote it. Human writers also sat down and penned the individual books of Scripture, but they did not sit alone. As they wrote, God wrote in and through them. It was a joint process that we call inspiration. "Inspiration" refers to the work of the Holy Spirit during the writing process. The Holy Spirit overshadowed and superintended the writing of each word that the human authors scratched onto parchment so that the words that were written were the words of God through human authors.

You don't have to belong to the Miami CSI lab to find both human and divine fingerprints on the documents of Scripture. The background and personality of the human authors are perfectly preserved in their writing. Yet God's work on these books is equally apparent. He is the one that ensured that all 66 books contain a consistent message, that every jot and tittle of the text was without error, and that every idea was exactly what the people of God would need to know until He returned. As Charles Hodge, the great Princeton theologian wrote, inspiration is "the supernatural influence of the Holy Spirit on selected individuals which rendered them the instruments of God for the infallible communication of his mind and will."[11] The Bible is more than just inspiring literature. It is inspired literature. It is God's word written.

This is why Peter said to the recipients of his second letter that

> First of all, you should know this: no prophecy of Scripture comes from one's own interpretation, because no prophecy ever came by the will of man; instead, moved by the Holy Spirit, men spoke from God.[12]

The importance of the doctrine of inspiration for the preacher cannot be overemphasized. The verbal and plenary inspiration of Scripture means that whatever the original author of the biblical text wrote to his original audience

---

[11] C. Hodge, *Systematic Theology*, vol. 1 (Grand Rapids: Eerdmans, 1981), 154.
[12] 2 Pet 1:20–21.

is true. It is utterly, totally, and completely reliable. As a preacher, this means that I can stake my personal reputation upon what it says. It means I speak with confidence and authority into the lives of my listeners as well as to society at large. Inspiration gives us a boldness that is critical to the preaching event.

As Donald Grey Barnhouse, founder and editor-in-chief of *Eternity* magazine and pastor of Philadelphia's historic Tenth Presbyterian Church for 33 years, said:

> The prime factor in expository preaching is the belief that the Bible is the word of God. I can speak of this only as I know it. When I take the Bible into my hands I think of it as originating with God, given by Him to man in the very order, terms, phrases and words in which He wanted us to have it.[13]

The doctrine of inspiration guarantees that as long as I restrict my preaching to what the Bible says, I will never be embarrassed. The halls of academia or the streets of common experience will never discover that what I said was wrong. I don't have to worry about whether my words may inadvertently injure my listeners. When my preaching is true to the biblical text it is automatically true to life. The Bible is the only book 100 percent guaranteed by the God who inspired it. The Bible is as true as God is.

Cornelius Plantinga Jr. puts it this way:

> What the Bible says, God says. That is why the Bible is an expert on how we must think and act. That is why the Bible has power to influence and help us. That is why the Bible has the right to give us orders that we must obey. God speaks through the Bible. And of course God is the supreme authority in the universe. After all, he thought it up in the first place.[14]

I preach because people have such a desperate need to know about God that God does everything possible to tell us about Himself. He pours out general information about Himself to all people everywhere and eternity, transforming information through a very special book—a unique book called the Bible that provides us with a completely trustworthy message to preach.

But in addition to being perfectly written, the Bible is incredibly valuable.

4. Because of the Value of God's Word

Is the psalmist exaggerating when he says, "Instruction from Your lips is better for me than thousands of gold and silver pieces"?[15] Is *any* book worth refinancing your house to purchase? Who needs this book? Everyone.

---

[13] D. G. Barnhouse, "On Expository Preaching," in *We Prepare and Preach: The Practice of Sermon Construction and Delivery*, ed. by Clarence Stonelynn Roddy (Chicago: Moody Press, 1959), 29.

[14] C. Plantinga Jr., *A Sure Thing: What We Believe and Why* (Grand Rapids: Bible Way CRC Publications, 1986), 67.

[15] Ps 119:72.

Unsaved People. The value of the Bible extends beyond the foyer of your church. It is a book that has enormous relevance for the entire world. The Bible's greatest value for the unsaved is to tell them why they need a savior and how they can be saved from their sin. Its value in leading people to salvation is undeniable. Paul underscores the importance of preaching to the unsaved when he tells the Christians in Rome:

> "Everyone who calls on the name of the Lord will be saved." But how can they call on Him in whom they have not believed? And how can they believe without hearing about Him? And how can they hear without a preacher? And how can they preach unless they are sent? As it is written: "How welcome are the feet of those who announce the gospel of good things!"[16]

Jesus personally underscores the value of preaching when he tells his disciples to "go into all the world and preach the gospel to the whole creation. Whoever believes and is baptized will be saved, but whoever does not believe will be condemned."[17]

Okay, so the Bible is important for Billy Graham and missionaries. But what about those of us who preach every week to Christians? Does the Bible have any value for those who have already accepted Christ as their Savior?

God's People. The Bible is critically important for all people—even for the people of God. The word of God nourishes the people of God. It feeds our souls. Scripture is to our souls what oxygen is to our bodies. We cannot live without it. And those who try to do so will perish.

God demonstrated the critical nature of His Word to Israel with a dramatic object lesson. We read about it in Deuteronomy 8 when Moses said to Israel:

> "You must carefully follow every command I am giving you today, so that you may live and increase, and may enter and take possession of the land the LORD swore to your fathers. Remember that the LORD your God led you on the entire journey these 40 years in the wilderness, so that He might humble you and test you to know what was in your heart, whether or not you would keep His commands. He humbled you by letting you go hungry; then He gave you manna to eat, which you and your fathers had not known, so that you might learn that man does not live on bread alone but on every word that comes from the mouth of the LORD."[18]

God sent Israel manna as a remedy for their spiritual arrogance. The humiliating act of daily gathering God's manna was intended to teach them a spiritual lesson. God wanted them to learn that they needed God's Word as much as

---

[16] Rom 10:13–15.
[17] Mark 16:15–16.
[18] Deut 8:1–3.

they needed His bread. Jesus underscores this lesson for us during His wilderness temptation when He reminds us, "Man must not live on bread alone but on every word that comes from the mouth of God."[19] The lesson is not to be missed. God's people need the Bible as much as they need bread. Your people cannot live without Scripture this week any more than they can skip eating. Why?

God's people need the spiritual nourishment of Scripture to grow into the mature Christians that God intends them to be. Pouring Scripture into our parishioners' hearts is like scooping food onto the dinner plates of our teenagers. It gives them what they need to grow into healthy mature people. This is why Peter said to the readers of his first epistle: "Like newborn infants, desire the unadulterated spiritual milk, so that you may grow by it in |your| salvation, since you have tasted that the Lord is good.[20]

There is no spiritual substitute for Scripture. On the dinner table you may be tempted to exchange Splenda for sugar or rice for pasta, but nothing can take the place of the Word of God. Only Scripture is capable of bringing people to maturity in Christ. This is why the apostle Paul reminded the young preacher Timothy, "All Scripture is inspired by God and is profitable for teaching, for rebuking, for correcting, for training in righteousness, so that the man of God may be complete, equipped for every good work."[21] The Bible has what the people of God need to become the people God wants them to be. No believer will be or do all that God intends for them if they are not nourished on the words of God. They cannot do it on their own.

This is why Paul could write to the church in Ephesus that God gifted

> some to be apostles, some prophets, some evangelists, some pastors and teachers, for the training of the saints in the work of ministry, to build up the body of Christ, until we all reach unity in the faith and in the knowledge of God's Son, growing into a mature man with a stature measured by Christ's fullness.[22]

Spiritual maturity results from the proclamation ministry involved in all of the offices listed by Paul. But note the special teaching emphasis of the pastor. While the English translation "pastors and teachers" could lead a reader to think that these are two separate gifts, in the original Greek they are arguably a single role. Paul is actually talking about pastor-teachers. You cannot be a pastor unless you are a teacher. Pastors teach the Scriptures. They must. Because only when they do what God intended them to do will their congregations be built up, unified, and mature.

---

[19] Matt 4:4.
[20] 1 Pet 2:2–3.
[21] 2 Tim 3:16–17.
[22] Eph 4:11–13.

The apostle Paul practiced what he preached. We get a glimpse of the prominent role that preaching played in his ministry when he wrote to the Colossians that

> We proclaim Him, warning and teaching everyone with all wisdom, so that we may present everyone mature in Christ. I labor for this, striving with His strength that works powerfully in me.[23]

Paul labors with his preaching to help bring his listeners to maturity in Christ. The great apostle gives his primary energies to preaching even though he is fully aware of the challenges inherent in the task. Paul has firsthand knowledge of how difficult it is to preach.

In secular Greek, the word that Paul used for the "labor" of preaching means "weariness as though one had been beaten," and the "exertion" or "trouble" which causes this state. In prose it was "the proper word for physical tiredness induced by work, exertion or heat . . . expressing severe labour."[24] Yet, because this word was not strong enough to express the effort that is involved in preaching well, Paul also uses the word "struggle." A literal translation of this word is "agonize." It was used to describe the work involved in physically "contend(ing) for victory in the public games . . . it also came to mean to take pains, to wrestle as in an award contest, straining every nerve to the uttermost towards the goal."[25]

Why does Paul give his best effort and energy to the task of preaching? Because it is a necessary ingredient of spiritual maturity. The people to whom he ministers cannot become spiritually mature without the faithful ministry of the word.

Please do not misunderstand me. Listening to sermons is not enough to become spiritually mature. There is not an absolute link between biblical knowledge and spiritual maturity. We all know spiritually immature know-it-alls. The Pharisees, for example, knew vast amounts of biblical data but were nowhere close to being spiritually mature. Bible knowledge alone does not guarantee maturity, in the same way that having flour does not mean that you have a cake. But you cannot have cake without flour. And you can't be spiritually mature without knowledge of the Bible. Biblical preaching is valuable because it helps give Christians the knowledge they need to become mature.

The reason why preachers are to occupy such a prominent role in the life of the church is because as the Word of God is preached, the listeners receive the spiritual food they need to become mature in Christ. Preaching is to the ministry of the church what spark plugs are to a car engine. Spark plugs are not the

---

[23] Col 1:28–29.

[24] G. Kittel, G. W. Bromiley, G. Friedrich, *Theological Dictionary of the New Testament*, electronic ed. (Grand Rapids: Eerdmans, 1964-c1976), S. 3:827–28.

[25] S. Zodhiates, *The Complete Word Study Dictionary: New Testament*, electronic ed. (Chattanooga: AMG Publishers, 2000, c1992, c1993), S. G75.

whole engine—and preaching is not all there is to ministry—but without the spark plugs the car will not work. The car cannot advance toward its destination. Without preaching, a church cannot advance toward its mandate of bringing Christians to maturity in Christ. In fact, the consequences of not preaching are far worse than spiritual stagnation. The absence of biblical preaching is catastrophic for the church. Just ask Hosea.

Hosea ministered to the northern kingdom of Israel just prior to its destruction in 722 BC. These were Israel's darkest days. Government-approved sacrifices and incense were openly offered to pagan gods. King Ahaz burned his son to death in a pagan sacrifice and looted the temple of God to find bribe money for the king of Assyria. What caused this tragic spiritual state? Hosea gives his diagnosis when he says,

> My people are destroyed for lack of knowledge. Because you have rejected knowledge, I will reject you from serving as My priest. Since you have forgotten the law of your God, I will also forget your sons.[26]

When we fail to preach to the people of God we fail the people of God. At the deepest possible level. God's people perish for lack of biblical preaching. They starve to death.

The silent priests of Hosea's day should have known better. They should have learned from a similar tragedy that occurred much earlier in their nation's history. We read in Judges 2 that

> The people worshiped the LORD throughout Joshua's lifetime and during the lifetimes of the elders who outlived Joshua. They had seen all the LORD's great works He had done for Israel.[27]

It is always difficult to lose a great leader, but what happened after Joshua's death was a far greater tragedy.

> That whole generation was also gathered to their ancestors. After them another generation rose up who did not know the LORD or the works He had done for Israel. The Israelites did what was evil in the LORD's sight. They worshiped the Baals and abandoned the LORD, the God of their fathers, who had brought them out of Egypt. They went after other gods from the surrounding peoples and bowed down to them. They infuriated the LORD.[28]

The greatest tragedy in this text is not the death of Joshua. The greatest tragedy is that the people of God lost their knowledge of God. The children who grew up after Joshua did not know the God of Abraham, Isaac, Jacob, Joseph, Moses, or Joshua. These were not bad kids, but they were theologically uninformed. And their lack of knowledge led them into a divine disaster. Igno-

---

[26] Hos 4:6.
[27] Judg 2:7.
[28] Judg 2:10–12.

rance led inevitably to sin, and sin led inexorably to judgment. Once again, the people of God were "destroyed for lack of knowledge."

Israel's preachers went mute. When they failed to preach to a generation they failed the generation. Ignorance is not bliss. It's the last stop before destruction.

It is common to hear jokes about preachers who preach too long. Probably because too many of us don't know when to quit! But when preachers choose to quit preaching altogether and walk away from their primary callings, or when you hear of people driving from church to church trying in vain to find one where God's Word can be clearly heard, the people of God are in deep trouble. Amos described such conditions with the terrible warning,

> Hear this! The days are coming—this is the declaration of the Lord GOD—when I will send a famine through the land: not a famine of bread or a thirst for water, but of hearing the words of the LORD. People will stagger from sea to sea and roam from north to east, seeking the word of the LORD, but they will not find it.[29]

I choose to embrace the hard work of preaching because of its inherent value. The whole world, saved and unsaved, desperately needs to hear God's Word. When we preach, destinies are changed. Eternity hangs in the balance. Every time the leaders of God's people have stopped preaching, the results have been catastrophic. *Every single time.*

As John Albert Bengel pointed out so many years ago:

> Scripture is the foundation of the Church: the Church is the guardian of the Scripture. When the Church is in strong health, the light of Scripture shines bright; when the church is sick, Scripture is corroded by neglect; and thus it happens, that the outward form of Scripture and that of the Church, usually seem to exhibit simultaneously either health or else sickness; and as a rule the way in which Scripture is being treated is in exact correspondence with the condition of the Church.[30]

I also choose to preach the Bible because of its inherent power.

5. Because of the Power of God's Word

If you want to make a substantive change in the lives of your people, and the world at large, I can think of no better way than to preach the words of God. Just ask Jeremiah.

In Jeremiah 1 God comes to Jeremiah and appoints him as "a prophet to the nations" (v. 5). Jeremiah's initial response to his new job was not excitement. His world, like ours, was in significant spiritual and moral disarray. What good

---

[29] Amos 8:11–12.

[30] J. A. Bengel, *Gnomon of the New Testament*, ed. A. R. Fausset, 5 vols. (Edinburgh: Clark, 1857–1858), 1:7.

could one man accomplish in a world gone so wrong? What good could he, a preacher, do with nothing but words? What impact could Jeremiah make by speaking little puffs of air? The problems are so big and words so weak.

We get a glimpse of how overwhelmed Jeremiah felt when he responded to God's appointment by saying: "Oh no, Lord GOD! Look, I don't know how to speak since I am only a youth" (1:6). "God," he is saying, "I don't have the experience. I don't have the training. I don't have the skill. I cannot arrange and speak my words with enough skill to fix the world into which you are sending me."

I don't think Jeremiah's heart was encouraged when we read in verse 10: "See, today I have set you over nations and kingdoms to uproot and tear down, to destroy and demolish, to build and plant." Look at the scope of the ministry that God gives him! There are six different verbs here, four of them destructive. God calls Jeremiah here to uproot and tear down, to destroy and demolish. God says, "I am calling you to lay waste to the strongholds of sin. I am calling you to do battle with the bastions of the evil one. I am calling you to destroy the inroads that Satan and his evil ones have made in the hearts of the people and the nations as a whole. And when that's done, I have more for you to do. I have two more verbs for you. I want you to build and to plant. I want you to nurture and grow and develop people. I want you to cause growth and healing."

I can see Jeremiah throwing up his hands in despair. How in the world could he accomplish such an ambitious agenda with his puny puffs of air? What can our words accomplish?

I agree with Jeremiah here. I think God's expectations for Jeremiah—and us—are unrealistic. It is impossible for our words to change our world unless we're given help, unless God gives us a tool to accomplish that impossible task. Notice what that tool is.

"You will go," God says to Jeremiah in 1:7, "to everyone I send you to and speak whatever I tell you." And then we read in 1:9, "Then the LORD reached out His hand, touched my mouth, and told me: 'Look, I have filled your mouth with My words.'"

In one of the most poignant descriptions of the preaching task, God says, "Jeremiah, you don't understand the task that I am asking you to do. I am not asking you to speak *your* words to this sin-twisted world. I am taking *My* words. I am placing My words in your mouth." It seems that it is God's words that make the difference. It is God's words that make a preacher powerful. Why?

William Barclay explains when he says, "In Jewish thought a word was more than a sound expressing a meaning, a word actually did things. The word of God is not simply a sound, it is an effective cause."[31] That's the word that Jer-

---

[31] W. Barclay, *New Testament Words* (Philadelphia: Westminster, 1974), 185.

emiah is given. God's word is fundamentally different from your word—from my word—from the word of a parent. God's word is effective.

If you are a parent you understand the weakness of your words. As a parent there are times in the morning when you speak words to your children. Words like: "Get up. Have breakfast," or "Do your homework." Sometimes those puffs of air leave your lips, hang suspended in time, and result in absolutely nothing. All too often, a parent's words fill the air, but they don't result in changed behavior. Zero.

But God's words are not like our words. God's words are impregnated with His power. And when God speaks, things happen. They are an effectual cause. When God speaks, results must occur. This is why Isaiah can say:

> For just as rain and snow fall from heaven, and do not return there without saturating the earth, and making it germinate and sprout, and providing seed to sow and food to eat, so My word that comes from My mouth will not return to Me empty, but it will accomplish what I please, and will prosper in what I send it to do.[32]

Because the power of God is resident in the words of God, it always accomplishes God's purposes—always. Consider the awesome and irresistible power of God's words.

One of the chapters where the power of God's word can be seen most clearly is in Genesis 1. In verse 3, for example, we learn that "God said, 'Let there be light,' and there was light." Think about that verse for a minute. With the power of just His word, God created the biggest bang that the universe has ever experienced. Suddenly, worlds and stars appeared out of nothing just because of the power of His spoken word. It took Thomas Edison more than 10,000 attempts before he managed to create a working electric lightbulb. And Edison was a bright guy! But God made light on His very first try. And He didn't need a fully equipped workshop either. Just His spoken word.

You can also see the immense power of God's word when God says, "'Let the water under the sky be gathered into one place, and let the dry land appear.' And it was so" (1:9). God spoke, and it was so. The text deliberately makes the creation of dry land sound easy. Effortless. But think for a moment about what must have occurred physically for that dry land to appear. Think of the geological plates shifting and moving and the unimaginable tectonic forces that this would have released. Imagine the towering tsunamis that would have swept across the planet. Think of the volcanoes that would have spewed forth their angry liquid into the hissing ocean, and the mountains being thrust upward toward the heavens as these continental plates smashed into each other. The geological forces that are released because of the words in this verse are humanly unimaginable. But they happened—because God said, "Let it be." This is the power of God's Word—immense and irresistible.

---

[32] Isa 55:10–11.

The heavens were made by the word of the LORD,
and all the stars, by the breath of His mouth. . . .
For He spoke, and it came into being;
He commanded, and it came into existence.[33]

At Your rebuke the waters fled;[34]

. . . long ago the heavens and the earth existed out of water and through
water by the word of God.[35]

The New Testament also speaks of the power of God's Word. Think of the
times when Christ spoke. Jesus sees the paralytic and He just says, "Pick up
your bedroll and walk!"[36] And he does. Even today the most talented and best
equipped surgeon cannot regenerate a dead spinal cord. But Jesus does. And
He does so with just the power of His word.

Jairus comes to Jesus. He says, "My little daughter is at death's door."[37] Jesus
later comes to her lifeless body and says, "Little girl, I say to you, get up!"[38]
With the power of just His words, life floods into the dead girl's body. Her
eyes are opened. And the first thing she wants is a milkshake. She can't wait
to eat. That's life—supernatural life that comes because God's power has been
infused through His words!

The writer of the book of Hebrews tells us that Jesus "sustains all things by
His powerful word."[39] Now that is a potent word!

When God asks us to speak He doesn't ask us to speak our words; He asks
us to speak His words. And when we speak His words, our words have a supernatural power and authority that they never could have otherwise. We don't
speak on our authority and our power; we speak with God's authority and
God's power. And we can accomplish things with His words that we never
could with our own. And all of God's preachers have known that.

Moses knew the power of God's words. He was a failed leader on the back-
side of nowhere, but God came and said to him, "I am sending you to Pharaoh
so that you may lead My people, the Israelites, out of Egypt."[40] An impossible
task if there ever was one. But Moses pulls it off! How? With the word of God.
Moses strides into the courtroom of the most powerful man in the world and
says what God told him to say, "Let My people go."[41] And Pharaoh did. He had
to. How could Pharaoh resist that kind of power?

---

[33] Ps 33:6, 9.
[34] Ps 104:7a.
[35] 2 Pet 3:5.
[36] John 5:8.
[37] Mark 5:23.
[38] Mark 5:41.
[39] Heb 1:3.
[40] Exod 3:10.
[41] Exod 5:1.

Nathan, the prophet comes to David and speaks the word of God to him. As he utters, "You are the man!"[42] David repents. A life is transformed. Sin is broken. Healing and growth begin to occur in the life of a fallen man of God because God's word was spoken.

Jonah goes to Nineveh. In obedience to God he says God's word, "In 40 days Nineveh will be overthrown!"[43] Not the most winsome sermon I have ever heard but it was God's word. And what happened? The nation repented. The destiny of a nation was changed because God's word was spoken.

When preachers stand to speak the words of God they are accessing the greatest resource of energy in the universe. Our puffs of air often accomplish little. But God's words are not our words. They are unstoppable. They can even transform sin-twisted lives like ours.

> "since you have been born again—not of perishable seed but of imperishable—through the living and enduring word of God. For

> "All flesh is like grass,
> and all its glory like a flower of the grass.
> The grass withers, and the flower drops off,
> but the word of the Lord endures forever."
> And this is the word that was preached as the gospel to you.[44]

The conviction that there is nothing more powerful than the word of God is critical for effective long-term preaching. The best way I can impact my world is by speaking the most powerful words in the universe. Knowing this keeps me preaching. As James Daane stated so well:

> Unless people perceive the mysterious creative power of the Word and recognize that when it is preached it *does* things and *creates* people who become doers of the Word, their desire to preach the Word in the pulpit . . . will not long endure.[45]

My words—my little puffs of air—often accomplish nothing. But God's puffs of air are irresistible. They have more impact than a category-5 hurricane. If my goal in ministry is to change my world for Christ, I can do no better than preach God's omnipotent words.

I preach because the God we must know has placed the highest possible priority on revelation, including giving us a trustworthy written record of who He is and how we should live in response to Him. This written record is a book filled with words so powerful that nothing in the universe can stop them from achieving their purpose. But that is not all. I also preach because as I do, I enter into a noble heritage.

---

[42] 2 Sam 12:7.

[43] Jonah 3:4.

[44] 1 Pet 1:23–25.

[45] J. Daane, *Preaching with Confidence* (Grand Rapids: Eerdmans, 1980), 3.

6. Because of the Examples in Scripture

Can you think of any preachers in the Bible? It does not take long to come up with a pretty impressive list. Names like Noah, Moses, Elijah, Jonah, Amos, Ezekiel, Jeremiah, Isaiah, and Malachi quickly spring to mind. And there are legions more. Are there preachers in the New Testament? Truckloads of them! All of the apostles were preachers. Even Jesus was a preacher. In fact our Lord took preaching so seriously that in Luke 4:42–44 we read:

> When it was day, He went out and made His way to a deserted place. But the crowds were searching for Him. They came to Him and tried to keep Him from leaving them. But He said to them, "I must proclaim the good news about the kingdom of God to the other towns also, because I was sent for this purpose." And He was preaching in the synagogues of Galilee.

Jesus would not be detoured away from His primary ministry. Even though the crowds were begging Him to stay and expand His healing ministry, and even though Jesus' popularity was skyrocketing, He would not give up preaching. He had to preach. That is why He was sent. Preaching was His purpose.

Almost everyone in the Bible who enjoyed a significant leadership role was a preacher. One of the distinguishing marks of these leaders is that they led by saying, "Thus saith the Lord." Their authority came from the word of God. They led with the Scriptures.

When we decide to preach we choose to walk a well-worn path, one worn smooth by the giants of the faith who have trod before us. We are in good company.

7. Because of the Commands of God

I preach because God does not speak of biblical proclamation as an optional extra. It was not a temporary activity. Scripture explicitly and implicitly commands us to proclaim publicly the word of God. We cannot choose not to preach. Jesus makes just this point after His resurrection when He speaks to a repentant Peter after cooking him a fish breakfast.

> When they had eaten breakfast, Jesus asked Simon Peter, "Simon, son of John, do you love Me more than these?" "Yes, Lord," he said to Him, "You know that I love You." "Feed My lambs," He told him. . . . He asked him the third time, "Simon, son of John, do you love Me?" Peter was grieved that He asked him the third time, "Do you love Me?" He said, "Lord, You know everything! You know that I love You." "Feed My sheep," Jesus said.[46]

In this emotionally charged passage, Jesus is not giving Peter advice in animal husbandry! Peter is not being instructed to drag hay bales to domesticated farm animals. Here Jesus, the Good Shepherd, is asking Peter to be an under-

---

[46] John 21:15–17.

shepherd for His flock. Jesus is asking Peter to look after those He just purchased through His death on the cross by feeding them. A shepherd's primary responsibility seems to be the feeding of the sheep.

We pastors are responsible for the spiritual nourishment of those sheep that God has entrusted to our care. Jesus is asking Peter—and us—to preach to His people. And as we do faithfully discharge our feeding/preaching responsibilities we demonstrate our love for the Chief Shepherd. Jesus calls us, as He did Peter, to preach to the people of God.

The early church certainly understood the importance of preaching. In Acts 6:2–4 we read,

> Then the Twelve summoned the whole company of the disciples and said, "It would not be right for us to give up preaching about God to wait on tables. Therefore, brothers, select from among you seven men of good reputation, full of the Spirit and wisdom, whom we can appoint to this duty. But we will devote ourselves to prayer and to the preaching ministry."

The apostles made a joint decision that it would be wrong for them to divert their attention away from the ministry of the word in order to wait on tables. The feeding of widows, as good and as important as that was, was not as important as the ministry of the word. The apostles thought it would be wrong to neglect the preaching of the word for any reason—even a good one. We pastors cannot do otherwise.

The apostle Paul communicates the critical importance of preaching in the way that he ministers to the church in Ephesus. This church had a special place in Paul's heart. He not only started the church during his first three-month visit,[47] but he returned the following year to begin an extended three-year ministry. Because of the unusual length of time that Paul invested in this church, we are able to see the apostle's ministry priorities in action. His parting comments to the church in Acts 20:25–27 reveal a startling emphasis on preaching.

> "And now I know that none of you, among whom I went about preaching the kingdom, will ever see my face again. Therefore I testify to you this day that I am innocent of everyone's blood, for I did not shrink back from declaring to you the whole plan of God."

Here the apostle defends his ministry from detractors on the basis of his extensive preaching ministry. "I am innocent of everyone's blood," he says, because I preached "the whole plan of God." By inference, therefore, we can say that if Paul did not preach the whole counsel of God, he would have the blood of innocent men on his hands. Paul knows that he would have sinned if he had kept silent. It was only by preaching the length and breadth of Scripture that Paul could faithfully discharge his pastoral call.

---

[47] Acts 18:19–21.

The priority that Paul placed on preaching in Ephesus cannot be construed as an isolated response to a localized problem. On the contrary, Paul writes to Timothy, a young pastor just beginning his ministry, that he too should give a high priority to preaching.

No one should despise your youth; instead, you should be an example to the believers in speech, in conduct, in love, in faith, in purity. Until I come, give your attention to public reading, exhortation, and teaching. . . . Practice these things; be committed to them, so that your progress may be evident to all. Be conscientious about yourself and your teaching; persevere in these things, for by doing this you will save both yourself and your hearers.[48]

It is hard to see how Paul could place greater stress on the critical importance of preaching in the life of a pastor. But he cranks it up another notch in his next letter to Timothy when he says:

Proclaim the message; persist in it whether convenient or not; rebuke, correct, and encourage with great patience and teaching. For the time will come when they will not tolerate sound doctrine, but according to their own desires, will accumulate teachers for themselves because they have an itch to hear something new. They will turn away from hearing the truth and will turn aside to myths.[49]

It is clear from Scripture that pastors must give priority to preaching. Of all the many tasks that we must perform in order to collect our paychecks, none is more important than the proclamation of the word of God. How tragic it is that so many preachers seem to have forgotten their primary calling! The symbol of pastoral office has shifted away from the Bible in favor of the cell phone and BlackBerry. Pastors are busier than ever. But their priorities are pulling them farther and farther away from the pulpits. As my former colleague David Wells said so well,

In this new clerical order, technical and managerial competence in the church have plainly come to dominate the definition of pastoral service . . . . The older role of the pastor as broker of truth has been eclipsed by the newer managerial functions.[50]

The more our priorities tilt away from "broker of truth," the more we slide into the role of executive director of a religious nonprofit organization. We risk losing the right to be called a pastor of God's sheep. God wants pastors to preach. It's a matter of basic obedience. Pastors who ignore the preaching of the Word or treat it lightly are being unfaithful to their calling.

I give my best pastoral efforts to preaching for theological reasons. But I also preach for historical reasons.

---

[48] 1 Tim 4:12–13, 15–16.

[49] 2 Tim 4:2–4.

[50] D. F. Wells, *No Place for Truth* (Grand Rapids: Eerdmans, 1993), 233.

Chapter 3

More Reasons for Preaching Today

Many of us have lived long enough to see fads come and go. Remember tie-dyed shirts, bell-bottom jeans, shag carpet, Cabbage Patch dolls, Rubik's cubes, and Pokemon? And, more recently, SUVs? Do you know anyone who wants to gas up a Hummer?

And think about all of the technological changes we have witnessed. How many "must-have" gadgets have you donated to landfill sites? Remember eight-track tapes, cassettes, vinyl records, and Sony Walkmans? How about CDs? Non-flat screen TVs? Telephones with cords? Typewriters?

In our rapidly changing world, how can we be sure that preaching is not going to go the way of the steam locomotive? How can we be sure that preaching is worth the discipline and energy that is required to master it? How can we be sure that preaching will not end up shelved next to our copy of *Evangelism Explosion*?

If the theological reasons we have considered have not already convinced you, perhaps the weight of history will persuade you.

Historical Reasons for Preaching

Many sports have built halls of fame to honor people who have made significant contributions to their sport by their play. Baseball has its hall of fame in Cooperstown, New York. There you can admire the accomplishments of some of the greatest baseball players of all time, including Hank Aaron, Ty Cobb, and Ted Williams. Hockey has its hall of fame in Toronto, Canada, where star players such as Henri Richard, Gordie Howe, and Wayne Gretzky are immortalized. If your preference is tennis, then the Tennis Hall of Fame and Museum in Newport, Rhode Island, is for you. Its museum boasts the world's largest collection of tennis memorabilia. And in its "Enshrinee Hall" you will find plaques honoring inductees such as Rod Laver, "Chrissie" Evert, and John McEnroe.

Preaching could also have a hall of fame. Through the history of the world God has chosen to use preachers to make a significant impact on the world to which they ministered. God has chosen to use the "foolishness of preaching" to change the world. There is a cause and effect relationship that exists between dramatic spiritual renewal and effective biblical preaching. In fact, "every renewal of Christianity has been accompanied by a renewal of preaching. Each renewal of preaching, in turn, has rediscovered biblical preaching."[1] When God chooses to do a significant work in this world, He chooses to use preachers.

Chrysostom

When God wanted to bring renewal to the early church, He placed His sovereign hand on John Chrysostom, one of the greatest preachers of all time. Schaff writes that Chrysostom is generally and justly regarded as the greatest pulpit orator of the Greek church.[2] He took the biblical text seriously, spoke in an engaging and conversational style, and filled his messages with vivid imagery. Fant and Pinson report that people were so interested in his sermons that pickpockets were able to operate with great success![3]

Selected as archbishop of Constantinople in AD 398, the "golden-mouthed orator" used his pulpit to bring the Bible to bear witness against the sins of the Roman Empire as well as the church. Chrysostom's sermons made a significant impact against the sexual sins of the clergy and the laity who lived lifestyles of extravagant excess. He was even so bold as to call his sinning empress a "Jezebel!" While his tenure as archbishop lasted only a few years, and his death was untimely, the influence of his preaching was vast. "Few preachers, ancient or modern, can rival him either in rhetorical eloquence or in passion for moral reformation and social justice."[4] John Chrysostom's preaching helped pull his church and society in the direction of holiness.

Augustine

Saint Augustine is one of the church's most significant figures. He is described in the *Stanford Encyclopedia of Philosophy* as "one of the towering figures . . . of philosophy"[5] and one of the most influential authors of all time.

---

[1] L. Keck, *The Bible in the Pulpit: The Renewal of Biblical Preaching* (Nashville: Abingdon, 1978), 11.

[2] P. Schaff, *History of the Christian Church*, (Peabody, MA: Hendrickson Publishers, 2006), 3:933.

[3] C. E. Fant and W. M. Pinson Jr., eds., *Biblical Sermons to Savonarola*, vol. 1, Twenty Centuries of Great Preaching; 13 vols. (Waco: Word, 1971).

[4] D. G. Hunter, *Preaching in the Patristic Age: Studies in Honor of Walter J. Burghardt, S. J.* (New York: Paulist Press, 1989), 119.

[5] http://plato.stanford.edu/entries/augustine/ (accessed 2/22/08).

Yet, as Peter Brown, the Rollins Professor of History at Princeton University points out:

> In his own lifetime, the letters and sermons of Augustine were just as important for his activity as a Catholic bishop. To be a preacher, a *seminator verbi*, a "sower of the Word of God" to his congregation, and not to be a theologian, was the job description of any late Roman bishop. Augustine was no exception. It is his letters and sermons that take us to the heart of his life as a Christian leader in North Africa.[6]

Augustine's commitment to preaching is evidenced in Book IV of his massively influential *On Christian Doctrine*, considered by many to be the most influential homiletical textbook ever written. The heart of Augustine's work, and one of the most significant ways that he influenced the world, was through his preaching.

More than a third of Augustine's works consists of sermons; he is credited with preaching some 8,000 sermons. "Possidius, Augustine's first biographer and friend for some forty years, had this estimate of Augustine's work: 'I believe . . . that they profited even more who were able to hear him preaching in church.'"[7] Augustine changed his world with his preaching. The same can be said about Martin Luther.

Martin Luther

Martin Luther's role in the Protestant Reformation cannot be overemphasized. Luther played a pivotal part in one of the most dramatic renewals that the Christian church has ever experienced. The reformation began with his concept of *sola scriptura* as the new rule for faith and practice. It is not surprising, however, to discover that his renewed priority on the Word of God should lead him to a heightened priority on preaching. As Kiessling pointed out:

> The sermons he thus evolved were as different from those of the later medieval preachers as the plays of Shakespeare are different from those of his predecessors. . . . His heart was filled to bursting with a great new idea that had remade his own life and was remaking the lives of many of his countrymen and contemporaries . . . . Preaching was never the same again . . . the new era began in that historic hour in which Luther . . . accepted the duty . . . [to] publicly . . . preach the Word of God.[8]

Martin Luther took preaching very seriously because, in Luther's opinion, preaching was the most effective way to reach people.

In a sermon delivered on July 21, 1532, Luther preached against the idea that people could profit as much from the private reading of Scripture as from

---

[6] http://www.ctinquiry.org/publications/brown.htm (accessed 2/22/08).
[7] G. Lawless as quoted in W. H. Willimon and R. Lischer, *Concise Encyclopedia of Preaching*, 1st ed. (Louisville: Westminster John Knox Press, 1995), 21.
[8] E. C. Kiessling, *The Early Sermons of Luther and Their Relation to the Pre-Reformation Sermon* (Grand Rapids: Zondervan, 1935), 146–47.

hearing it proclaimed from the lips of a preacher. "Even if they do read it . . . it is not as fruitful or powerful as it is through a public preacher whom God has ordained to say and preach this."[9] In his comments on Malachi 2:7, Luther further defended preaching by saying that:

> The Word is the channel through which the Holy Spirit is given. This is a passage against those who hold the spoken Word in contempt. The lips are the public reservoirs of the church. In them alone is kept the Word of God. You see, unless the Word is preached publicly, it slips away. The more it is preached, the more firmly it is retained. Reading it is not as profitable as hearing it, for the live voice teaches, exhorts, defends, and resists the spirit of error. Satan . . . flees at the speaking of the Word.[10]

Luther took preaching seriously because he wanted to make a serious mark on his world. And it worked. Lutheran scholar Daniel Olivier asserts that "Luther's influence was due to the wide-ranging character of his evangelical preaching."[11] Martin Luther's preaching helped remake the lives of countless individuals. And we are the glad beneficiaries of his work in the pulpit.

John Calvin

John Calvin, another towering figure of the Protestant Reformation, is best known for his peerless theological work *Institutes of the Christian Religion*. What many do not know, however, is that Calvin gave his best energies on a regular basis to the pulpit of his church in Geneva. Calvin preached two different sermons every Sunday, plus every day on alternate weeks (6:00 a.m./7:00 a.m. in the winter). He averaged 170 sermons per year.[12] Olivier Fatio affirms the central role that preaching played in Calvin's ministry: "In the city's three churches [his preaching] sounded forth every day of the week . . . with sermons that lasted for more than an hour."[13]

Why did Calvin give preaching such emphasis? Because for him, preaching "was like a 'visitation' from God, through which He reaches out His hands to draw us to Himself"; Calvin was convinced that "the preacher's primary task was to expound Holy Scripture, which is, so to say, the voice of God himself."[14] John Calvin changed his world for the glory of God. And preaching played no small part in this transformation.

John Wesley

Consider John Wesley, the founder of Methodism. In the early part of the eighteenth century, England was in moral trouble. "Popular amusements were coarse, illiteracy widespread, law savage in its enforcement, jails stunk of disease and

---

[9] M. Luther, et al., *Works*, American ed. (Saint Louis: Concordia Pub. House, 1955), 64, n. 66.

[10] Ibid., 401, n. 18.

[11] D. Olivier, *Luther's Faith: The Cause of the Gospel in the Church* (St. Louis: Concordia, 1982), 110.

[12] R. Reymond, *John Calvin: His Life and Influence* (Evangelical Press), 84.

[13] O. Fatio, *Christian History* (vol. 5, no. 4): 10.

[14] T. H. L. Parker, *Calvin's Preaching* (Louisville: Westminster John Knox Press), 17.

iniquity. Drunkenness was more prevalent than at any other period in English history."[15] England needed help, and help arrived in the person of John Wesley.

The fifteenth of nineteen children, John Wesley was educated at Oxford where he formed a "holy club" whose members earned the campus nickname of "Methodists" because of their regular religious practices. In 1739, when the Church of England refused to allow Wesley to preach inside their church buildings, Wesley, with the encouragement of George Whitefield, began preaching to the English masses outdoors. And not just to handfuls of people. "On his first occasion of field-preaching on April 2, 1739, he preached to 3,000 persons—on a Monday! By June of that year he was preaching to nearly 14,000 of Blackheath."[16]

Of all of his remarkable achievements, perhaps the most phenomenal aspect of Wesley's life was his rigorous preaching schedule. He is estimated to have journeyed more than 200,000 miles on horseback in England, Scotland, and Ireland, and to have preached some 42,000 sermons. The impact of Wesley's sermons is undeniable. When he died in London in 1791, his work "had largely revolutionized the religious condition of the English lower and middle classes."[17] Yet the impact of Wesley's preaching went beyond just spiritual reformation. Wesley's denunciation of miscarriages of justice in the court system, poor prison conditions, corrupt election practices, government policies that hurt the poor, as well as his calls for education reform and the elimination of slavery and the slave trade transformed British society. Historian Earle E. Cairns acknowledges the enormous impact of John Wesley's preaching when he points out that:

> historians readily acknowledge that Methodism ranks with the French Revolution and the Industrial Revolution as one of the great historical phenomena of the century, and some subscribe to the idea that Wesley's preaching saved England from a revolution similar to that of France.[18]

Not bad for a preacher. When God wanted to transform England he sent a preacher named John Wesley. When God wanted to do a similar work in America, he sent a preacher named Jonathan Edwards.

Jonathan Edwards

While the American colonies may have been settled by deeply spiritual Puritans who wanted to build a "city set on a hill," that would be a moral and spiritual beacon for the entire world, this early spiritual zeal did not last. By the 1700s America was not gripped with a desire for righteousness. Historian J. Edwin Orr describes this period of America's history as decadent. At this time, church attendance was even low. More children were born out of wed-

---

[15] W. Walker, *A History of the Christian Church*, 4th ed. (New York: Scribner, 1985), 596–97.

[16] P. S. Wilson, *A Concise History of Preaching* (Nashville: Abingdon, 1992), 130.

[17] Walker, *A History of the Christian Church*, 605.

[18] E. E. Cairns, *Christianity through the Centuries: A History of the Christian Church*, rev. and enl. ed. (Grand Rapids: Zondervan, 1981), 382.

lock than with the benefit of a two-parent family. Alcoholism was so rampant, and the church so enfeebled, that many pastors had difficulty finding their pulpits Sunday mornings. It was in this environment that a tall, skinny, myopic, brilliant pastor named Jonathan Edwards walked to his pulpit in Northampton, Massachusetts. The sermon he preached July 8, 1741, was entitled, "Sinners in the Hands of an Angry God." One of the most famous sermons in American history, this sermon was used by the Holy Spirit to transform hundreds of lives and spark the Great Awakening. This revival was fanned by the work of fellow preacher George Whitefield, and the impact was undeniable.

> Out of a population of 300,000 in New England, 30,000 new converts were added to the churches. . . . 150 new congregations were formed by Congregational pastors alone in twenty years. The moral improvement in New England towns was generally recognized. A historian called the work "the most glorious and extensive revival of religion and reformation of manners" the country had ever known. . . . The Awakening had an immediate effect on education . . . [for the education of ministers]. . . . Nine university colleges were established in the Colonies during the thirty years following 1740, and six of them directly or indirectly sprang from the Awakening: Brown, Columbia, Dartmouth, Pennsylvania, Princeton and Rutgers. The first five presidents of Princeton were outstanding evangelists. . . . Missionary concern was furthered by the Awakening, and the movement stirred up sacrificial efforts to evangelize the aboriginal Indians and the enslaved Negroes . . . . Anti-slavery sentiments of evangelical origin, assisted by the forces of liberal humanitarianism finally triumphed over religious and secular reaction."[19]

It is hard to overestimate the revolutionary impact that the Great Awakening had on the United States of America. Compared to the many nations of the world who have not experienced such a mighty moving of God, America, for all of its flaws, is still considered to be a Christian nation. The legacy of the Great Awakening continues today. And it was all started by a pastor in his pulpit.

When God wants to change the world, He sends a preacher to speak his all-powerful word. God's word has shaped human hearts and history in the past and will continue to do so in the future. The strength of the sermon can be seen both theologically and historically. The way that you and I can have the most significant impact on our world is by opening our Bibles and speaking it.

But if theology and history are not enough to get you to give your best efforts and energies to the task of preaching, perhaps pragmatism will. I preach for theological and historical reasons, but I also preach for pragmatic reasons. Preaching works.

---

[19] J. E. Orr, *The Re-study of Revival and Revivalism* (Pasadena, CA: 1981), 6–7.

Pragmatic Reasons for Preaching

My good friend and colleague at Talbot School of Theology, Donald Sunukjian, wrote in one of his doctoral theses that:

> Oral discourse is the most effective medium for religious communication, and . . . nothing, however able and effective, in the way of print, radio, pastoral work, or liturgical worship will ever take the place of the preacher.[20]

Is Sunukjian correct? Or is he guilty of overstating the case for preachers? Think about his assertion for a moment. He is not saying that these other forms of religious communication are not valid or profitable. He is saying that no other form of communication is as effective as a preacher personally speaking the word of God. This is a bold statement. Is it true?

After all, books speak their messages longer than flesh and blood preachers can. DVDs never get too tired to preach in multiple worship services and multiple locations. And radio signals can penetrate to parts of the world where you and I cannot get visas to enter. Liturgical worship can be breathtakingly significant. What can a local preacher do that a high definition video podcast on an iPhone cannot do, even when it's equipped with the latest software?

Preaching Is Incarnational. Preaching is the killer "app" because it is *incarnational* communication. The very best way to communicate a message is to do so in person. I say this because live personal communication is the way that God chose to express Himself. The God who can do anything chose to communicate incarnationally.

My response to those who question the value of incarnational communication is to ask, "Why didn't Jesus just come to earth for a long weekend?" If the only reason for Jesus becoming human was to die on the cross, why didn't He just come to this dusty planet for a four-day weekend? That would have been plenty of time for Jesus to die on the cross and rise on the third day. The sacrificial atonement on the cross could have been satisfied in short order.

So why did Jesus share the planet with us for 33 years? What was His purpose for staying so long? Was He bored of heaven? Did He enjoy the stresses and strains of peasant life in the first century? Hardly.

When God wanted to express Himself most clearly, He incarnated—He came in person. Jesus, the image of the invisible God, came in the flesh in order to show us the invisible God. This is why Jesus said, "The one who has seen Me has seen the Father."[21]

When God wanted to communicate the most important message in history He used the most effective communication strategy: incarnational communication. Why is incarnational communication so effective?

---

[20] D. R. Sunukjian, "The Homiletical Theory of Expository Preaching" (unpublished Ph.D. diss; University of California, 1974), 36.

[21] John 14:9.

37

1. Sermons given in person are laden with personal credibility. When you deliver a message in person, you stand as a living embodiment of your message. Who you are matters. It changes how people receive the message that they hear. That is why most people would believe a message delivered by General Colin Powell over Richard Nixon. That is why you believe your best friend over a stranger at a bus stop.

   The respect that your congregation has for you covers your sermons like paint on a bedroom wall. Who you are colors everything you say. You are not a disembodied electronic representation of a stranger in a distant location, like hucksters on the home shopping network. When you stand flesh and blood in front of people you know and people who know you, you are giving your personal guarantee to the truthfulness of your message. Your integrity guarantees the integrity of your sermon.

   We are far more likely to trust people we know well rather than airbrushed strangers who grin at us from the back of magazine covers. People trust messages spoken by people they know.

2. Incarnational communication is audience adaptive. When I preach to people in person—as opposed to on CD or DVD—I can see and hear the extent to which people understand and agree with my message. I can "fine tune" what I am saying to a given audience based on their immediate response. If they don't seem to grasp a part of my sermon I may give an additional metaphor I was not planning on giving, or take additional time to explain the original context of the biblical passage. When I am present with the people who are hearing my message, I can adapt my message for maximum effectiveness.

   Audience adaptation cannot take place on the radio because radio speakers cannot receive simultaneous feedback from their audience. Nor can audience adaptation be done on a DVD or CD. The mediums require that the present hearers receive a stagnant presentation that was delivered to a different audience (or none at all!) at a different place and time. Generic-sized clothes fit very few people well. Generic sermons suffer from the same deficiency. We prefer customized sermons, knowing that the preacher is speaking specifically to us, just like we prefer custom tailored clothes. We buy clothes that fit our bodies, and we buy into messages that fit our life situations.

3. Your presence gives evidence of how valuable you think your audience is. It is pretty easy to make a phone call. It is even easier to fire off a mass e-mail. But when you want the person to whom you are speaking to know that you value them, and if you think it is critical that they understand and respond to your message, you have to show up in person.

Send flowers if you like, but nothing says that you love your mother more than singing happy birthday in person, even if you are off key! The communicators we respond to the best are those that we can see, hear, and touch. We respond because they cared enough to come.

It is impossible to deny the value of incarnational communication. Certainly the secular world recognizes the value of person-to-person communication. Why else, in our day of sky-high energy prices and increasingly costly air travel, would successful companies spend the huge amounts of money to send a salesperson across the globe? Because they want to seal the deal. And they know that the most effective communication is person-to-person communication. If the client is valuable, they send a person, not an email, to seal the deal.

How else do you explain the phenomenon of rock concerts? A couple of years ago my wife, Nola, bought us a couple of tickets to a local Paul McCartney concert. I am a Paul McCartney fan (much to the chagrin of my sons!) and have most of his CDs. On the way to the concert, Nola and I listened to his latest album in our small SUV, and I have to say that the sound quality in our vehicle was outstanding. So was the comfort. When we walked into the Honda Center for the concert, there was no question that the sound quality would suffer. This was a hockey rink! It was not designed for acoustic excellence. What is more, the seats were hard and had very little legroom. And being surrounded by 17,000 screaming fans is not likely to improve the sound quality! So why go hear songs I already know—that will not sound better than what I experienced in my car? Because I wanted to see Paul McCartney in person. I wanted to actually see him pick up his guitar and play "Yesterday." As anyone who has been at a concert can tell you, there is nothing like seeing a band live!

I am further convinced of the value of incarnational communication after watching the most recent presidential campaign. Why didn't Hillary Clinton, John McCain, and Barack Obama rely on e-mails and TV advertising to try and win their elections? Why did they spend millions of dollars flying to every state in the union? Why did they push themselves to the edge of exhaustion trying to shake the hand of every voter in the country? Because they knew that if you heard them speak and looked in their eyes as they did, you would be far more likely to believe their message. They knew that if you saw them and shook their hand you would be more likely to vote for them. That's the power of presence, the power of incarnation, a power that every married couple has experienced.

If you are married, there was a time when either you or your spouse decided to "pop the big question." Tell me, how did that happen? How did the "big question" get asked? Did you do it via e-mail? Write a postcard? Make a phone call? Not likely. It is pretty rare for anyone to ask, long distance, if someone would be their spouse. Why? Why, whenever possible, do we choose to show up in person to ask such an important question? Because you want the answer to be "yes." Because you know intuitively that the most effective form of communication—the best way to get a positive response to your important question—is to ask it person to person.

By showing up you personally guaranteed the authenticity of your words. Your presence said that you meant what you were saying. Because you showed up you could also adapt your message depending on the response. Do you have to say more? Have you said enough? You wouldn't know if you had arranged for an electronically prerecorded message to be delivered. Showing up to ask the question also communicated how much you valued your future life partner. You were saying nonverbally that nothing and no one else was more important to you than them. The best way to communicate important messages successfully is to do so incarnationally. That is true in matters of romance as well as faith.

The apostle Paul was convinced that preaching had a unique ability to accomplish spiritually what no other form of communication could do. That is why he wrote to the church of Rome, "I am eager to preach the good news to you also who are in Rome."[22] Don't miss the obvious here. Paul wrote this verse as part of inspired Scripture—a truly effective form of spiritual communication if there ever was one. Yet, according to the apostle Paul, preaching has an ability to communicate truth that cannot be replaced—even by holy writ! There is no substitute for the incarnational power of a real person speaking God's word to real people. Don Sunukian was right, "oral discourse is the most effective medium for religious communication."[23]

I know we are living in a day when an increasing number of churches are choosing to "preach" electronically in remote locations. The reason I hear given for this trend is that the prerecorded preacher is so good, no local preacher could match their skill. But let's be careful about turning to electronics as a long-term solution to the shortage of quality preachers. I suggest that a better use of our resources is the development of more good preachers. Effective preachers who speak in person have a greater potential for changing lives than wide screen monitors. Just think about it. Do you think Billy Graham gets a greater response when he does a "live" crusade or when a prerecorded crusade airs on TV? The most effective preachers are the ones who show up for their congregations.

The best sermons preached this Sunday won't be delivered by airbrushed superstars via satellite to a waiting world. The sermons that will touch lives most significantly this weekend will be preached by local church pastors who know and are known by their congregations, who stand and give their personal guarantee to the message they speak, tailor their message for their unique congregation, and demonstrate their love for their people by being with them.

Preaching Works

Haddon W. Robinson often says, "Something is not true because it is in the Bible. It is in the Bible because it is true." By this he means that when God

---

[22] Rom 1:15.
[23] See note 20 above.

40

commands or forbids various attitudes or actions, He is not being arbitrary or capricious. When God directs us toward or away from something in the Scriptures He is acting in our best interests. God's commands come from the heart of the One who only and always wants our best. While this is true for all of life, it is also true for preaching.

I preach in order to be obedient to the Scriptures as a pastor of Christ's church. But I also pour my best energies into preaching because I know that it works. The burden of preaching becomes much lighter when one is convinced that preaching is the best use of my time. It is easier when I am convinced that preaching is not only true to Scripture but truly effective in ministry. God calls pastors to preach the Scriptures because it is the best use of our time and energy. This is very clear when you examine the results of a new study that asked people new to church why they joined.

In 2005–2006 my Talbot School of Theology colleagues Michael Anthony and Gary McIntosh conducted a study among 1,081 people who joined an evangelical church within the previous two years. The people they studied came from 741 churches: 55 percent of them were in the Baptist tradition, 16 percent from the Wesleyan tradition, and 29 percent from other evangelical traditions. The tested group was 40 percent male and 60 percent female. They also represented a wide spectrum of ages.

- Builders (before 1945)   17%
- Baby Boomers (1946–1964)   47%
- Generation X (1965–1983)   40%
- Millennials (after 1984)   6%

The 1,081 people they studied came from a wide spectrum of locations

- Metropolis   7%
- Large city   8%
- Medium city   28%
- Small city   40%
- Small town   15%
- Rural   2%

Why did these 1,081 decide to attend the church that they did? Surprisingly, 51 percent of the respondents said that the location of the church was not important. What was important? Here are the top five reasons.

1. Preaching of the pastor
2. Church's theological position
3. Style of music and worship
4. Other
5. Age group programs

When these 1,081 people were asked specifically if the pastor's preaching was an important factor in their decision to attend their church, 91 percent said that it was. The overwhelming factor in the growth of the church today is the preaching of the pastor.

The Anthony-McIntosh study is not the first to affirm the importance of preaching. In 2001 the Presbyterian Church (USA) collected data from more than 300,000 people in the U.S., who worshipped for one weekend in 2001 within 2,200 congregations of more than 50 faith groups. They claim to have conducted the largest survey of worshippers ever developed in the U.S. The goal of their "U.S. Congregational Life Survey" was to identify the key factors related to church growth. As part of it, they interviewed "new people" and asked them what impressed them and made them want to come back. The quality of the sermon ranked number one.[24]

Pastors, please take note and comfort in these studies. They are telling you that there is nothing you can do that has a greater positive impact on the health and growth of your church than to preach—and preach well. They are telling you that God's command for you to preach is not just true because it is in the Bible; it is in the Bible because it is true. God chooses to use the foolishness of preaching to grow His church.

Preaching is not something that we can discard like the tie-dyed t-shirts and bell-bottom jeans of the 1970s. Preaching is not a fad. It is as central to the mission of the church as prayer and evangelism. Preaching is a pastoral necessity.

God uses preachers as bulldozers to remove mountains of sin. God uses preachers as thoracic surgeons to repair wayward hearts. God uses preachers as cheerleaders to encourage those growing weary in His service. God uses preachers to accomplish His purposes.

Why do I preach? I preach for theological reasons, historical reasons, and pragmatic reasons. I preach because as "difficult and challenging as preaching in today's world may be, it remains central to the cause of the kingdom of God, to the health of the church, and to the fulfilment of the minister."[25]

I preach because "preaching is indispensable to Christianity. Without preaching a necessary part of its authenticity has been lost. For Christianity is, in its very essence, a religion of the Word of God."[26]

---

[24] See U.S. Congregations, *U.S. Congregational Life Survey*, ed. Research Services Presbyterian Church USA (2001), http://www.uscongregations.org (accessed July 19, 2008).

[25] J. C. Barry, *Preaching in Today's World* (Nashville: Broadman Press, 1984), 7.

[26] J. R. W. Stott, *Between Two Worlds* (Grand Rapids: Eerdmans, 1982), 15.

Start with Your Heart

A good man produces good out of the good storeroom of his heart.
An evil man produces evil out of the evil storeroom,
for his mouth speaks from the overflow of the heart.[1]

The implications of Jesus' words for the preacher are immense. They mean that who we are impacts how we preach. The character of the preacher has a profound impact upon the content of the sermons that they preach.

Deep sermons cannot be preached by shallow people. Profound sermons only come from people who enjoy a profound relationship with God. Like it or not, the condition of our personal relationship with God will control our public ministry for God.

The Santa Ana winds of Southern California blow into Orange and Los Angeles Counties with a heat and ferocity that has to be experienced to be believed. They are hot hurricanes that leave you feeling like you are standing near the business end of an enormous hair dryer. The reason why they are so hot—and cause so many wild fires—is obvious. The wind is blowing through the funnel shaped canyons from the desert into the city. Santa Ana winds are very dangerous because they come from the Mojave Desert.

Likewise, cold climates create cold winds. The winds that blow south from the Canadian arctic are freezing cold because they pass over miles of frozen snow and ice.

---

[1] Luke 6:45.

Sermons have similar origins. The words of every sermon that is preached come from the heart of a preacher. The temperature of the preacher's heart will determine the temperature of their messages. Frozen hearts will always create an atmosphere of frigid spirituality. But preachers' hearts that have been "strangely warmed" create a pleasant atmosphere that stimulates the spiritual growth of everyone who lives within its influence.

Great preaching begins with a great relationship with God. It is impossible for a preacher to compensate for a relationship that has gone cold, for the "mouth speaks from the overflow of the heart."

So let me ask a very personal question. What is your spiritual temperature? Where are you with God? How would you describe your relationship with your heavenly Father? What metaphor would be most accurate? The second commandment might help you understand where you are spiritually.

Who Is God to You?

On the surface, the second commandment seems very distant to us.

> Do not make an idol for yourself, whether in the shape of anything in the heavens above or on the earth below or in the waters under the earth. You must not bow down to them or worship them; for I, the LORD your God, am a jealous God, punishing the children for the fathers' sin, to the third and fourth generations of those who hate Me, but showing faithful love to a thousand generations of those who love Me and keep My commands.[2]

I rarely meet people who struggle with the temptation of burning incense or bowing down in worship to carvings of bulls, eagles, or monkeys, so how relevant can it be for us? This commandment seems best directed toward distant times, cultures, and shores, rather than toward the affluent, educated, twenty-first-century people to whom we often speak. But what is idolatry?

At its core, an idol is a representation of God. It is an attempt to capture His essence. And, since no one physical or mental image can fully capture God's full character, idolatry always leads people into thinking less of God than He really is. Idolatry is a diminished view of God. Thought of this way, idolatry does not seem so distant from us. Many of us suffer from a diminished view of God. How do you view God?

Some people think of God as a GPS. For them, God has a mission for them to fulfill and a destination for them to reach. And He sits on the dashboard of their lives telling them what to do: "Turn left here. Proceed 500 feet and turn left. Then go 21 miles and exit on the right." To these individuals, God has a job for us to do, and our job is simply to do what we are told.

While it is true that we are to obey God, God wants far more from us than just blind obedience. God chooses to use us for His glory and promises to

---

[2] Exod 20:4–6.

direct our paths, but we are not just worker bees in God's hive. And God does not want us to be His drones.

Other people think of God as the "Bible God," bound by leather and covered in dust. Once again, these people are partly correct. God has given us the Bible, but God is not the Bible. We know God through the Scriptures, but God is not contained within the Bible. It is wrong to think that we can master God by mastering the content of His book. Godliness is not measured by verses memorized and theological books mastered.

Knowing stuff about God does not mean that you know God. Satan has good theology, too, but he is very far from God. God is not the Bible. God wants us to know Him as a person, not as a subject in school.

Still other people's image of God is like a bad British car. I love British cars, but not all of the cars that come from that country are worthy of our admiration. As a teenager I had a friend who had a Triumph TR6. He loved that car! It was beautiful to look at and wonderful to drive. The problem came when he decided to "upgrade" to a Triumph TR7. That car was a loser. It broke his heart as well as his bank account.

The TR7 was a blast to drive but rarely worked. Its electrical system caught fire and had to be replaced at least twice! My friend loved the car so much that he would go to the mechanic and say: "What do I have to do to make this car work? I will do (and pay for) whatever you ask!" People think God is like that car. They come to God and say, "God, what do I need to give You to make my life work? What do I need to give You so that my life can move forward? Do You want more money? More prayer? Volunteer work in the nursery? I will do whatever You ask." But God is not a temperamental car. He doesn't want us to lay down our stuff in order to please Him. God asks for more—far more.

Who is God? It is so easy for us to settle for an idolatrous image of God that is far less than who He really is. It is easy for us to adopt an image that whittles God down to an acceptable size and shape. But how do we avoid the dangers of idolatry that have plagued the people of God throughout all of recorded history? How can we accurately and adequately wrap our minds around the person of God?

Let me suggest that you adopt a different image of God. He is not a GPS or a book or a British car. Let me suggest one of the dominant images used for God in the Scriptures. I suggest that you begin to think of God as your lover.

The Divine Lover

The image of God as divine lover saturates the Bible. Consider Hosea. When God wanted to communicate to a people of God who had fallen deeply into idolatry, God sent the prophet Hosea to the northern kingdom with the mandate to communicate God via words and deeds. In order to help this wayward nation rediscover the true God, God asked Hosea to marry a prostitute.

Hosea's marriage was to exemplify the kind of relationship that God wanted to have with the people of the northern kingdom. God was saying to this prophet, "I want you to love this woman; be passionate about this woman so that these people will see how deeply I love them and how passionately I want them to love Me in return."

> Then the LORD said to me, "Go again; show love to a woman who is loved by another man and is an adulteress, just as the LORD loves the Israelites though they turn to other gods and love raisin cakes." So I bought her for 15 shekels of silver and five bushels of barley. I said to her, "You must live with me many days. Don't be promiscuous or belong to any man, and I will act the same way toward you."[3]

God's passionate love for His people is like a bridegroom's passionate love for his wife. In fact, the word translated as "man" in the final verse above is often best understood as "husband."

> One of the most common usages . . . is in the sense of "husband." The word begins to achieve significance in this sense first in Gen 2:23–24 where the origin of woman is described. While the derivation of *iššâ* from *iš* suggested by this passage is difficult philologically (there may be no more than a word play), there is no question that the words "This . . . is bone of my bones . . . She shall be called woman because she was taken out of man" (v. 23), communicate a close and intimate relationship that Adam could not find apart from one who shared his own station and nature; indeed, his own life. It reflects God's desire to provide man with a companion who would be his intellectual and physical counterpart.[4]

God is saying here that He wants to be in a relationship that is at least as passionate and intense and consuming as that which Adam and Eve enjoyed with each other as they romped through the Garden of Eden.

God is not a remote and distant God who operates like a divine supercomputer. He is not our grandfather, our uncle, or our boss. He is our lover. God loves His people with an intense, almost embarrassing ardor. And He wants His people to respond in kind. Hear the unmitigated infatuation in God's voice as He calls out to His people through Hosea:

> Therefore, I am going to persuade her, lead her to the wilderness, and speak tenderly to her. There I will give her vineyards back to her and make the Valley of Achor into a gateway of hope. There she will respond as she did in the days of her youth, as in the day she came out

---

[3] Hos 3:1–3.

[4] R. L. Harris, G. L. Archer, and B. K. Waltke, *Theological Wordbook of the Old Testament*, 2 vols. (Chicago: Moody Press, 1980), 38.

of the land of Egypt. In that day—the LORD's declaration—you will call *Me*: My husband, and no longer call Me: My Baal.

I will take you to be My wife forever. I will take you to be My wife in righteousness, justice, love, and compassion. I will take you to be My wife in faithfulness, and you will know the LORD.

I will sow her in the land for Myself, and I will have compassion on No Compassion; I will say to Not My People: "You are My people," and he will say: "You are My God."[5]

If this sounds like a suitor wooing his bride, it should. Here God is enticing His people to surrender to His advances. He is seducing her into a more intense relationship with Him, the kind of intimacy that once existed between God and humanity in the Garden of Eden.

Creation testifies to the passion that God wants to have with us. How else do you explain God creating such an achingly beautiful world? God certainly wasn't required to do so. He was not forced to create an almost limitless variety of trees, shrubs, and flowers. He didn't have to fashion so many different birds, animals, and reptiles that no zoo in the world is capable of holding a specimen of each species. He didn't have to create the stunning landscapes that cover our world—mountain ranges, deserts, rain forests, and prairie. But He did. God lavished His limitless resources and creativity to produce a planet that is the envy of the entire universe. And at the center of it all was a garden called Eden. Here, God cultivated a garden that was as refined in its beauty as the rest of the world was rugged in its majesty.

Why did God go to such extraordinary lengths to make such a breathtakingly beautiful world and garden? Passion.

God worked on the world for the same reason a jeweler works on the setting of a ring: to hold and display an even more valuable jewel. We are the apex, the diamond of God's creation. We are the most precious of God's creations, created in His own image. He placed us as a jewel in a setting that He custom designed for us, the beauty of which displays the passion of His love.

God made a spectacular world and garden because it was to be the home of His bride. In the same way that in ancient Israelite culture a husband-to-be would work during his one-year engagement period to build the home to which he would bring his betrothed after their wedding day, so God prepared a gorgeous world to house the people He loved.

God did not create our world with minimalist efficiency. He did not give us a stripped-down, bare bones, bottom-of-the-line starter home. Like any man who is infatuated with his bride to be, God provides the very best to the ones

---

[5] Hos 2:14–16, 19–20, 23.

He loves the most. The beauty of creation demonstrates the depth of God's passion for His people. So also does God's behavior in the garden.

In Genesis 3:8 we discover that it was God's habit during this honeymoon period to come for "[a walk] in the garden at the time of the evening breeze," whereas after their sin "they hid themselves from the LORD God among the trees of the garden." They had not previously been running away from God. They had been walking with Him. It seems that, in old-fashioned southern style, God was in the habit of "coming to call" on His lover. God was dating Adam and Eve. They went on dates, walking and talking and enjoying each other's fellowship. God is passionately in love with us and wants us to return His affection. He is our lover. Nowhere is this better seen than on the cross.

Mel Gibson got it right when he titled his film on the death of Jesus as *The Passion of the Christ*. If the cross communicates anything, it communicates passion. After all, why would God decide to come in the flesh and allow sinful humanity—the very people He had come to save—to spit upon His flesh, to whip His flesh, to impale His flesh, and to pierce His flesh? God's decision to come and save a people as sorry as us is not reasonable. A good accountant would have told God to cut His losses, declare us bankrupt, and go start fresh on a new planet with a fresh creation. So why didn't God declare chapter 13 and move on? Passion. Irrational, unexplainable passion.

God loves us the way a wife may choose to love an unfaithful husband. Yes, she could move on. Yes, she could declare the marriage over. Yes, the unfaithful spouse is unworthy of her continued love. But for passion's sake, some spouses have made a way for their wayward partner to come back. They have made it possible for the relationship to be restored, just like God did. Love is as powerful as it is inexplicable. And this is the kind of love that God has for you.

If we don't get this, we don't get God. We don't understand Him at all, and will not be used by him. We will be like the Pharisees.

The Pharisees gave God everything but their passion. They reduced their relationship with God to mechanical obedience. They were content to know God abstractly and theologically rather than personally. And Jesus responded to these religiously impressive but passionless people with some of His most caustic words. He called them whitewashed tombs and a brood of vipers. Jesus rejected those who would not give Him their hearts. And they rejected Him.

The People God Uses

The people God chooses to use for His glory are people who not only know about God but are passionate about Him. He uses people who love Him with an irrational obsessive desire. Consider Moses, David, and Paul.

Moses was greatly used by God. He spearheaded Israel's rescue from Egypt, gave them their religious and societal structure, and did everything necessary to prepare them for entrance into the promised land. Why? Why did God choose to use Moses in such significant ways? Certainly God did not *need* Moses. God does not need anything or anyone. So why did God *choose* to use him? I think we see the answer played out in Exodus 33.

In Exodus 33 Moses has just returned from scaling Mount Sinai and entering the presence of God. As he made his way back down to Israel, he discovered that during his absence they had abandoned the God who had just saved them in favor of full-blown idolatry. After appropriate punishment had been meted out on Israel, God made an unusual offer to Moses.

> The Lord spoke to Moses: "Go, leave here, you and the people you brought up from the land of Egypt, to the land I promised to Abraham, Isaac, and Jacob, saying: I will give it to your offspring. I will send an angel ahead of you and will drive out the Canaanites, Amorites, Hittites, Perizzites, Hivites, and Jebusites. Go up to a land flowing with milk and honey. But I will not go with you because you are a stiff-necked people; otherwise, I might destroy you on the way."[6]

God's solution to the sin of Israel was very personal. He would send them on with an angel to get the promised land He had promised, but He would not go with them. They could enjoy God's stuff but not God. They would be accompanied by one of God's angels but not God. Moses's response was a clear "no."

Moses pleads with God saying, "If Your presence does not go . . . don't make us go up from here."[7] Moses is desperate for God Himself. He wants to enjoy time in God's presence. He wants the person of God, not just the presents He gives. Blessings are fine, but Moses will not trade the friendship he enjoys with God (Exod 33:11) for the trinkets that God has offered. Moses wants to know God in increasingly deeper and more profound ways. Moses is passionate about God. That is why he goes on to make an astounding request for God to show him His glory: "If you are pleased with me, teach me your ways so I may know you and continue to find favor with you."[8]

It is interesting that the verb translated here as "know" in verse 13 is the same one used in Genesis 4:25 to describe when Adam lay with his wife—or knew her—in a physical/sexual sense. It is a word that describes the deepest possible intimacy that human beings can share. This is how close Moses wants to be with his God. He wants to mingle his soul with God's. He wants his God like a bride wants her husband. This is passionate love at its purest. And God responded.

God placed Moses in a cleft in the rock, shielded him with his hand, and allowed Moses to view His back as He passed by. God gave Moses the desire of his heart. God allowed Moses to know Him as deeply as humanly possible.

---

[6] Exod 33:1–3.
[7] Exod 33:15.
[8] Exod 33:13a, NIV italics added.

No human can fully comprehend God, anymore than any person can fully consume the water of the Great Lakes or suck all the oxygen in the earth's atmosphere into their lungs. God is far too vast, too immense, but the people that He uses want as much of Him as their hearts and heads can handle.

Do you want God or God's blessings? Do you want personal advancement or personal intimacy with God? Your honest answer to these questions will have a major impact on how you preach. It will determine whether you preach deeply or whether your sermons skim off the lives of your listeners, i.e. whether you preach evangelical clichés or share profound insights into the character of God.

The people God uses in significant ways always want Him and refuse to trade His presence for cheap carnival prizes like larger salary, fame, or larger ministries. No, when these people turn their eyes upon Jesus, they find that the things of earth become strangely dim. This was true of Moses. It was also true of King David.

Like Moses, David's shadow across the pages of Scripture is immense. He is a central figure in God's redemptive story. Why did God use David so significantly? Not because he was the biggest, strongest, or most gifted person in Israel. He wasn't. God used David because "Man does not see what the LORD sees, for man sees what is visible, but the LORD sees the heart."[9] We get insight into David's heart in Psalm 27:4:

> I have asked one thing from the LORD; it is what I desire: to dwell in the house of the LORD all the days of my life, gazing on the beauty of the LORD and seeking Him in His temple.

David has passion. For David, God is obviously not a subject to be mastered or a possession to be obtained and shelved. On the contrary, David is actively and continuously seeking God. Not that God is playing hard to get. There is no divine hide-and-seek going on here. It is just that David, like any lover, wants more of his lover than he has ever had before. Notice the words that are used here.

David wants to "dwell" in God's presence. He wants to linger and enjoy Him. He wants to savor God's company. He also wants to "dwell" in God's house—not just visit it on Sabbaths and during ceremonial functions. He wants to move in so that he can gaze "on the beauty of the Lord."

If these words don't sound like love to you, then you are in desperate need of some romantic therapy! Here David is not yearning for personal marital bliss or a strategic military success or a foreign policy triumph. No, the passion of David's heart is to know God more intimately. This is why David would write in verse 8, "In Your behalf my heart says, 'Seek My face.' LORD, I will seek Your face."[10]

David's passion for God reminds me of Psalm 42:1–2,

---

[9] 1 Sam 16:7b.
[10] Ps 27:8.

As a deer longs for streams of water,
so I long for You, God.
I thirst for God, the living God.
When can I come and appear before God?

The passion of the psalmist is particularly poignant here. The image used is of an animal sweltering under the desert sun, an animal so parched that it knows it will perish unless it can find satisfaction by consuming water. The natural streams have gone dry, and the animal knows that it will die without water. What will an animal that knows it will perish without water do to get to the water it needs? Anything. There is no enemy that the animal will not attack, no barrier it will not try and go over or around. It will do whatever it takes to get to the water it needs.

Have you ever been that thirsty? The answer is probably not like this. We have a Starbucks on almost every street corner and a 7–11 in between. We cannot fully relate to the psalmist's image here. To get closer, think instead about a drug addict.

Have you known a friend or family member who has been addicted to drugs? If you have, you will know that the addiction started with very little "need" for the drug of choice. Over time, however, a physiological change occurred. They become "hooked" when their bodies think that they require the chemical ingredients of the drug to survive. As they go into withdrawal their skin crawls, their body shakes, their eyes are crazed, and they become extremely agitated. What will an addict do to get a "hit" of the drug that they are convinced they need to survive? Anything. Addicts will do anything to get their drugs—lie, steal, cheat, prostitute themselves. Anything. The only thing that matters is that they get their drugs. This is the kind of intensity being described by the psalmist.

The psalmist cries out to God like an addict. He says, "I must have you or I will die." He does not say, "Gee, I would like to read the latest book or download the latest Christian CD from iTunes when I get around to it." No, the psalmist is convinced that God is essential for his very survival, not an optional extra. This man is addicted to his God and will not allow anything or anyone to separate him from God. This is passion—the kind of passion we see in the life and ministry of Paul.

In Philippians 3 the great apostle Paul, the one who planted and grew churches everywhere he went, the man who wrote inspired and inspiring literature, wrote:

> But everything that was a gain to me, I have considered to be a loss because of Christ. More than that, I also consider everything to be a loss in view of the surpassing value of knowing Christ Jesus my Lord. Because of Him I have suffered the loss of all things and consider them filth, so that I may gain Christ.[11]

---

[11] Phil 3:7–8.

Again, these are not the words of someone who is "kind of fond of God," the kind of person who will frequently select God if He happens to be on the menu. God is as important to Paul as oxygen is to a deep-sea diver. He is essential to life. He is his very breath. Compared to Christ, everything else in life is like freeway trash. What is more, Paul goes on in verse 10 to assert, "My goal is to know Him and the power of His resurrection and the fellowship of His sufferings, being conformed to His death."

Paul does not just want to know Christ in a detached, abstract, academic fashion. On the contrary, he wants to press himself into the person of Jesus as a child presses his face into the skirt of his mother. He wants to "know" Christ in the most personal and intimate way possible. Nothing is more important than this to Paul. Nothing.

Paul wants to intermingle his life with Jesus' to such an extent that they share everything—even their destinies. He wants to share in His sufferings, becoming like Him in His death. Do you? This is not cold, hard logic. This is red-hot passion.

God is our lover. We are told that "God loved the world in this way: He gave His One and Only Son."[12] Wow, that is extreme! I may give a few dollars to a person who is down on their luck. But would I give that person my car? My house? My firstborn? Hardly. My accountant would say that such acts of generosity would be foolish and ill-advised. But God did not heed her advice. And neither do those who God chooses to use in significant ways.

God uses people who reject moderation and reflect His passion back to Him. God refuses to use individuals or groups who are not passionate about Him. Consider the church in Ephesus.

> I know your works, your labor, and your endurance, and that you cannot tolerate evil. You have tested those who call themselves apostles and are not, and you have found them to be liars. You also possess endurance and have tolerated many things because of My name, and have not grown weary.

> But I have this against you: you have abandoned the love you had at first. Remember then how far you have fallen; repent, and do the works you did at first. Otherwise, I will come to you and remove your lampstand from its place—unless you repent.[13]

God threatens to shut down an active church planted by the apostle Paul. Why? Because God does not want people who just work for Him. And while God appreciates the fact that you refuse to bend to the ongoing attacks of a godless culture and admires your insistence on theological orthodoxy, that too is not enough for Him. What is God's nonnegotiable? Love. And not just any kind of

---

[12] John 3:16.
[13] Rev 2:2–5.

love, but first love. God is our lover and wants us to love Him with the intensity of a honeymoon bride.

I find it fascinating that the New Testament never refers to the church as the wife of Christ, only the bride of Christ. That is because in typical husband-wife relationships the sparks that mark the start of a relationship often subside over time. We say that a couple's love has "matured," but God says He does not want us to develop this kind of maturity. He wants our raw teenage passion. He never wants us to stop romancing Him. When we try and substitute sweat for scented candles, orthodoxy for Friday night date nights, and endurance for weekend getaways, we are farther from God than we realize. God does not use pastors or churches that are not passionately in love with Him. The prerequisite to deep preaching is a deep and passionate relationship with the God for whom we speak.

Too many preachers treat sermons as lectures or term papers. Too many preachers view God as a subject to be understood, analyzed, and discussed. They cut God open on an autopsy table and wonder why their sermons are dead. Their congregations gather to hear about a living, loving God that is larger than the universe and instead hear discourses suitable for a dead local deity. They are zombie preachers: the living dead.

Where are you with God? How hot is your relationship with Him? Are you enjoying a torrid affair with your Savior? Like it or not, you are as close to God as you choose to be.

Mel Shareski, a former pastor of mine who is now with the Lord, told the story of a man who was driving his wife to an appointment. The two sat in silence for a number of miles until the wife turned to her husband and began complaining about the lack of fire in their relationship. She bemoaned the fact that they no longer enjoyed the passion that they had in earlier days. To illustrate the distance that had crept into their relationship she pointed out that in years past they used to sit right next to each other, their legs touching and hands clasped as they drove. "Look at us now," she said, "there is at least two feet of space between us!" It was then that the husband looked at his wife from behind the steering wheel and said as kindly as he could, "I am not the one who moved."

This is what God says to us. He has not moved. He has not changed. He is just as passionate about us as the day He brought us to Himself. If there is distance in our relationship with Christ, we are the ones that created it. To us, like the church in Ephesus, Christ says: "Remember then how far you have fallen; repent, and do the works you did at first."[14]

What Is Your Goal?

In his best-selling book, *Into Thin Air*, John Krakauer tells the story of the ill-fated expedition to the summit of Mount Everest in 1996. In the book he mentions a member of the expedition named Yasuko Namba. Ms. Namba was a 46-year-old Japanese FedEx employee with a passion for climbing. She was

---

[14] Rev 2:5.

an accomplished climber, having reached the summits of seven of the largest mountains on the planet. The only one left for her to conquer was Everest, the tallest in the world. She desperately wanted to get to the top of Everest as well. This was her goal. So much so that Krakauer, who was also a member of the expedition, tells how "Yasuko was totally focused on the top. It was almost as if she was in a trance. She pushed extremely hard, jostling her way past everyone to the front of the line. She wanted to get to the top of Everest." Later that day, she made it. She accomplished her goal. She was the oldest person ever to make it to the highest point in the world.

Later that afternoon, however, Yasuko and a number of other climbers were caught in a terrible blizzard. And as the icy winds blew, Yasuko succumbed to the exhaustion of her climb and froze to death. Yasuko Namba died agonizingly close in time and location to where she had gained her greatest prize. This helps explain her tragic mistake.

According to Krakauer, Yasuko's fatal flaw was that she adopted the wrong goal. Yasuko's goal had been to get to the top of the mountain. What she wanted the most was to stand at the top of the world, and all of Japan cheered her when she did. But this was the wrong goal, and a frequent and sometimes fatal mistake that climbers make. The goal of climbing should never be to get to the top of a summit. Successful climbers know that the goal is not to get to the top—it is to get back down to the bottom.

The tragedy is that Yasuko accomplished her goal. Against incredible odds she made it to the top of the mountain. But as she poured out her energy to get to the top, she did not save enough strength to make it back down. Yasuko failed because she adopted the wrong goal. Many preachers make the same mistake. If we adopt the wrong goal, we can fail even though we accomplish our objective. It is *critical* that we preachers focus our energy on the correct goal.

Great Ministry?

The goal of the preacher must not be to have a successful ministry. It is not wrong for people to swell and applaud your ministry, but it is dangerous when they begin to distract you from what is most important. When some measure of fame comes knocking, it often holds the door open for pride to pay you a visit. When your ego gets tied up with the success of your ministry and popularity begins to become important to you, you are in serious trouble.

We cannot allow our ministries to be about advancing ourselves. Whatever happens, we must not allow what we do on the platform to become more about us than it is about God. If our reputation becomes a greater concern to us than God's reputation, then God is no longer being glorified. And God will not honor our ministries, for He refuses to share His glory with another.

Pride is the Achilles heel of many preachers. I have not met many preachers who, like John the Baptist, are happy to walk away from a significant high-profile ministry. By default, most of us want to go to larger churches rather than smaller ones. By default, most of us want more visibility rather than less visibility and more influence rather than less influence. Not many of us find it easy to say along with John the Baptist that "He must increase, but I must decrease."[15] Most of us are at least as interested in building our own careers as we are in advancing God's kingdom. This is why Jesus asks His disciples to pray a disciples' prayer that includes the words "*Your* kingdom come. *Your* will be done."[16] We need to remind ourselves constantly that we minister for Him and for His glory, not for our own. It is about God and His glory and His kingdom, not us. We need to keep our eyes fixed on the proper goal. It is never our ministry.

Great Sermon?

The goal of the preacher must not be to preach a great sermon. It is wonderful if you do, and we should always strive to do our very best, but if your goal is a well-received sermon, you will face two temptations. The first temptation that arises when your goal is to preach outstanding sermons is to cut the cloth of your sermon to accommodate the preferences of your listeners. You will be sorely tested to say in God's name what you know will get a good response, even if the sermon doesn't quite square with the Scriptures. If your ear is tuned to the applause of people as you preach, you will be tempted to sacrifice content for response.

The second temptation that results from a goal to preach great sermons is the enticement to preach above your heart. You will be tempted to fake it—to be a hypocrite. In other words, you will pretend that you have an intimacy with God that you don't really enjoy.

Preachers whose goal is to preach great, deep sermons out of shallow hearts discover that it cannot be done. And they quickly turn to plagiarism in order to fake it.

They are like those would-be entertainers who try and develop an international reputation as singers even though they have only mediocre talent. Such singers quickly discover they have no choice but to lip-sync. They have no alternative but to fake it by mouthing other people's words. The same thing is true of preachers. If you are not enjoying a deep relationship with your heavenly Father—and you want to preach deeply—then you have to fake it. You have to find other people's voices and mouth their words. You will become the churches' answer to Milli Vanilli.

Milli Vanilli was a pop and dance music project formed in 1988 that starred Fab Morvan and Rob Pilatus. Their debut album earned them a Grammy Award for Best New Artist in 1990. They sold more than 30 million singles, 14 million albums, and became one of the most popular pop acts in the late 1980s and early 1990s. As you may recall, however, their success turned sour when it was discovered that the vocals were not the voices of Morvan and Pilatus. Their

---

[15] John 3:30.
[16] Matt 6:10, italics added.

Grammy was revoked. In 1998, ten years after Milli Vanilli's debut, Pilatus was found dead in a Frankfurt hotel of an apparent drug overdose.

When you want a reputation for singing that is greater than your talent, you have no choice but to lip-sync. When you want a reputation as a deep preacher—when you are not in a deep and passionate relationship with your Lord—you will be sorely tempted to fake it.

Singers who lip-sync eventually get caught. So do preachers. Preachers who pretend to be deep will eventually be exposed for what they are—posers, wannabes, glory-seekers.

In order to preach a deep sermon you need to be like Moses, David, and Paul. You need to begin with a passion for God. Your ultimate goal has to be God Himself, to know Him. Only those who know Him intimately can communicate Him accurately. Only if your hunger and thirst for Him has been satisfied will you be able to set a homiletical banquet for His people. You cannot preach deep sermons if you don't know God deeply. He must be your ultimate ambition.

Keep Your Eyes on the Prize

When one of my sons was learning to drive he had problems staying in the middle of his lane. As he drove our pickup he would weave back and forth across his lane in a way that was disconcerting for his passengers as well as for surrounding drivers. As I watched him drive, however, I discovered his error. He was looking down at the yellow line at the side of the truck, thinking that if he remained at a constant distance from the line beside him, he would drive straight. It was hard for him to learn not to look down at the pavement where you are, but to look up at where you want to go. You will not get to where you are going in a vehicle if you do not fix your eye on your destination. You will not get to where you are going in the pulpit if you do not fix your gaze on your ultimate destination. As a preacher, your focus must be solely and exclusively on God. If He is not your goal then you, like my son, will be prone to wander.

The only way that we can significantly communicate God to the people He made is by making and keeping God as the ultimate priority of our lives and ministries. As A.W. Tozer, a deep preacher par excellence once said,

> If . . . your soul cries out to God, for the living God, and your dry and empty heart despairs of living a normal Christian life . . . then I ask you: Is your desire all absorbing? Is it the biggest thing in your life? . . . If your heart cries "Yes" to the questions you may be on your way to a spiritual breakthrough that will transform your whole life.[17]

This kind of breakthrough could transform your preaching and those who listen to it because preaching comes from your heart.

---

[17] A. W. Tozer, *Keys to the Deeper Life*, rev. and expanded ed. (Grand Rapids: Zondervan, 1984), 38.

Chapter 5

Get the "Big Idea"

I n his book, *Ideas that Changed the World*, Felipe Fernández-Armesto asks
the question, how does human change happen?

> Contrary theories of how history happens litter the literature. . . .
> This book takes a different approach. The pages that follow are about
> history that happens first in the mind: history driven by ideas. This
> could be the reason why our human record teems with change. Com-
> pared with other species . . . we have enormously complex facilities
> for thinking. New thoughts are destabilizing, even dangerous. . . . I
> think most historical change has intellectual origins and that ideas
> are at least as powerful agents for change as material exigencies, eco-
> nomic needs, environmental constraints and all other proposed deter-
> minants.[1]

I think Fernández-Armesto is right. More than any other single factor, the
history of the world has been influenced by the ideas that it has held. Humans
are rational creatures. We act in harmony with the concepts we hold dear. People act according to their beliefs. There is a cognitive congruence between our
minds and our hands. If you change how people think, you will change how
they act. The destiny of nations and individuals is determined by the ideas that
they hold. Consider some of the ideas that have powerfully shaped our world.

---

[1] F. Fernández-Armesto, *Ideas that Changed the World* (New York: DK Pub., 2007), 6.

The Power of Ideas

Darwin proposed in his writings that all species of life evolved over time from common ancestors through the process he called natural selection. He rejected the idea that God directly created people and things, and proposed that the "origin of the species" resulted from a combination of time, chance, and natural selection. The impact of Darwin's idea has been breathtaking. Without God, there is no basis for ethics. In a "dog-eat-dog" world, the big dog is allowed to do whatever he wants. Might makes right, and the strong abuse the weak under the guise of "natural selection." And if God did not uniquely create humanity in His image, we are just one animal among many, so who cares? There is no reason why people should be valued above other living creatures. Dead people are the moral equivalent of dead cats. Abortion and euthanasia become acceptable options. Morality is determined on the sliding scale of relativism. There is no all-powerful God to provide absolute truth. Darwin changed our lives and those of countless others on this planet. He used an idea as a lever to alter the course of history.

Karl Marx was a relatively obscure nineteenth-century philosopher, political economist, and sociologist. While he did not change the world during his lifetime, his idea would. Marx's idea that world history is the story of economically based class struggles, and his subsequent call for a classless society through economic restructuring, permanently altered the political landscape of the world. *The Communist Manifesto* that Marx wrote changed the destiny of billions of people. Lenin took Marx's idea and ran with it.

In 1998 *Time* magazine tried to help its readers understand the forces behind the century that was quickly coming to an end.[2] *Time's* editors identified Vladimir Ilyich Lenin as one of the major leaders of the twentieth century. Why?

> A bookish man with a scholar's habits and a general's tactical instincts, Lenin introduced to the 20th century the practice of taking an all-embracing ideology and imposing it on an entire society rapidly and mercilessly; he created a regime that erased politics, erased historical memory, erased opposition. In his short career in power, from 1917 until his death in 1924, Lenin created a model not merely for his successor, Stalin, but for Mao, for Hitler, for Pol Pot.[3]

Ideas are not neutral. They can be powerful forces for evil as well as good.

The United States of America is itself a testament to the power of ideas. The signatories of the Declaration of Independence began their historic document on July 4, 1776, by stating that:

> We hold these truths to be self-evident, that all men are created equal, that they are endowed by their Creator with certain unalienable Rights,

---

[2] April 13, 1998.
[3] D. Remnick, http://www.time.com/time/time100/leaders/profile/lenin.html (accessed 8/13/08).

that among these are Life, Liberty and the pursuit of Happiness.—That to secure these rights, Governments are instituted among Men, deriving their just powers from the consent of the governed,—That whenever any Form of Government becomes destructive of these ends, it is the Right of the People to alter or to abolish it, and to institute new Government, laying its foundation on such principles and organizing its powers in such form, as to them shall seem most likely to effect their Safety and Happiness.

The opening statements of the Declaration are filled with powerful ideas. Ideas like: God gave all people basic rights that no government can abrogate. And, the idea that a government's authority is derived from the people they govern. So that if the citizens of a country do not think that their government is acting in their best interests, they are entitled to change governments.

These ideas galvanized the colonists and led to their rebellion against England and the creation of a new and great nation. What is more, they have inspired countless others to embrace democracy. The ideas of this document changed history.

Never underestimate the power of an idea. Ideas change the destiny of nations as well as individual lives. Good ideas make life much better. Bad ideas make life infinitely worse. Consider the horror and the heroism that took place on September 11, 2001.

On that infamous day the world's attention was gripped by two very different groups of people. At first we couldn't take our eyes off the destruction caused by nineteen Al Qaeda terrorists who hijacked four commercial airliners, crashing two of them into the Twin Towers of the World Trade Center, a third into the Pentagon, and a fourth into a field in Pennsylvania. But as the smoke from these horrors filled the skies, our eyes were drawn to the heroism of the first responders. We were transfixed by the images of men and women risking and giving their lives to try and help the victims trapped within the burning buildings.

On that day we saw the stark difference between the terrorists who were willing to sacrifice their lives to accomplish their goal of murdering innocent people, and the members of the fire and police departments who were willing to sacrifice their lives to accomplish their goal of saving innocent people. The contrast between the terrorists and the first responders could not have been greater. The source of the contrast lay in the ideas that they held.

The idea that drove al Qaeda was a divine imperative to establish "pure" Islamic rule worldwide. All people and cultures that hindered their goal were considered enemies of Allah and needed to be treated accordingly. For the terrorists, the 9/11 victims were enemies of Allah and they were willing to give their lives to destroy them.

What caused New York City firefighters, police, and paramedics to rush into burning and collapsing buildings? The idea that the trapped people are precious and their deaths would be a terrible loss. For the first responders, the 9/11 victims were such valuable people that they would give their lives trying to save them. The tragedy of September 11, 2001, was a clash of ideas. Ideas change the course of history.

The destiny of all people—including those to whom we preach—is determined by the ideas that they hold. Our mothers were wrong when they told us that "we are what we eat." We are what we think. Our lives are a direct result of the ideas we believe. Your life is an expression of your ideas.

Preachers are in a battle for the minds and destinies of their listeners. The only way we can significantly influence the lives of those listening to us is by changing the ideas to which they hold. Ideas are the hinges of history. Our destinies swing on what we believe.

All week our culture is bombarding our listeners with false and potentially destructive messages. Ideas pour forth out of magazines, television shows, radio talk shows, Web sites, billboards, music, and theater. We preachers have just one hour a week to challenge the false ideas that have crept into our congregants' minds and try to replace them with the truth of God's ideas.

Can an Idea Change My Sermon?

A proper appreciation of the power of an idea will make two critical contributions to your sermons. The first contribution is *simplicity*. When you understand the enormous power that resides within an idea, you will not put more than one of them in a sermon.

Every sermon gets its own idea for the same reason that every thoroughbred racehorse gets its own stall. If you place them too close together they will hurt each other. And neither will win the race.

An inverse relationship exists between a sermon's effectiveness and the number of ideas it contains. The more ideas you pile onto a sermon the less impact it has. The law for deep preaching is simple. Less is more!

Like simultaneously pushing and pulling a stalled car, trying to communicate two different ideas in the same sermon takes a lot of effort . . . and doesn't get you very far! If you want deeper sermons you will need to put yours on a strict diet. No more than one idea per sermon!

A sermon that tries to explain why God's people should pray *and* how to discover the will of God for your life *and* why we should tithe will accomplish nothing. When you aim in every direction you don't hit anything. Sermons that include multiple ideas are too long, too complicated, and try to accomplish too much. They collapse under their own weight. The narrower your focus, the greater your impact.

Preachers who deliver multiple-idea sermons resemble carpenters who pick up a handful of nails and throw them at a wooden door as hard as they can.

What happens when all those nails hit the wood? They fall to the floor almost as quickly.

The same thing is true of sermons that contain a handful of ideas. Multiple-idea sermons strike the minds of their listeners with a flurry but quickly drop away. The only way to make a nail stick deeply into a wooden door is for a carpenter to grasp a single nail and hammer it individually into the door. In the same way, an effective preacher will grasp a single idea and pound that single idea into their listeners mind. Nails that are hammered this way—and sermons that are preached this way—will remain for a lifetime.

Preachers who understand the power of an idea will preach sermons that are simple. And their messages will stick for a lifetime.

Appreciating the power of an idea can make a second contribution. It helps preachers create sermons that are *focused*. One of the greatest temptations that preachers face is to include interesting but unnecessary information. But preachers who have learned to preach deeply have learned to resist this temptation. While their sermons do communicate content, they realize that background information about the Babylonians or first-century Ephesus is secondary to the idea of the text. Deep preachers know that Bible facts, by themselves, do not save anyone. Scores of atheists know the content of the Bible and continue to walk away from God. Even Satan can quote Scripture!

Biblical knowledge should never be our goal. In an age of information overload, it is more important than ever for us to communicate significant ideas. It's time to move beyond "sword drills" and Bible trivia contests. It is time to preach ideas. Don't complicate your sermons with unnecessary religious "stuff." Preach sermons that are focused upon a central idea. Shave off any and all extraneous data. Keep the main idea the main point of your sermon.

The impressive sight and sound of a missile being launched can be deceptive. To the untrained eye, that which dominates the senses appears to be what is most important. But it's not. The most important part of a missile is not what belches fire and smoke. The most important part of a missile is its payload, the warhead that explodes upon impact. The missile does not make a difference. The payload does.

The payload of a sermon is its idea. The idea is the critical payload that explodes in the minds and lives of those who hear it. What makes a sermon powerful—and deep—is not the biblical data it contains but the biblical idea that it delivers to its target.

Design your sermon in the same way that a military scientist would design a missile: include the design elements necessary for the payload to reach its intended target and eliminate anything that could throw it off course.

To achieve an effective missile design engineers must achieve efficient aerodynamics, and this is only possible by reducing unnecessary drag. Effective sermon design is similar. To achieve effective sermon design, preachers must streamline their messages. The only way to achieve efficient sermon aerodynamics is by shaving off all extraneous data.

Focus on what is necessary to communicate God's idea in your sermon. And scrape all information that is not exactly on point into your office wastebasket. Refuse to chase factoids down rabbit trails. Say only what needs to be said. Focus your sermon on its main idea.

Whose Ideas Should You Preach?

We spend our lives swimming in an ocean of ideas. Which ones are worth preaching? Which ones should never be preached? Of all the good ideas that exist, how do you decide which one to preach to your particular church, on this particular week? Making this decision makes you feel like a parent.

"What will I serve for dinner?" Parents ask this question on a daily basis. "Should I microwave some TV dinners or make a salad? Or maybe I'll boil some spaghetti and open a jar of sauce. Oh forget all that . . . the traffic is terrible, I think I will just get some Taco Bell take out."

The decision about what to serve for dinner every night is significant. Your menu choices affect the long-term development of every member of your family. Healthy choices help families thrive. Menu plans littered with take-out burgers, Kraft dinners, and Pizza Hut will result in long-term problems.

Pastors make similar decisions for their church families on a weekly basis. Every week, every pastor wonders, "What's for dinner?" What spiritual food will I serve up to my congregation this week? The decision about what to preach is not incidental. Your choice impacts the spiritual health and development of the people you lead.

How do you decide what to preach? What criteria guide your decision? Even if you are committed to preaching Scripture, the question remains. What portion of the Bible will you preach this week, month, and year? What parts will you not preach? Why?

Many preachers regularly decide to preach topically, to bring Scripture to bear on a subject that a biblical author never specifically addressed. Topical sermons on "how to date" or "how to handle stress" can be helpful and biblical. Topical sermons are not necessarily second-rate sermons. In more than 25 years of being a pastor, however, I have chosen not to feed my congregations a steady diet of topical preaching. My practice has been to preach through the books of the Bible. I have chosen to preach the ideas that the biblical writers have placed within the natural units of the Scripture they were inspired to write. Why?

Got a Good Idea?

I preach through books of the Bible because *I'm not that smart*. Some preachers seem to overflow with penetrating and insightful series ideas that perfectly fit with the unique needs of their audience. Not me. I try to know my people well, and I will occasionally preach topical sermons that I believe are both relevant and necessary, given a particular cultural or congregational situation. At their best, such sermons seem highly effective. But every week?

To my mind, it seems presumptuous for a preacher to claim to have perfect clarity into what their congregation needs to hear next. I struggle to understand what my own heart needs; how do topical preachers possess such tremendous spiritual clarity into the unique needs of their local congregations? I've come to realize that many don't.

A significant number of topical preachers do not wrestle with God to understand the unique and deeply significant truth that their flock needs to hear. On the contrary, it seems to me that many preachers preach topically in order to hit "hot" topics that will "boost their ratings."

If the major benefit of topical preaching is the opportunity it provides to bring the mind of Christ to bear to a specific congregation at a unique time, how do you explain that so many topical preachers across the continent are all preaching the same topic?

A few months ago I drove past a church in my town whose sign caught my eye. On the sign the new pastor was announcing a new sermon series entitled: "Desperate Households." The series was an obvious play on the hit TV show *Desperate Housewives* and was so cute and clever that it sent my mind racing. I was instantly thinking about how I could piggyback on the idea. I started indentifying the topical sermons I could preach as part of a similar sermon series in my own church.

I was impressed that the pastor of a church in my small town had the creativity to come up with such a great title for a sermon series . . . that must be touching an urgent need in that particular church. Or was it? I began to wonder if it was too creative. So when I got home I googled the pastor's sermon series title. Guess what I found? Hundreds of pastors across North America were preaching the exact same series. It was for sale on the Internet. So also were sermons designed for this "creative" title, as well as PowerPoint slides, posters, and banners. The whole thing was for sale as a complete package. *Please.*

There is no problem with preaching an expository topical sermon that meets a pressing need of your congregation. But those who purchase or steal other people's preaching topics defeat the main reason for preaching a topical sermon in the first place. Preachers that purchase "hot topics" to preach seem to resemble TV executives trying to guess what the next hit TV shows will be. Their selection criterion is ratings. They will give the nod to whatever will boost their ratings the most.

By the way, I recently drove by that same neighborhood church. This time I saw a fancy banner announcing a new sermon series entitled: "CSI: Crime Scenes in the Bible." Give me a break. We have enough CSI TV shows on the airwaves. I don't think we need more in church. Unless you have an urgent congregational need to address, I recommend that you preach the ideas that God thought were important enough to inspire in Scripture.

Will You Create Godliness?

I preach through books of the Bible because *I'm not that holy*. Sin is the best-proved doctrine of the Christian faith. I see it in my culture. I see it in myself. I am convinced that every part of my being has been warped by sin, including my ability to select sermon topics. I am convinced that left on my own I would spend far too much time riding around on my favorite hobby horses.

When an invitation to preach as a guest somewhere includes the words "share whatever is on your heart," what do you choose to preach? If you are like me, you will gravitate toward those ideas that resonate with you and away from those ideas that make you feel uncomfortable. If I am struggling with a particular sin, I will usually try and avoid preaching on it. It makes me feel too uncomfortable. If I am angry at someone in my church or about a difficult situation taking place in my church, I can select a sermon topic that advances my personal agenda.

Do you really want to select every idea you preach? I don't. I'm sinful. I can think of no more effective way to transform God's people into my image rather than His. Preaching books of the Bible helps me make sure that God's agenda, not mine, is accomplished in the lives of my people.

Will the Bible Be Respected?

I preach through books of the Bible because *I'm busy*. Is it possible to preach an expository topical sermon? Of course. But it does take a lot of work. If you have three points in your topical sermon you have to do at least three times the exegesis required to preach a single biblical passage. It gets worse. Topical preachers typically decide what they want to say and then go looking for passages that say what they want to say. But this process may force you to exegete a number of passages before you find one in which the original author intended to say what you want to say. As many of my students can tell you, finding biblical passages in which the authorial intent meshes with the preacher's intent is not easy. And when time is short it is very tempting to preach in God's name what God did not say.

When I preach through books of the Bible, I only have to exegete one passage at a time. As I work my way through a book of the Bible, it is far easier to understand a text in its context. The exegesis I do for one week's sermon always contributes to next week's message. Preaching consistently through a book of the Bible is an effective use of my time. I choose to preach through books of the Bible not just because exegetical topical preaching is so hard, but it also makes good pastoral and theological sense to me.

Will Biblical Tensions Be Preserved?

I preach through books of the Bible so that I can *maintain balance* in my preaching.

God often presents His truths in tension. Prayer versus God's sovereignty. Election vs. free will. Suffering versus blessing. One of the benefits of preaching through the Bible is that it makes it harder for me to "shave" off unpalatable passages. I cannot skip over sections that do not fit my personality or doctrinal system. God's canon becomes my canon. Preaching through books of the Bible helps me preserve the doctrinal tensions that God intentionally placed in His Word. Our people would have a more balanced personal theology if we preached the whole counsel of God. We might also reduce the frequency and intensity of denominational doctrinal wars. A little balance goes a long way.

Will You Be Predictable?

I preach through the books of the Bible because I want *to be creative* in the pulpit. Cooking the same kind of food every day will bore the people who sit around your dinner table. Preaching the same kind of sermons every week will have a similar effect.

As a rule, topical sermons are very predictable. They even sound similar. Most of them begin with a question and have a number of points—usually two or three—that answer the question. Why should we pray? Let me give you three answers. How can I have a great marriage? Let me give you three answers. Why are missions important? Let me give you three reasons. How can you have a great sex life? Here are the three keys.

Give your listeners a break from the monotony. Give them a little variety by preaching through the books of the Bible. How does preaching through books of the Bible enhance creativity? Because God did not just inspire the words of Scripture; He also intertwined those words with an inspired genre. It was no accident that Psalm 23 was written as a song or that the truths of Galatians were written as an epistle. God's inspiration of Scripture extends to the literary genre as well as the words themselves. God selected the perfect combination of word and genre to communicate His meaning. Word and genre fuse to form God's idea.

Many of us were taught in seminary to respect the genre of biblical text as we interpret it. To be consistent, however, we need to be just as respectful of genre in our communication of the biblical text. Our sermons should reflect both the form and the words of the biblical text. When they do, our sermons will be as varied as the Bible.

The decision to preach the books of the Bible—and fully respect its inspiration as you do so—will force you to expand your homiletical creativity. Your homiletical repertoire will have no choice but to expand to match the genres found in Scripture. You will have to fall into step with the creativity of God Himself.

No longer will you preach a psalm the same as you would preach the book of Revelation. Or Proverbs like Romans 5. The different forms of literature in the Bible will force you to learn new sermon forms. The very nature of God's inspired Word forces preachers out of their topical comfort zones and demands inspired creativity in the pulpit.

Will You Feed What They Need?

I preach the books of the Bible to ensure that my preaching is *nourishing*. How do you know if your preaching is providing your congregants with the spiritual nutrients they need for healthy growth? If "all Scripture is inspired by God and . . . profitable . . . so that the man of God may be complete, equipped for every good work" (2 Tim 3:16–17), then my congregation needs all of Scripture in order to be equipped thoroughly. If they don't get all of Scripture, they will not be getting what they need to grow. Since the books of the Bible are enriched with all the nutrients necessary for spiritual maturity, I have decided to stick with God's menu plan. I intend to say what God said.

Will You Be Significant?

I preach the books of the Bible because I want my sermons to make *a big difference* in the lives of my listeners.

Let me be blunt. You cannot blow up a mountain with firecrackers or build skyscrapers with toothpicks. Nor can you make a deep impact on people's lives with lightweight ideas. Insignificant ideas make insignificant changes in people's lives. One of the reasons why so many churches are hearing shallow sermons is because so many preachers are preaching shallow ideas. When all you have to work with are firecrackers and toothpicks, you are not likely to make much of a difference!

Archimedes said, "Give me a lever long enough and a fulcrum on which to place it, and I shall move the world." He knew that the key to changing the world was an adequate-sized tool. We preachers could learn from this ancient Greek and refuse to enter our pulpits without an idea that is adequate for the job.

Where do small ideas come from? From us. When the ideas we preach originate from our own wisdom—or a Google search—we greatly increase the likelihood that the fulcrum of our sermon will prove hopelessly inadequate to leverage deep change in the lives of our listeners. Significant change can only be accomplished with a significant idea. This is one of the dangers of a heavy reliance upon topical preaching.

A twelve-week sermon series on "How to Handle Stress in the 21st Century" is not likely to result in a significant increase in sanctification. Nor will four weeks on "How to Find a Good Wife." The best way to make sure that you have an idea significant enough to leverage deep change is to start with the authorial intent of a passage of Scripture. If, in God's opinion, an idea was significant enough to place into Scripture, we can be confident that it has the leverage needed to accomplish significant change.

When deep preachers do the grammatical-historical study in the text necessary to discover the original idea that the biblical writers intended to communicate to their original audiences, they will have an idea they can use to leverage significant change. My ideas can suck like a straw. God's never do.

Paul said to the church he pastored in Ephesus that he was "innocent of everyone's blood, for I did not shrink back from declaring to you the whole plan of God" (Acts 20:26–27). Whatever form of preaching we may prefer, let's make sure we can say the same thing.

Understand the Ideas that God Put in the Bible

Preachers that recognize how ideas reshape lives will make sure that the ideas that they pound home are God's ideas.

One of the most significant differences between a motivational speaker and a preacher is the source of the ideas they communicate. Motivational speakers skillfully arrange their speaking material around an idea of their own choosing. Preachers are different. As spokespeople for God, we arrange the content of our sermons around God's ideas. Motivational speakers sell their audiences their ideas. Preachers persuade people to adopt God's ideas.

The goal of the biblical preacher must be first to understand the idea that the biblical author was intending to communicate to his original audience. They ask themselves: What was God saying, through the biblical writer, to the original recipients of this portion of Scripture? One of the first and most critical steps in deep preaching is to understand the authorial intent of a passage of Scripture.

Determining authorial intent is not easy. It requires extensive training in biblical exegesis and continual effort to apply those seminary-acquired skills to the biblical text on a weekly basis. It is not unusual for well-trained pastors to labor for 15 hours or more a week in hard exegetical work in order to determine the authorial intent of a passage. Why?

Why is it so critical for deep preachers to understand the original idea that the ancient biblical writers intended to communicate to their original audience? The first reason is a matter of basic integrity. If we do not say what God inspired, we will be saying in God's name what God never intended to say. We will be signing God's name to a check that He did not write. This is fraud. And, understandably, God is not pleased when people say in His name what He did not say.

God's low opinion of those preachers who falsely claim to speak His words is crystal clear. As He said to the false prophets in Jeremiah's day:

> This is what the LORD of Hosts says: "Do not listen to the words
> of the prophets who prophesy to you. They are making you worth-

less. They speak visions from their own minds, not from the LORD's mouth.

> For who has stood in the council of the LORD to see and hear His word? Who has paid attention to His word and obeyed?

> I did not send these prophets, yet they ran with a message. I did not speak to them, yet they prophesied. If they had really stood in My council, they would have enabled My people to hear My words and would have turned them back from their evil ways and their evil deeds.[4]

Preachers who do not do their best to communicate God's ideas are not true prophets. They are certainly not deep preachers. They are just motivational speakers in costume.

If the wayward prophets of Jeremiah's day had preached God's truth they would have turned their listeners from their evil ways and deeds. Because they failed to say what God said, they failed to make an impact on the lives of those to whom they preached. God says to these fraudulent preachers:

> You used the words, "This is the oracle of the LORD," even though I told you that you must not claim, "This is the oracle of the LORD." Therefore, I will surely forget you and cast you out of my presence along with the city I gave to you and your fathers. I will bring upon you everlasting disgrace—everlasting shame that will not be forgotten.[5]

It is a grave sin to preach what God has not said. That is why James warns us that "Not many should become teachers, my brothers, knowing that we will receive a stricter judgment."[6]

To make a deep impact in the lives of our listeners for the glory of God our sermons need to build upon the solid foundation of an exegetically accurate understanding of what God was saying through His human writers to their original audiences. Faithful preachers pass on God's ideas to their listeners. They are biblical plagiarists. To do otherwise is to display a shocking lack of integrity—and to invite the judgment of God.

Anatomy of an Idea

What is an idea? If you were to place a peach on the cutting board in your kitchen and slice through it with a sharp knife, you would discover that a peach has four major components: skin, soft flesh, a pit, and, inside the pit, a seed. Biblical passages are similarly constructed. If you were to slice open a biblical passage you would see four major elements: a natural unit, a topic, a subject, and a complement.

---

[4] Jer 23:16, 18, 21–22.
[5] Jer 23:38b-40, NIV.
[6] Jas 3:1.

First, take note of the "skin" or circumference of a passage. The skin of a peach is what gives unity to the fruit. The skin separates one peach from another and allows you to savor each peach separately. Every peach has its own skin.

Biblical passages also have "skin." In exegetical terms, the "skin" is the *natural unit* of Scripture.

In order to find the big idea of a text, you must first find the skin of your text: you need to determine the natural divisions of the Scripture passage with which you are working. The size of a natural unit can vary according to the biblical literature with which you are working. Some narratives, for example, can encompass multiple chapters.[7] In epistolary literature, the smallest unit of Scripture is a paragraph. Psalms are best interpreted individually. The individual proverbs are probably the only biblical literature that should be preached as individual verses. It is critical that you properly identify the "skin" that surrounds your text. I find it helpful to read through a biblical book numerous times in order to gain an overview of what the author is saying and how he is putting his book together.

Please do not skip this step! As with peaches, if you don't properly separate the units of Scripture you will be preaching, you will have a mess on your hands! Failure to divide the word properly will preclude you from finding the big idea of the biblical author. Once you have identified the natural unit you will be preaching, however, you can begin determining the topic of your text.

The *topic* of a passage is like the flesh of a peach. Like the flesh of a peach, the topic of a passage is most accessible to us. The topic of a passage is the *broad subject* that the original author was addressing. Some simple questions I often ask to help me identify the topic of a passage are: "Is this passage talking about divorce? Nuclear warfare? If not these topics then what?" You have to know the general topic that is being discussed by the biblical author. Is he talking about prayer or money? If you cannot answer this question ask yourself "Why not? What is keeping me from understanding this passage?" Then go back to your passage and do the exegesis necessary to answer these questions. If you have done a reasonable amount of exegetical work and properly identified the natural unit of your text, however, the topic is usually easily accessible. It should be fairly easy to "sink your teeth" into the topic.

The problem with topics, however, is that while identifying them is a helpful step in the preparation of a sermon, they are impossible to preach. Like the

---

[7] For more detail on how to interpret and communicate biblical narratives, see J. K. Edwards, *Effective First-Person Biblical Preaching: The Steps from Text to Narrative Sermon* (Grand Rapids: Zondervan, 2005).

flesh of a peach, topics are too big to get your mouth around. A topic is too large to preach in a single sermon. It is impossible, for example, to preach a sermon on prayer. The topic of prayer is as large as the ocean. How could we reduce something this large down to a single serving? Will you talk about the reasons for praying? The challenges of praying? The benefits of prayer? You certainly cannot say everything about prayer in a single sermon. You will have to narrow the focus of your sermon in order for it to have maximum impact. The way to narrow a topic down to "bite-size" portions is to identify the subject of the passage you are preaching.

The *subject* of a passage, like the pit of a peach, holds everything together. It is the core of your message. The subject answers the question: "What is the author saying about his topic?" What is he talking about? Is the author answering the question: "Why should we pray?" or "When should we pray?" or perhaps "How should we pray?" No single piece of communication could answer all of those questions, so the preacher must identify the one single question that best summarizes what the original author is saying about his topic.

The process of correctly identifying the core or subject of a natural unit of Scripture will be significantly easier if you follow two simple rules. First, always form your subject into a question. The grammatical process of forming a question will help sharpen your thinking. Second, whatever question you form, make sure that it begins with a single interrogative: who, what, where, when, how, or why. Forming this question is not easy. In fact, the fashioning of it has often proved to be enormously frustrating to me. But when I cannot write out the single question that lies at the heart of a natural unit of Scripture—as a peach pit lies at the core of a peach—I ask myself "Why?" What is keeping me from understanding what this passage means? My questions spur me on to additional exegesis.

To determine the meaning, or idea, of a passage we begin by writing the subject of a natural unit of Scripture in the form of a question. But we can't stop there. We need to answer the question we just asked. In addition to a topic and subject, we need to find a complement in our natural unit of Scripture.

A *complement*, as the word implies, completes a subject. It answers the question that was asked by the subject. Complements nestle inside their subject like a peach seed into its pit. The two are organically connected and found within the flesh of the text.

Since deep sermons communicate God's thoughts, the only complements or answers we will use in our sermon are the complements that the original author included in his writings.

How many complements should a sermon have? It has as many as are in the text. Just make sure that you understand the biblical genre with which you are working.

If, for example, you are working with narrative literature, you will discover that narratives have only one complement.[8] Epistolary literature, on the other hand, almost always contains multiple complements. Just make sure you preach the complements that are found in the natural unit of Scripture you are preaching. Don't make stuff up!

Finding the Idea

How do we find subject and complement in a biblical text? Let's see how this works with an actual text. Let's look at Romans 5:1–5. This is a natural unit of Scripture. As a rule, the smallest unit of thought in an epistle is a paragraph. So while you can choose to preach larger natural "chunks" of an epistle, you won't want to go smaller. You need to have a natural unit of Scripture to have an idea.

Take a moment to read through the passage.

> Therefore, since we have been justified through faith, we have peace with God through our Lord Jesus Christ, through whom we have gained access by faith into this grace in which we now stand. And we rejoice in the hope of the glory of God. Not only so, but we also rejoice in our sufferings, because we know that suffering produces persever-ance; perseverance, character; and character, hope. And hope does not disappoint us, because God has poured out his love into our hearts by the Holy Spirit, whom he has given us.[9]

Since this is epistolary literature, the topic is fairly easy to determine. Epis-tles are similar to a contemporary essay in structure, and good essays always begin a paragraph with a topic sentence. In the first sentence of this paragraph the topic is introduced.

> Therefore, since we have been **justified through faith,** we have peace with God through our Lord Jesus Christ, through whom we have gained access by faith into this grace in which we now stand. And we rejoice in the hope of the glory of God. Not only so, but we also rejoice in our sufferings, because we know that suffering produces persever-ance; perseverance, character; and character, hope. And hope does not disappoint us, because God has poured out his love into our hearts by the Holy Spirit, whom he has given us.[10]

The topic that Paul is talking about in this natural unit of Scripture is justifi-cation by faith. But what is Paul saying about justification by faith? He cannot say everything about this subject. What particular question is he asking here? Since epistolary literature is so dense and complex, I find it helpful to re-

---

[8] Stories always have a point, but they don't have points. There is always "a moral to the story" but not morals. For more discussion on narrative, see *Effective First-Person Biblical Preaching*, ibid.

[9] Rom 5:1–5, NIV.

[10] Ibid., boldface font added.

write an epistolary passage in a way that exposes its dominant and subordinate clauses. I write the most dominant thoughts on the far left of my paper and the more subordinate clauses on the far right. I find this a helpful tool to help me distinguish the subject and complements of epistolary literature.

Here is what Romans 5:1–5 looks like when I rewrite it to expose its dominant and subordinate thoughts.

Therefore, **since** we have been **justified through faith,**
>> **we have peace with God**
>>>> through our Lord Jesus Christ,
>>>>>> through whom we have gained access by faith
>>>>>>>> into this grace in which we now stand.
And **we rejoice in the hope of the glory of God.**
>>>>>> Not only so,
but **we also rejoice in our sufferings,**
>>>> because we know that suffering produces perseverance;
>>>>>> perseverance, character; and
>>>>>> character, hope.
>>>>>>>> And hope does not disappoint us,
>>>>>>>>>> because God has poured out his love into our hearts
>>>>>>>>>> by the Holy Spirit, whom he has given us.*

---

* Rom 5:1–5, NIV

The topic of this passage is justification by faith. What is the subject? In the form of a question, the subject is "What are the benefits of justification by faith?" In this passage, Paul is explaining to the Christians in Rome the tangible benefits that result from being declared legally and morally innocent by the Holy God. What are these benefits? How has life changed for the Roman Christians as a result of being justified by faith? Now that the text has been rewritten to reveal the dominant and subordinated thoughts, the complements are pretty easy to see.

Topic: Justification by faith.

Subject: What are the benefits of being justified by faith?

Complement: We now have peace with God, hope of the glory of God, and the perspective we need to rejoice in our sufferings.

How do you know that you have properly identified the correct "big idea" of a natural unit of Scripture? When your subject and complement explain, or connect, all of the details of the biblical text. I have used the metaphor of a wagon wheel to explain how this works.

The rim of the wheel is the natural unit of Scripture. The spokes of the wheel are the exegetical details contained within that unit of Scripture. The hub of the wheel is the "big idea." This is the central idea of the biblical text. The job of the preacher is to identify the "big idea" that connects all of the information contained within a natural unit of Scripture into a single satisfying question and answer.

If you create a "big idea" that does not make sense out of significant elements of your text, then you cannot be correct. You need to go back to your exegesis and do the work necessary to enable you to move forward. Ask: "What do I need to understand about this text? What would help me write a subject and complement that connects all the spokes of this passage?"

I realize that this is easier said than done. The first few times I try and craft a "big idea" for a passage of Scripture I am usually wrong. My early ideas often connect a few of the facts of the passage but miss others. I have worked for many hours trying to articulate the idea that connects all of the details of the biblical text. But I can no more preach an idea that does not connect with the facts of my natural unit of Scripture than I can ride a bicycle with half the spokes not connected to the wheels. If I try to move forward without attaching the spokes, disaster is inevitable.

Don't give up. There is an idea at the core of every natural unit of Scripture . . . just like there is a peach pit at the center of every peach. My job, as a communicator of Scripture, is to find it. Deep sermons begin with the careful exegesis of Scripture, and the goal of exegesis is the author's intended "big idea." As Fee and Stuart said so clearly:

> Exegesis is the careful, systematic study of the Scripture to discover the original, intended meaning. . . . It is the attempt to hear the Word as the original recipients were to have heard it, to find out what was *the original intent of the words of the Bible.*[11]

The conviction that an idea lies inside every natural unit of Scripture is enormously helpful as you struggle to connect the spokes of a passage to a big idea.

---

[11] G. D. Fee and D. K. Stuart, *How to Read the Bible for All Its Worth: A Guide to Understanding the Bible*, 2nd ed. (Grand Rapids: Zondervan, 1993), 19.

But don't think it's easy. Sometimes a passage is like a Golden Retriever that rolls on its back begging you to scratch its stomach. It yields without effort. But other times the text resembles a grizzly bear defending her young. You enter the battle more than a little unsure that you are going to win.

John Henry Jowett was right when he said that

I find the getting of that sentence the hardest, the most exacting, and the most fruitful labour in my study. To compel oneself to fashion that sentence, to dismiss every word that is vague, ragged, ambiguous, to think oneself through to a form of words which defines the theme with scrupulous exactness—this is surely one of the most vital and essential factors in the making of a sermon: and I do not think any sermon ought to be preached or even written, until that sentence has emerged clear as a cloudless moon.[12]

Doing the hard exegetical work necessary to identify the authorial intent of a natural unit of Scripture in the form of subject and complement is a necessary step in the creation of deep sermons. But it is not the last step. There is a long, long way to go.

To be biblical, every sermon needs to have an exegetically sound idea at its core. This is the starting point of a sermon. But it is not the destination. Far from it.

For deep preachers, a biblical idea is like freshly harvested grape juice—clean, cool, and refreshing, but a long way from what it could be. With expert care and sufficient time, this juice could become fine wine. It could do more than just quench a temporary thirst; it could explode on your palette with a bouquet of flavors that take your breath away.

What else is there to do? What remains after the exegesis has been completed? Much, much more. So far you have used your resources. Now you need to allow the Holy Spirit to do His work. Now you need to go deep.

---

[12] J. H. Jowett, *The Preacher, His Life and Work* (New York: Doran, 1912), 133.

Chapter 6

Take God's Idea
into Your Closet

I'm not very smart. God reminded me of this a few months ago. I was in a desperate struggle to determine the big idea of the passage I was going to preach that Sunday, when God showed me how ignorant and intellectually arrogant I really was. He revealed my limitations to me.

I was sitting on the couch in my family room at the time with my Mac laptop open and working full tilt. In addition to having four or five windows open to the Internet, my MacBook Pro had the latest version of PowerPoint humming in the background, as well as a copy of Microsoft Windows, within which I was running four of the most respected Bible study programs available today. At the nudging of the Spirit I began to reflect on the amazing amount of computing power and Bible reference tools contained within the shiny slab of metal and plastic that rested on my lap. And the questions that flooded my mind were, "Why does God need me? What 'value added' do I bring to the exegetical process? Why am I even needed?"

The programs on my laptop can exegete a text more effectively than I can. They have a far superior knowledge of the grammar of the ancient languages than I do—or ever will. And they can instantly refer to and cross-reference thousands of electronic books loaded on the hard drive and access the virtually limitless informational resources of the Internet. Unlike me, these programs never forget what they have been taught and can compute data with the speed of an electron. Who am I? I can't even function before my morning coffee!

To make matters even worse, unbelievers also eclipse my exegetical skills. I can go to any secular university and find a faculty member whose facility in the original languages far exceeds my own. So why doesn't God use pagans to communicate Scripture? Some of the most gifted linguists have not been converted. Neither have some very respectable archaeologists. In fact, I have quite a few exegetical tools on the shelves of my library authored by people who have refused to trust in Jesus Christ alone for their salvation.

The question that haunted me was "Why does God need me to interpret the Bible?" I'm clearly not the sharpest tool on His workbench, so why doesn't God just use my laptop or an unbelieving linguistic scholar? Why does God need me? Or you?

The Holy Spirit Teaches Us

The reason that God chooses to use you and me to interpret and communicate His book is because only we can adequately understand His book. Only people who are spiritually alive and enjoy the work of the Holy Spirit in their lives can properly understand God's book, because God's book is unlike any other book ever written. God's book has both a human and a spiritual dimension because it has dual authorship. Scripture consists of the exact words that its human authors chose to write. Scripture also consists of the exact words that the Holy Spirit chose to write. Men and God equally wrote the Bible. Both writers fully accomplished their purposes as they penned it. As the apostle Peter pointed out:

> First of all, you should know this: no prophecy of Scripture comes from one's own interpretation, because no prophecy ever came by the will of man; instead, moved by the Holy Spirit, men spoke from God.[1]

Christians are not necessarily the best interpreters of Ernest Hemingway, William Wordsworth, or Sinclair Lewis. But when it comes to Holy Scripture, however, Christians have a clear edge. Because unlike laptops and atheists, Christians have the Holy Spirit, the Bible's coauthor, residing within us. And one of the things that the Holy Spirit does is give us insight and understanding into His Word.

Jesus knew that we needed more than a seminary education with a high GPA to adequately understand Scripture. This is why He promised His disciples in John 14 that

> "I will ask the Father, and He will give you another Counselor to be with you forever. He is the Spirit of truth. The world is unable to receive Him because it doesn't see Him or know Him. But you do know Him, because He remains with you and will be in you."[2]

---

[1] 2 Pet 1:20–21.
[2] John 14:16–17.

What will the Spirit of truth do? One of His primary ministries is to reveal the truth of His Word. He teaches. The Holy Spirit gives a depth of understanding into the Word of God that cannot be achieved by raw human intellect or Pentium computer processing alone.

"I still have many things to tell you, but you can't bear them now. When the Spirit of truth comes, He will guide you into all the truth. For He will not speak on His own, but He will speak whatever He hears. He will also declare to you what is to come. He will glorify Me, because He will take from what is Mine and declare it to you. Everything the Father has is Mine. This is why I told you that He takes from what is Mine and will declare it to you."[3]

Jesus realized that, as consistently and as effectively as He taught His followers the Scriptures, much more instruction would be required after His ascension. According to Jesus, the Holy Spirit would pick up where Jesus left off. What Jesus did with His disciples on the road to Emmaus, so the Holy Spirit will do for us. Our hearts can also burn with supernatural insight into the biblical text. The joy that all the disciples experienced when the resurrected Christ "opened their minds to understand the Scriptures"[4] can be ours via the teaching ministry of the Holy Spirit.

The Holy Spirit does for us what Jesus did for His disciples. The Spirit helps us cognitively to extend beyond the capacity of our human exegetical skills.

Computer programs and well-educated pagans are capable of understanding the rudimentary elements of a biblical text. They can decline the nouns and parse the verbs just fine, but it takes the supernatural enabling of the Holy Spirit to move beyond mere exegesis to the fuller understanding of Scripture that God intends for his children. It requires the supernatural enabling of the Holy Spirit for us to comprehend and receive all that God intended when he inspired Holy Writ.

As John Calvin pointed out in his *Institutes*,

The testimony of the Spirit is superior to reason. For as God alone can properly bear witness to his own words, so these words will not obtain full credit in the hearts of men, until they are sealed by the inward testimony of the Spirit. . . . For though [Scripture] in its own majesty has enough to command reverence, nevertheless, it then begins truly to touch us when it is sealed in our hearts by the Holy Spirit.[5]

I agree with Millard J. Erickson that the Holy Spirit assists the believer to comprehend the meaning of the biblical text. Insufficient understanding of God's truth is a consequence of sin. Sin inhibits our ability to fully interpret

---

[3] John 16:12–15.
[4] Luke 24:45.
[5] *Institutes* 1:7, 4–5.

Scripture. Sin clouds our vision and injects unconscious presuppositions that bias our understanding of Scripture. Only the Spirit can overcome these noetic effects of sin.[6]

It is impossible to adequately understand the Bible without the assistance of God's Holy Spirit. Human intelligence is not enough. No software is adequate. The Holy Spirit is a critical component of the biblical interpretive process.

The apostle Paul certainly realized the importance of the illuminating work of the Holy Spirit. As undeniably brilliant as he was, Paul knew that his intellect was inadequate for the rigors of biblical interpretation. He knew that nobody is smart enough to understand Scripture on their own. This is why Paul wrote in 1 Corinthians that "the natural man does not welcome what comes from God's Spirit, because it is foolishness to him; he is not able to know it since it is evaluated spiritually."[7] Spiritual insight is required for us to get a grip on what God is saying in His Word. We need God's Holy Spirit to help us wrap our minds around it.

Paul understood that, in addition to our natural faculties, we also need the supernatural faculties of the Holy Spirit. He emphasized the critical role that the Holy Spirit played in his exegesis when he wrote:

> . . . we speak God's hidden wisdom in a mystery, which God predestined before the ages for our glory. None of the rulers of this age knew it, for if they had known it, they would not have crucified the Lord of glory. But as it is written:
>
> "What no eye has seen and no ear has heard,
> and what has never come into a man's heart,
> is what God has prepared for those who love Him."
>
> Now God has revealed them to us by the Spirit, for the Spirit searches everything, even the deep things of God. For who among men knows the concerns of a man except the spirit of the man that is in him? In the same way, no one knows the concerns of God except the Spirit of God. Now we have not received the spirit of the world, but the Spirit who is from God, in order to know what has been freely given to us by God. We also speak these things, not in words taught by human wisdom, but in those taught by the Spirit, explaining spiritual things to spiritual people.[8]

Paul understood the limitations of human-powered exegesis. He had specialized in it before his dramatic confrontation with the risen Christ. He remembered what it was like to study the Scriptures without the assistance of the Holy Spirit. And he wants none of it. The results of human exegesis prac-

---

[6] M. J. Erickson, *Evangelical Interpretation: Perspectives on Hermeneutical Issues* (Grand Rapids: Baker, 1993), 44–45.

[7] 1 Cor 2:14.

[8] 1 Cor 2:7–13.

ticed by the Pharisees were not pretty, and did not lead to godliness. The fruit of their work in the text was soul-deadening. Exegesis that is done without the illuminating work of the Holy Spirit results in the interpreter manipulating the Word rather than allowing God to shape the life of the interpreter. It ultimately leads people away from God rather than toward Him.

It is clear that as he wrote to the Corinthians, the apostle Paul had come to practice a different form of exegesis. Now Paul allows the Spirit to be his teacher. Now he allows the Spirit to instruct him in the Scriptures. It is because of the illuminating work of the Holy Spirit in his intellect that Paul can say in 1 Corinthians 2:16, "For: 'who has known the Lord's mind, that he may instruct Him?' But we have the mind of Christ."

Paul also makes it clear that the illuminating work of the Holy Spirit is to be enjoyed by more than just the apostles. This was clear when Paul wrote to the church in Ephesus that

> I pray that the God of our Lord Jesus Christ, the glorious Father, would give you a spirit of wisdom and revelation in the knowledge of Him. I pray that the eyes of your heart may be enlightened so you may know what is the hope of His calling, what are the glorious riches of His inheritance among the saints.[9]

Paul prayed that the Holy Spirit would teach the laypeople of this church. The letter he was writing was intended to give them important theological information from which they could gain a level of understanding based on their past training. But Paul knew that they needed more than human ability. This is why he was praying that the Holy Spirit would teach them. They needed the Spirit of wisdom in order to know God better, to know God deeply.

People who are aided by the Holy Spirit think differently when they study the Bible. They can understand the Scriptures in ways that laptop computers and secular linguistic scholars will never know. They are led into a fuller comprehension of the biblical text by the author of Scripture.

The Holy Spirit Helps Us Comprehend the Bible

Please do not misunderstand me. I am *not* saying that the Holy Spirit will teach us new truths outside of Scripture. In the Bible, God has given us His complete and sufficient revelation, and none of us should be looking for 3 Corinthians or 1 and 2 Los Angeles. The canon is closed. I take the apostle John's warning in Revelation 22 very seriously.

> I testify to everyone who hears the prophetic words of this book: If anyone adds to them, God will add to him the plagues that are written in this book. And if anyone takes away from the words of this pro-

---

[9] Eph 1:17–18.

phetic book, God will take away his share of the tree of life and the holy city, written in this book.[10]

We do not need additional revelation. Paul was correct when he wrote, "All Scripture is inspired by God and is profitable for teaching, for rebuking, for correcting, for training in righteousness, so that the man of God may be complete, equipped for every good work."[11] The Bible does not lack anything. It is complete.

God's Spirit does all things well, including book writing. When the Holy Spirit inspired Scripture He not only wrote the best-selling book of all time, and the only error-free book ever written, but He also wrote a complete book. His book contains everything He knew we needed to become fully mature in Christ. The Bible was written by the Holy Spirit to teach us who God is and how to live in response to Him. And like most published teachers, the Holy Spirit chooses to use the book He authored as our spiritual textbook.

The Holy Spirit will not lead us away from Scripture. He wrote it to give us the truth He knew we needed. The Bible contains all we require to live in deep relationship with our heavenly Father.

The Holy Spirit Helps Us Comprehend What the Bible Means

The fact that the Holy Spirit is your teacher does not mean you can skip the hard exegetical work in the text that is necessary to determine the authorial intent of the text you will preach. All sermons must be grounded in Scripture. If they aren't, they aren't biblical sermons.

All sermon preparation must begin with a thorough grammatical-historical analysis of a natural unit of Scripture in order to determine the main idea that the original human author and the Holy Spirit placed there. The Holy Spirit extends your mental faculties; He does not replace them.

The Holy Spirit will not teach you what the original author did not intend to communicate to his original audience. To be truly biblical, all exegesis must have as its goal the objective truth that is contained in the biblical text. Haddon Robinson is correct when he says, "A text cannot mean what it never meant."

If Moses were listening to a sermon you were preaching from the book of Exodus, he should not be surprised by your exegesis. If Moses is startled by what you say, then you are not preaching a biblical sermon. The Holy Spirit will not guide you to an interpretation that He did not intend.

I agree with G. B. Caird:

> We have no access to the mind of Jeremiah or Paul except through their recorded words. A fortiori, we have no access to the word of God in the Bible except through the words and the minds of those who claimed to speak in his name. We may disbelieve them, that is our

---

[10] Rev 22:18–19. John was speaking about the book of Revelation when he wrote these words; however, the principle can be extrapolated to apply to the whole of Scripture.

[11] 2 Tim 3:16–17.

right; but if we try, without evidence, to penetrate to a meaning more ultimate than the one the writers intended, that is our meaning, not theirs or God's.[12]

Intimacy with and reliance upon the Holy Spirit will not eliminate the hard exegetical work in the text. Far from it.

But exegetical work alone is inadequate. It is only the first step in the interpretive process. And, as challenging as this first step may be, it is often the easiest step. Deep preaching requires that you have Holy Spirit-assisted insight into the Scriptures you preach. Deep preaching requires more. Much more.

The Homiletical Help of the Holy Spirit

My growing appreciation of the teaching work of the Holy Spirit has led me to rethink and adjust the homiletics process I teach and employ. I used to view the preaching process as outlined below.

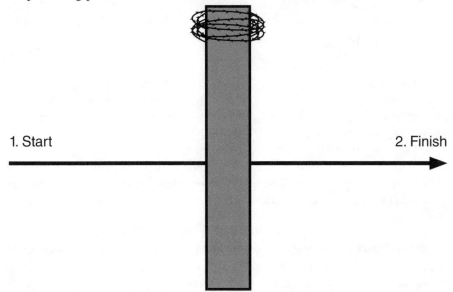

1. There is a time when the preaching event starts. This is when you first learn that you will be preaching on a certain date. At that moment the preaching process begins.

2. There is a time when the sermon is over. This is when the final prayer is given, the final song is sung, and everyone makes his or her way out of the auditorium. Your final responsibility as the preacher is to stand in the foyer and greet the people and respond to the comments of your congregants. At this point there is nothing you can do to change the sermon. It's finished.

---

[12] G. B. Caird, *The Language and Imagery of the Bible* (Philadelphia: Westminster Press, 1980), 61.

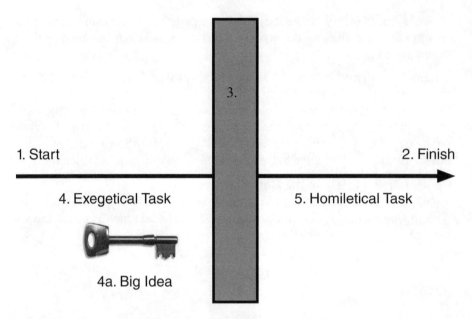

3. It is critical to note, however, that there are two discreet tasks in the process of creating a sermon. I put a vertical wall across this path (with razor wire on top) to show that this process must be bisected into two discreet parts: the exegetical task and the homiletical task.

4. The exegetical task is, as we have seen, to identify the main idea that the original author intended to communicate to the original audience. This idea should be expressed in the form of subject and complement: question and answer. The goal of the exegetical task (4a) is a correct *understanding* of the text.

5. The homiletical task is very different from the exegetical task. On this side of the wall we determine the most effective way to retransmit the idea of the biblical author. Here we ask questions such as: "What do I have to explain about this text to my audience?" "How should I apply this text for my audience?" "What is the most effective way to arrange my material?" The goal of the homiletical task is *communication*.

The reason this diagram has a wall with razor wire separating the exegetical tasks is to emphasize that these tasks must be kept discreet. It is imperative that they not overlap. A common mistake of those who have preached regularly for a few years is the tendency to look at a passage and immediately try and identify the homiletical structure that they could use to preach it. This is a major mistake. Why? Because it is far too easy for preachers to rush at a text, and in their haste to get a sermon for Sunday end up bending the text to say what the author did not originally communicate.

In order to do justice to the text, I find it critical first to spend a significant amount of time in the text doing exegetical work—while I pretend that I will never have to preach it. I tell myself that this is just an academic exercise. I pretend that I am back in seminary writing a paper. I know that my professor doesn't care what idea I present in the conclusion of my paper, as long as I can prove exegetically that it is the main idea of the biblical text.

My sole focus at this stage is to determine the idea that the original author intended to communicate to the original audience. Nothing else. Only when this has been accomplished can I move on. By keeping this single-minded focus I allow the biblical author to control the content of the sermon.

The subject and complement of the natural unit of Scripture becomes the key I use to open the door in the wall. Only when I have the idea firmly in hand can I open the door and cross the barrier to begin the homiletical process.

For many years I have been very happy with the preaching process I have just outlined. I felt that it did justice to the entire preaching process. It treats the exegetical and homiletical tasks with the integrity they deserve. It helped produce sermons that were faithful to the biblical text and relevant to the listeners. I am not alone.

A significant number of preaching books urge their readers to employ a similar methodology. Evangelical homileticians frequently employ some variation of this methodology to teach aspiring ministers how to preach.

The problem I have discovered with this homiletical model, however, is that it doesn't adequately allow for the teaching role of the Holy Spirit. It does not outline how I can enjoy the supernatural input I need to fully proclaim the Word of God.

But what model is better? How can I, as Paul prayed in Ephesians 1:18, have the eyes of my heart supernaturally enlightened as I prepare to preach? How do I open myself to the teaching ministry of the Holy Spirit without sacrificing my respect for the objective meaning of the biblical text?

These questions led to the development of the model below.

Allowing the Holy Spirit to Help Us Comprehend

In the preaching model diagrammed below, the primacy of Scripture is maintained. It does not jettison Scripture in favor of some Gnostic-ish divine knowledge that arrives directly and privately communicated from God to the preacher. It takes J. I Packer's warning of the "insufficiency" of either the

Spirit without the Word or the Word without the Spirit very seriously.[13] The "Deep Preaching" model outlined below recognizes the importance of both Scripture and Spirit.

In this model the exegetical and homiletical tasks retain their integrity by remaining separate. The exegetical task remains the first task of the preacher. There is no sidestepping of the grammatical-historical interpretation of the biblical text in favor of a "mystical" meaning. The goal of the exegetical process remains the identification of the big idea of the biblical text and requires rigorous work in the original languages and culture. This big idea must be the same idea that the original author intended to communicate to his original audience. Any big idea that cannot be sustained by rigorous application of the grammatical-historical examination of the text should not be preached. We must not say in God's name what God did not say.

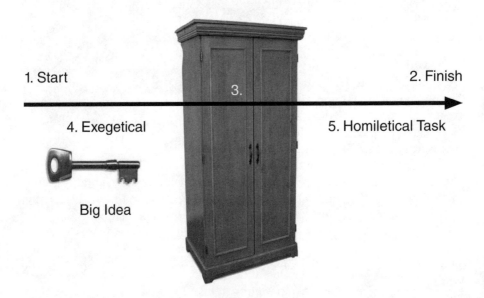

The obvious change in the model is that the wall has been replaced with a closet. Why a closet? This metaphor is borrowed from Jesus' teaching in the Sermon on the Mount where, in His comments on spiritual disciplines, He tells His disciples that when they pray they are not to be like the hypocrites: "But when you pray, go into your private room, shut your door, and pray to your Father who is in secret. And your Father who sees in secret will reward you."[14]

---

[13] "Endless possibilities of self-deception and Satanic befoulment open up the moment we lay aside the Word to follow supposedly direct leadings of the Spirit apart from the Word." J. I. Packer, "The Holy Spirit and His Work," *International Council on Biblical Inerrancy Update* (August 1985): 3.

[14] Matt 6:6.

Deep preaching requires that the preacher take the idea of the biblical text into a place of solitude and intentionally invite the Holy Spirit to participate. The closet is where the preacher shuts the commentaries and listens to God.

The closet is where the Holy Spirit helps us move beyond the elementary understanding of a biblical text. Here the Spirit gives us a fuller comprehension of the biblical text than we could ever accomplish with human energy and ability alone.

What does the Holy Spirit do with us in the closet?

- Closet Work does for the exegete what a supercharger does for a commuter car. It radically improves our exegetical performance.
- Closet Work helps us move beyond the grainy black and white picture of a TV circa 1950 to the breathtaking clarity of a digital high-definition image on a studio quality plasma screen. We see what God is saying in the biblical text with far more clarity than ever before.
- Closet Work allows the Holy Spirit to do for us what an audio headset does for a visitor to a museum. The museum visitors who take advantage of the audio headsets will see the same exhibits as everyone else, but their comprehension of those exhibits will be far better. The visitors with the headsets have the added benefit of having the curator of the museum whisper into their ear about the displays they are looking at. Only those who use the headsets will fully appreciate the displays at which they are looking. Those who decide to do it on their own will gaze admiringly but uncomprehendingly at the wonders that surround them.

  During Closet Work the Holy Spirit whispers in our ears about the wonders of Scripture that surround us. Closet Work gives us a fuller understanding of what we see in the biblical text.

- With our own exegetical resources we stare at the Bible like tourists in downtown Denver looking at the Rocky Mountains. By ourselves all we can see is that there are mountains in the west. But during Closet Work, the Holy Spirit picks us up like a helicopter and takes us to downtown Vail.

  The Holy Spirit will never take us to different mountains than what we saw in the Bible. But the Spirit will help us see those mountains with a clarity that we could never have experienced on our own. With the Holy Spirit's help we can fully comprehend what we saw at a distance.

  During our Closet Work the Spirit takes us by the hand and gives us a guided tour through His creation. We stroll hand in hand with Him through the high meadows, smell the flowers, feel the warmth of the sun, splash in a stream, and taste the ice of a glacier.

As we leave the closet we will say, "On my own I knew that there were Rocky Mountains out there. But I now fully understand these mountains. The abstract has become real. What was distant has become personal. I am comfortable living here."

Any well-educated pagan can understand the grammar of a passage of Scripture. But we need the Holy Spirit in order to adequately comprehend what a text means.

A. W. Tozer understood this. He spoke strongly against the intellectual arrogance of human textualism. Tozer understood textualism as

the belief that the human mind is the supreme authority in the judgment of truth . . . it is *confidence in the ability of the human mind to do that which the Bible declares it was never created to do and consequently is incapable of doing.* . . .

The inward kernel of truth has the same configuration as the outward shell. The mind can grasp the shell but only the Spirit of God can lay hold of the internal essence. Our great error has been that we have trusted to the shell and have believed we were sound in faith because we were able to explain the external shape of truth as found in the letter of the Word.

From this mortal error fundamentalism is dying.[15]

I'm suggesting that you heed Tozer's warning. I urge that you deliberately utilize the Holy Spirit in your preaching by taking the idea of the biblical text into a place of solitude. Go into your spiritual closet, where, alone with God, you use the classic spiritual disciplines of meditation, prayer, and fasting to invite the Holy Spirit to speak. This is what I call homiletical "Closet Work." And it is a deliberate break from the modernistic mind-set of the past.

While I am not a great fan of postmodernity, it does teach us two important lessons. First, that no one is entirely objective. All of us approach issues—and biblical texts—with something less than absolute neutrality. None of us is completely unbiased. Our individual perspective necessarily slants our views. A second lesson of postmodernity is the limitation of rationalistic modernity. In the modern age people believed that they were smart enough to solve the problems of the world. With the right technology and enough education, modernists believed that there was no problem they could not conquer. "We can solve anything and everything." Postmodernists listened to modernity's audacious claims and looked at the evidence. They looked at the fruit of

---

15 A. W. Tozer, *God's Pursuit of Man* (Camp Hill, PA: WingSpread Publishers, 2007), 79–80.

modernity—nuclear terror, global warming and massive economic disparity—and stated the obvious: modernity is bankrupt. It did not deliver what it promised.

Postmoderns point out that people are not smart enough to cure the world's problems. Human intelligence has serious limitations. It is the height of arrogance for us to pretend that we have the resources to solve the big issues of life. Our human limitations cry out for help.

When we go into our closet we are acknowledging our human limitations. In humility we walk away from the modernist façade that purports by its practice that seminary education is all that is required to fully understand God's divine book. The closet is an acknowledgment of our limitations and a cry for help. It is a request for the Holy Spirit to be our Bible teacher.

Closet Work embraces the humility that postmodernity has taught us. We are not omni-competent. We need help to grasp the big ideas of Scripture. It is an acknowledgment that the only way we can adequately understand the meaning of a passage of inspired literature is by asking the God who inspired it.

Avoid the temptation to rush toward outlines, illustrations, and the like. Until your "Closet Work" is completed, don't do any homiletical work. Don't think about how you will arrange your material before you comprehend what you are going to say.

The Holy Spirit Takes Us Deep

The secret of "Deep Preaching" is the Holy Spirit. Those preachers who allow the Holy Spirit to be their teacher are able to plumb to the depths of the ocean of God's Word and enter into a wonderfully richer understanding of Scripture. Those who rely exclusively on their own exegetical expertise stay stuck on the surface of the Bible's meaning. They bob about on the surface of the biblical text trying vainly to peer below its surface into the wonders below. As regenerate exegetes, we have an amazing intellectual resource! The Holy Spirit wants to teach us. He wants to click on His light in our mind and let us see more fully what is written on the pages of Scripture.

Yet how infrequently do I rely on the Holy Spirit to teach me? And how easy do I find it to fire up my laptop, open a word study book, or crack a commentary? Why do I not take the teaching ministry of the Holy Spirit as seriously as Jesus and Paul did? What would happen if I relied upon the Spirit as much as I did my exegetical training? What would this do to my understanding of Scripture? My relationship with God? My preaching?

The illuminating work of the Holy Spirit made a significant difference in Paul's preaching. The Spirit enabled Paul to go deep in two ways. First, He enabled Paul to see deeply into the content of the Scripture he was preaching. This is why Paul could comment on his own preaching in 1 Corinthians 2:13, "We also speak these things, not in words taught by human wisdom, but in those taught by the Spirit, explaining spiritual things to spiritual people."

Paul's sermons were not strung together clichés sung to familiar tunes. Like Jesus' teaching, Paul's sermonic material was fresh and authoritative, because God taught him the truths directly.

The Holy Spirit's work of illumination had a second influence on Paul's preaching. In addition to influencing directly the content of Paul's sermons, the Holy Spirit also directly influenced the *response* of those who listened to Paul's messages. The Holy Spirit-inspired sermons that Paul preached received a dramatic response by those who heard them. Positively or negatively, few people walked away bored from the apostle Paul's preaching. The Holy Spirit so worked within the truth of the sermons He had illuminated that people were forced either to accept completely or dramatically reject what they heard. And Paul knew this. He said to those to whom he preached in Thessalonica, "For our gospel did not come to you in word only, but also in power, in the Holy Spirit, and with much assurance."[16]

Paul was not surprised that his sermons elicited such dramatic response. Why wouldn't they? God has always used His Word to make a dramatic difference in His world and in the lives of those who populate it.

The unusual power of Paul's sermons stemmed from their unusual source. Unlike most of the preachers of his day, Paul preached what the Holy Spirit taught him from the Word of God and watched God use His words to transform lives. Paul says in Colossians 1:28, "We proclaim Him, warning and teaching everyone with all wisdom, so that we may present everyone mature in Christ." Paul preached with the confidence of a person who knows that what they were saying came straight from the mind of Christ.

What is surprising, however, is that the illuminating work of the Holy Spirit is not restricted to apostles. We can all enjoy the mind of Christ in our sermon preparation process. In fact Paul wants every believer, ordained and lay, to enjoy the illuminating work of the Holy Spirit. This is especially clear in his letter to the Colossians. He wants these believers to know that

> since the day we heard about you, we have not stopped praying for you and asking God to fill you with the knowledge of his will through all *spiritual wisdom and understanding.*[17]

And he exhorts these dear people to

> let the word of Christ dwell in you richly as you teach and admonish one another with all *wisdom,* and as you sing psalms, hymns and spiritual songs with gratitude in your hearts to God.[18]

The illuminating work of the Holy Spirit is available to all believers. It is available to you. Take advantage of it.

---

[16] 1 Thess 1:5.

[17] Col 1:9, NIV, emphasis added.

[18] Col 3:16, NIV, emphasis added.

Ask for Help

When the only exegetical tools you use to understand Scripture are dusty books written by long-dead scholars, it should be no surprise that your sermons have a musty odor. If the software embedded within your plastic laptop dominates your sermon preparation, your sermons will sound faked. When we limit ourselves to human exegesis, we choose to deliver messages of clay.

I am convinced that much of the shallow preaching pervading America can be traced to exegesis that has been done in the power of the flesh. Anemic sermons flow from our refusal to allow the Holy Spirit to teach us. Please don't try and "go it alone."

The Holy Spirit was not only personally involved in the inspired writing of Holy Writ, but He continues to personally help His children comprehend what He wrote. He inspired Scripture in the past and illuminates it in the present. Why not ask the author of the book you are preaching to help you understand what He wrote?

Don't rush your exegetical idea to the pulpit. First go to your closet and invite the Holy Spirit to speak. Ask Him to help you gain a greater comprehension of His word. And listen to what the Holy Spirit whispers back to you.

You are not smart enough to preach a deep sermon. No one is. We need the Holy Spirit to help us.

Chapter 7

Grasp the Grandeur

On a beautiful evening in 1901, a cowboy working in New Mexico named Jim White noticed something strange rising out of the ground up into the sky. At first he thought it was a column of smoke, but there was no fire. What was it?

As Jim would later recount: "During my life on the range I'd seen plenty of prairie whirlwinds, but this thing didn't move: it remained in one spot, spinning its way upward. I watched it for perhaps a half hour until my curiosity got the better of me. Then I began investigating."

What Jim White found was a large hole in the ground and a countless number of bats flying up into the night sky. "I . . . sat for perhaps an hour watching bats fly out. I couldn't estimate the number, but I knew that it must run into millions. The more I thought of it the more I realized that any hole in the ground which could house such a gigantic army of bats must be a whale of a big cave. I crept between cactus until I lay on the brink of the chasm, and looked down. During all the years I'd known of the place, I'd never taken the trouble to do this. There was no bottom in sight! I shall never forget the feeling of aweness it gave me."[1]

The "aweness" of peering into the mouth of the large cave grew exponentially when he was able to climb underground. What Jim White saw below the surface changed the course of his life.

"I returned to the cave with some crude tools and a kerosene lantern. I cut sticks of wood from nearby shrubs and built a rope ladder in order to descend into the mouth of the cave." When White ran out of rope, he lit his lantern and

---

[1] http://www.pbs.org/weekendexplorer/newmexico/carlsbad/carlsbad_white.htm (accessed 9/27/08).

saw a tunnel off to his right about 20 feet down. Holding onto the wall, he descended into a huge chamber.

"I explored the tunnel to the left first, finding the bat cave. Returning to the large room, I headed for the tunnel to the right where I saw a wonderland. Enormous stalagmites rose from the floor, clusters of stalactites in a variety of colors hung from above and onyx-lined pools full of pure water sparkled brilliantly on the floor."

Jim White had discovered the Carlsbad Caverns. He came back to the caves again and again, often staying as long as three days within the caves. In time he decided to devote his life to exploring their beauty. The years he spent in their depths made Jim the foremost authority on the caverns.

But the cowboy didn't want to keep his find to himself. The more he saw below the surface the more he wanted to show others.

He built and installed a series of ladders and pathways that made the caves more accessible. He even invented a "bucket elevator" to give visitors an opportunity to fully access the wonders that lay below the surface. And those who had no money got their tour for free. Jim White couldn't help himself. He felt compelled to show people the beauty he had discovered below the surface, to help people appreciate the grandeur beneath their gaze.

Deep preachers do with the biblical text what Jim White did with the Carlsbad Caverns. Like Jim White, we are not content to lie on the surface of the text. Deep preachers climb down into it and spend time personally exploring its breathtaking beauty. We are not satisfied with reading books and watching documentaries about other people's explorations. We expend our own time and energy to encounter personally the depths of God's wonders for the benefit of others.

Deep preachers grasp the cavernous grandeur of God's Word so that others can gape openmouthed at what God hath wrought.

The tools we need to climb down into the richness of God's Word are not rope ladders and lanterns. Our explorations require the use of the classic spiritual disciplines. Closet work is a prerequisite to deep preaching. \|

Closetphobia

Many of us suffer from a deeply personal fear of spiritual closets. "Closet-phobia" does not stem from claustrophobia, because Closest Work doesn't require that you sit in an actual closet! Closetphobia arises from a fear of still-ness. We fear Closet Work because we are so unfamiliar with solitude. |

Bernie Krause is a bioacoustician. He records natural sounds such as ani-mals, thunderstorms, waves breaking on the beach, leaves blowing in the wind, and the like. In a 2007 interview Krause said, "fully 30 percent of my library from 30 years of work comes from extinct habitats. Habitats we can't record anymore, because there's no natural sound." What happened to the natural sound? It was destroyed by noise pollution. Our world is becoming increas-ingly noisy. For a person trying to record just a robin singing—without a car or jackhammer in the background—this can be a real problem. "When I started in 1968, it used to take me 14 or 15 hours of recording to get an hour of usable material (undefiled by background noise.) Now it takes me a year to get that same amount of material."[2]

Bernie Krause spends his life tramping to and around remote locations try-ing in vain to find the sound of silence. If it takes him a year to collect an hour of silence, what are the chances that you and I are going to stumble across silence this week? We are inundated by noise. We live in a cacophony of clat-ter. When do we power down our iPod and remove the battery from our cell phone? Does God ever get a chance to speak softly into our lives, or do our noisy lives drown Him out?

| Silence is not the only aspect of our spiritual closet that frightens us. We also fear its ability to force us to focus. A spiritual closet not only shuts out the noise of life, but it is the only place where we cannot do two, three, or four things at once. The closet forces us to focus on just one thing. And that feels strange.

Multitasking defines life in the twenty-first century. We do not know how to do one thing at a time. We prize efficiency and value "using our time twice." Why just drive when you can also catch up on your phone calls? Take your iPhone to the staff meeting; if things go slow you can respond to the emails piling up in your inbox. Stuff your BlackBerry into your beach bag. Write a memo in the evening with the TV on.

> Working parents spend a quarter of their waking hours multitasking. Grafted to our cell phones, we drive like drunks; even if it kills us, we get that call. Instant-messaging's disjointed, pause-button flavor makes it the perfect multitasking communications medium. More than

---

[2] http://emusician.com/em_spotlight/bernie_krause_interview/ (accessed 9/29/08).

half of instant-message users say they always Web surf, watch TV, talk on the phone, or play computer games while IM'ing.[3]

We spend our lives like air traffic controllers, splitting our attention between a hundred distractions circling overhead, seldom concentrating on a single task. Our cultural aversion to silence and focus keeps us out of our spiritual closets.

We would do well to learn from the priority that Jesus placed on finding places of solitude to focus on the things of God. "Jesus made silence and solitude his special companions. . . . His hectic teaching and ministering was constantly punctuated by these times of withdrawal."[4]

Jesus began His ministry in the wilderness.[5] He chose His disciples after spending a night alone in prayer.[6] Jesus sought the solace of solitude after John the Baptist's death.[7] And Jesus wouldn't face the horrors of the cross without first having some serious alone time in Gethsemane.[8] All through His life Jesus made sure that He set aside serious "face time" with His God. And He taught His disciples to do the same.

To become a deep preacher you will have to become more like Jesus and less like the cultural norm. Deep preaching requires you to be countercultural. It requires you to embrace the quietness and focus that wait in your spiritual closet.

What will you take with you into your quiet closet? Forget the latest gadgets that clutter and distract you. All you need for Closet Work are the classic spiritual disciplines.

Understanding the Spiritual Disciplines

The Bible assumes that the people of God regularly practice spiritual disciplines. These are the private ordinances that *ought* to be part of every Christian's life but *must* be part of a preacher's life. If your listeners fail to practice the disciplines, they impoverish their own spiritual lives. But if you fail, the entire congregation suffers.

While discussion continues regarding the merits of some of the more contemporary spiritual exercises, the value of the basic disciplines is unquestionable. The spiritual disciplines of meditation, prayer, and fasting have an indisputable place in the Christian life. While some may argue that the list of disciplines could be expanded, no one suggests that it should be shortened. Meditation,

---

[3] M. Jackson, *Distracted: The Erosion of Attention and the Coming Dark Age* (Amherst, NY: Prometheus Books, 2008), 74.

[4] D. Runcorn, *A Center of Quiet: Hearing God When Life Is Noisy* (Downers Grove, IL: InterVarsity Press, 1990), 4.

[5] Matt 4:1–11.

[6] Luke 6:12.

[7] Matt 14:13.

[8] Matt 26:36–46.

prayer, and fasting are foundational practices of the Christian life. They must be grafted into your life.

Meditation

Biblical meditation is not exegesis. It is not trying to understand what the grammar of a biblical text is communicating. Meditation begins when exegesis is finished.

The basic meaning of the Hebrew words translated into English as meditation is "a low sound, characteristic of the moaning of a dove (Isa 38:14; 59:11) or the growling of a lion over its prey (Isa 31:4)."[9] To meditate is to "growl" over a text as a lion would over the carcass of its prey. Lions growl with satisfaction over the carcass of their victim after a successful hunt. They purr with self-congratulation every time they take a bite. A lion exults in its position as the conquering "king of the jungle" every time he savors the taste of his quarry. And the growling continues as long as the meal—sometimes for days or even weeks. God calls us to meditate over Scripture the way that the lion growls over its prey.

To understand how meditation works, try imagining a marine serving his country at some distant overseas posting. Suppose that marine decided in the loneliness of his barracks to write a letter to his high school sweetheart—and to ask for her hand in marriage. How much time do you think he would take to compose that letter? Twenty hours? Thirty? And during that time, how many times would he rewrite it? A dozen times perhaps? But every time he put his pen down he would obsess anew over what he had written. Did he say it correctly? Could it be phrased better? How will she hear this? It may take an entire week of obsessing over this letter until he was satisfied with that single sheet of paper. What that marine did when he wrote his letter is what we are to do when we read God's letter. What that marine called obsession, the Bible calls meditation. It means to think and consider from every possible angle.

Biblical meditation means that after we have subdued the meaning of a biblical passage, we take the time to murmur over it. Meditation means taking the time, effort, and energy to linger over what God is saying—to murmur about it the way a teenager will murmur after being told that they must vacuum the house before they can go out with friends. What do teenagers do when parents ask them to do such an "onerous" task? They meditate on what they have just been told. They push the vacuum cleaner while mumbling under their breath—and the noise of the vacuum—how unjust the whole situation is. For the entire time it takes to complete the chore they mumble under their breath things like:

---

[9] R. L. Harris, G. L. Archer, B. K. Waltke, *Theological Wordbook of the Old Testament*, electronic ed. (Chicago: Moody, 1980; repr. 1999, c1980), S. 205.

I'm sure that nobody else's parents are as mean as mine.
I just vacuumed last weekend!
My brother gets easier chores than I do.
I wonder if my friends will wait for me?
The rugs don't even need vacuuming. They look fine!

Biblical meditation involves taking the time to examine a biblical truth from every angle to consider its implications, to review, reflect, and feel the text, and to enter into the emotion of the text.

When God called Ezekiel to minister to the Israelites, he handed Ezekiel a scroll of His words. But God's command to His prophet was unlike any seminary syllabus I have ever read. God did not tell him to exegete the scrolls or to memorize them or to compare and contrast their wording with other ancient scrolls. Instead,

> He said to me: "Son of man, eat what you find here. Eat this scroll, then go and speak to the house of Israel." So I opened my mouth, and He fed me the scroll. "Son of man," he said to me, "eat and fill your stomach with this scroll I am giving you." So I ate litl, and it was as sweet as honey in my mouth.[10]

Biblical mediation involves an academic understanding of a text but goes beyond that. It means that we internalize the text. We ingest it. We allow it to become part of who we are. Meditation goes beyond distant objectivity. When we meditate we take truth out of the exegetical petri dish and put it on our tongue.

When we meditate we treat the truth of Scripture as a child would devour a homemade popsicle. When I was a child my mother would make popsicles by pouring juice into a Tupperware mold and letting it solidify in our kitchen freezer. We couldn't wait for the "frozen juice on a stick" to emerge from the freezer so that we could take our time and enjoy it. We didn't just chew it; we sucked it. We would suck the top of the popsicle as hard as we could. We sucked until all of the color and the taste was gone. We sucked until nothing was left on the plastic stick but a column of ice. We invested the time and energy necessary to extract every particle of flavor that my mother had put in.

This is what God wants us to do with His Word. He wants us to suck on it, to extract everything He put in. He wants us to roll its truth around on our tongue, to fully experience all that a passage contains. This is what the psalmist is talking about in Psalm 1.

> How happy is the man who[se] . . . delight is in the LORD's instruction, and he meditates on it day and night. He is like a tree planted beside streams of water that bears its fruit in season and whose leaf does not wither. Whatever he does prospers.[11]

---

[10] Ezek 3:1–3.
[11] Ps 1:1–3; insert mine.

The happy man is the one who "delights" in the Lord's instruction. It is not a duty for him to read Scripture. It is not a burden for him to exegete a unit of Scripture. It is a joy—a delight. It is so delightful that he meditates on it "day and night." The happy man cannot keep himself from thinking about what he has discovered. He growls over it as he drives to work. He contemplates it as he grabs lunch. He sucks on it like a frozen treat in a summer heat wave.

> *What does this mean about the way I work?*
> *Should I change my investments?*
> *Why would God say this?*
> *Is it in my best interest to obey this truth?*

In a later chapter I will give you a series of questions that you can use to guide your meditation, but for now just realize what God is asking when He asks us to meditate. He is asking us to ruminate on His Word and to probe it from every possible angle.

God personally emphasized the importance of biblical meditation to Joshua. After the death of Moses, God came to Israel's new leader and promised to help him in his new role. How comforting it must have been for Joshua to hear God say, "No one will be able to stand against you as long as you live. I will be with you, just as I was with Moses. I will not leave you or forsake you."[12]

At the same time, however, God outlined to Joshua the part he was to play in their new relationship. Joshua's responsibility was to meditate on Scripture.

> Be strong and very courageous. Be careful to obey all the law my servant Moses gave you; do not turn from it to the right or to the left, that you may be successful wherever you go. Do not let this Book of the Law depart from your mouth; meditate on it day and night, so that you may be careful to do everything written in it. Then you will be prosperous and successful.[13]

Notice, once again, that meditation is, by definition, an extended process. The standard way that many of us were taught to have our "devotions" do not come close to what the Bible means by meditation. Meditation cannot be accomplished in "Seven Minutes with God." Those seven minutes may be wonderful and beneficial, but they do not include meditation. Meditation starts in solitude, but it does not stop there. We carry our Spiritual Closet with us as we go through life. Meditation occurs as we reflect on Scripture throughout our day. We are never to stop thinking about it.

Those who meditate on Scripture will reap a significant harvest. Meditation gifts its practitioners with twin rewards: intellectual and moral.

Intellectually, meditation gives you a superior grasp—a *deeper understanding*—of the biblical text. The psalmist points this out in Psalm 119:97–99,

---

[12] Josh 1:5.
[13] Josh 1:7–8, NIV.

> How I love Your teaching!
> It is my meditation all day long.
> Your command makes me wiser than my enemies,
> for it is always with me.
> I have more insight than all my teachers
> because Your decrees are my meditation.[14]

According to the psalmist, the best way to understand the Bible is to consider it from every angle, to mull it over, to incubate its precepts until they hatch. If you do, your biblical insight will exceed that which lies on the tongues of your teachers—or on the library shelves of the schools that employ them.

Consider this the next time you quickly run toward the commentaries on your shelf or your hard drive. When you skip meditation you miss out on the depth of insight that the Holy Spirit wants to give you. But meditation promises to improve more than just your intellect.

Meditation also results in *moral transformation*. The Scriptures we mutter make an indelible mark on our lives. As the psalmist continues his comments on meditation in Psalm 119:100–102, his comments move from head to feet. It seems that as our understanding of Scripture grows, the prospects for godliness enjoy a commensurate improvement.

> How can a young man keep his way pure?
> By keeping Your word.
> I have sought You with all my heart;
> don't let me wander from Your commands.
> I have treasured Your word in my heart
> so that I may not sin against You.[15]

The more time that we spend in meditation the deeper its truths are pressed into our lives. Meditation does for your soul what stain does for raw wood. If you are a woodworker you know that you have options when it comes to stain. You can pour stain onto a piece of unfinished furniture and immediately wipe it off. If you do this, the impact of the stain is slight. Stain that does not stay long does not make a significant change in the color of the wood. If, however, you take the stain and spend hours with a cloth rubbing it deep into the wood, the effect is entirely different. When you invest a significant time and "elbow grease" the stain doesn't just sit on the surface. The stain is pressed down deeply into the grain of the wood.

As you spend time meditating on the truth of Scripture you are rubbing it deeper and deeper into your soul. You are deepening the patina of your life. You are taking on the hue of your Savior. You are becoming increasingly godly. And the results will be lasting.

---

[14] Ps 119:97–99.

[15] Ps 119:9–11.

Please don't make the mistake of thinking that the spiritual discipline of meditation is an onerous or unpleasant assignment. Nothing could be farther from the truth. Meditation on Scripture leads to increased understanding, which leads to increased obedience, which leads to increased success in life. In fact the psalmist declares in Psalm 19:9b–10 that

> the ordinances of the LORD are reliable
> and altogether righteous.
> They are more desirable than gold—
> than an abundance of pure gold;
> and sweeter than honey—
> than honey dripping from the comb.

The psalmist discovers in his time of mediation what Ezekiel found out; that the Scriptures are delicious! It is a treat to be able to bite down on God's ideas because we can chomp with confidence. Not only does God give us exactly what we need, but His ideas will never hurt you. On the contrary, they will enrich your life beyond your wildest imagination. In keeping them there is great reward! The writer of Psalm 1 agrees, "Whatever [the person who meditates] does prospers."[16]

Meditating on Scripture has been likened to a cow chewing its cud, and it turns out that the analogy works! According to Donna M. Amaral-Phillips, the Extension Dairy Nutritionist at the University of Kentucky, when a dairy cow chews her cud, she is regurgitating, rechewing, and reswallowing food that was eaten earlier. As unappetizing as this sounds, cows work very hard to make sure that they reap all of the nutritional benefits out of the food they eat. How hard? "Dairy cows spend almost 8 hrs a day chewing their cuds for a total of almost 30,000 chews daily."[17] That is a lot of chewing!

While I prefer to eat my meals just once, we could learn a thing or two from our four-legged friends when it comes to Scripture. Too often we gulp down the truths of Scripture as quickly as 99-cent hamburgers at a fast food joint. How much better off would we be—as well as our listeners—if we were to slow down and chew on the truth we exegeted? It's time we gave serious thought about the truth we preach. It is time we brought the classic spiritual discipline of meditation back into the sermon preparation process.

How much time should we spend in meditation? It all depends. When my wife realizes that a cut of meat is particularly tough, she allows it to marinate longer. Her rule is: the tougher the meat, the longer it needs to be in the marinade. The same principle applies to meditation. The tougher a passage is for you to get your mind and heart around, the more time you will need to set aside.

---

[16] Ps 1:3; insert mine.

[17] D. M. Amaral-Phillips, Extension Dairy Nutritionist, University of Kentucky http://www.uky.edu/Ag/AnimalSciences/dairy/extension/nut00014.pdf (accessed 9/29/08).

It is worth noting, however, that both Psalm 1:2 and Joshua 1:8 speak of meditating "day and night." These passages do not refer to just a set "meditation" time blocked off in our daily schedule. That would be a good idea, but it would not exhaust the instruction of these passages. In Psalm 1 and Joshua 1 we are urged to go through our days in a spirit of meditation. After our exegesis is complete we are to suck on the biblical truth as if it were a piece of hard candy. Let it sit on your tongue all day and coat you with its flavor. Mull it over. Mutter about it. Chew on it. And you can do this as you commute, cut the grass, or clear the dishes. Spend your days meditating on truth.

This is what Moses was telling Israel to do when he told them, "Impress these words of Mine on your hearts and souls, bind them as a sign on your hands, and let them be a symbol on your foreheads."[18] Don't just read your Bible chapter for the day and go on for the day. Keep what you have read before you all through the day.

Is meditation worth all the effort? Before we start short-cutting around the discipline of meditation, we would be wise to hear the words of the respected Puritan William Bates.

> ✟ If I should be asked what do I think is that best means and way to advance the Faculties, to make the Ordinances Fruitful, to increase Grace, to enlarge our Comfort, to Produce Holiness and the like, I should answer, Meditation, Meditation, Meditation.[19]

For the sake of our own souls, as well as those who will come to hear us preach, we would be wise to meditate on the Scripture passages we will preach.

Prayer

Writing to preachers about prayer is like speaking to bankers about money. Because our profession requires us to handle it on a daily basis we think we have mastered it.

We pray in the pulpit. We pray when we take parishioners out for lunch. We pray during hospital visitation. Through the years we have preached many sermons on "the need for prayer," "the power of prayer," and "how to pray." We've quoted James 5:16, "The intense prayer of the righteous is very powerful" so many times it rings in our ears like a cliché. We've preached about Elijah's display of prayer on Mount Carmel with great enthusiasm. Our parishioners consider us prayer experts. And sometimes we agree with this perception. But do we pray? Do *you* pray?

---

[18] Deut 11:18.

[19] W. Bates, *A Discourse of Divine Meditation*, in *The Works of the Late Reverend and Learned William Bates* (London: For B. Alymer and J. Robison, 1700; Ann Arbor: University Microfilms, 1981, microfilm), 893 as quoted in G. K. Daniel, "The Puritan Ladder of Meditation" (unpublished M.A. diss.; Trinity Evangelical Divinity School, 1993), 34.

I am not asking you if you "say your prayers." I'm pushing beyond a "check-up" of your devotional life. I'm asking if prayer is a distinguishing element of your life.

We know from the Gospels that Jesus' life was seasoned with prayer, and that prayer characterized the early church. What we may have overlooked, however, is that in the New Testament, prayer was not limited to specific times and locations. While there were special places and times set aside for prayer, prayer was not quarantined within those places and times. Christian prayer bursts the boundaries of time and space. The New Testament church prayed constantly. And so should we.

The word most commonly used by the writers of the New Testament to express the continual nature of Christian prayer is *proskarterō*. The term was regularly used in everyday first-century speech. According to Kittel's *Theological Dictionary of the New Testament*:

> its basic meaning is "to stay by," "to persist at," "to remain with."
> 1. In connection with persons it means "to be loyal to someone," . . .
> 2. In connection with objects it means a. "to occupy oneself diligently with something," "to pay persistent attention to."[20]

In Romans 13:6 *proskarterō* is used by the apostle Paul to explain why we pay taxes to the state. According to Paul we should pay taxes because "the authorities are God's servants, who give their *full time* to governing."[21] Paul's argument is that we need to pay the wages of civil servants because they don't have time to earn money any other way. They are fully and constantly engaged in their governmental responsibilities.

The word *proskarterō* is used by Jesus in Mark 3:9 when "he told his disciples to have a small boat ready for him, to keep the people from crowding him" (NIV). Why did Jesus ask for the boat? The consensus among commentators is that "it appears to be simply a means of temporary physical escape"[22] in case the crowds became threatening. The boat was Jesus' escape plan in case He was mobbed. The boat was for Jesus what a get-away car is for a bank robber. In Mark 3:9 Jesus asks the disciples to keep the boat in a *constant* state of readiness. Jesus' command meant that the disciples *continued* at "red alert" status with the boat while Jesus preached.

This is how we are to pray—full time, constantly, unceasingly, without a break. The word *proskarterō* is used ten times in the New Testament, mostly in the context of prayer.

---

[20] G. Kittel, G. W. Bromiley, G. Friedrich, *Theological Dictionary of the New Testament*, electronic ed. (Grand Rapids: Eerdmans, 1964–c1976), S. 3:618.

[21] Rom 13:6, NIV; italics added.

[22] R. T. France, *The Gospel of Mark: A Commentary on the Greek Text* New International Greek Testament Commentary (Grand Rapids/Carlisle: Eerdmans/Paternoster, 2002), 154.

In Acts 1:14 we learn that the very early believers "were continually (*proskarterō*) united in prayer, along with the women, including Mary the mother of Jesus, and His brothers."[23] Here *proskarterō* is used in reference to prayer. The emphasis that Luke is giving to the prayer life of these people is obvious. These people were not just having devotions, they were giving themselves to constant prayer. And this was not a temporary state of affairs.

We read in Acts 2:42 that "They were continually (*proskarterō*) devoting themselves to the apostles' teaching and to fellowship, to the breaking of bread and to prayer."[24] Here Luke emphasizes the continual nature of their actions. The post-Pentecost church that we admire so highly was very serious about prayer. These people were not satisfied with just "going to church"; they took church with them as they went through life.

In case you are tempted to think that this constancy in prayer was just an early church aberration—like how a contemporary teenage crush often results in a temporarily stratospheric number of cell phone calls and text messages—the apostle Paul moves this emphasis on prayer from the descriptive to the prescriptive.

In Romans 12:11–12 Paul tells his readers, "Do not lack diligence; be fervent in spirit; serve the Lord. Rejoice in hope; be patient in affliction; be persistent (*proskarterō*) in prayer."[25] He underscores the importance of placing this priority on prayer in Colossians 4:2 when he instructs us to "Devote (*proskarterō*) yourselves to prayer; stay alert in it with thanksgiving."[26] This is a double-stacked emphasis on the importance of placing special focus on prayer. He is calling for constant, continuous prayer.

Paul knew the implications of placing such high expectations on the prayer lives of his listeners because he practiced what he preached. He lived the life of prayer that he asks us to embrace.

In Ephesians 1:15–19 Paul wrote,

> This is why, since I heard about your faith in the Lord Jesus and your love for all the saints, I **never stop** giving thanks for you as I remember you in my prayers. I pray that the God of our Lord Jesus Christ, the glorious Father, would give you a spirit of wisdom and revelation in the knowledge of Him. I pray that the eyes of your heart may be enlightened so you may know what is the hope of His calling, what are the glorious riches of His inheritance among the saints, and what is the immeasurable greatness of His power to us who believe, according to the working of His vast strength.[27]

---

23 Greek word inserted.
24 NASB; Greek word inserted.
25 Greek word inserted.
26 Greek word inserted.
27 Emphasis mine in bold.

The word translated as "stop" in the HCSB means "to come to an end, take one's rest, a willing cessation."[28] According to Paul's own words, he has *never stopped* praying for his friends in Ephesus. He *continually* remembers them before his heavenly Father. Is Paul's closet confession to the church in Ephesus the exception rather than the rule? Is it an anomaly to his typical practice? I don't think so.

Colossians 1:9–10 reverberates with the same sentiment.

> For this reason also, since the day we heard this, we **haven't stopped praying** for you. We are asking that you may be filled with the knowledge of His will in all wisdom and spiritual understanding, so that you may walk worthy of the Lord, fully pleasing to Him, bearing fruit in every good work and growing in the knowledge of God.[29]

Paul didn't just say his prayers at the end of his day. He prayed until the end of his day. He lived in constant prayerful contact with the God he loved. He talked to God as constantly as some of us text our BFF. And Paul asks us to imitate his exemplary prayer life.

Paul is clear in the epistles that his pattern of unending prayer is to become our practice.

> Pray in the Spirit on all occasions with all kinds of prayers and requests. With this in mind, be alert and *always keep on praying* for all the saints.[30]

> Don't worry about anything, but *in everything, through prayer and petition with thanksgiving, let your requests be made known to God.* And the peace of God, which surpasses every thought, will guard your hearts and your minds in Christ Jesus.[31]

> Rejoice always! *Pray constantly.* Give thanks in everything, for this is God's will for you in Christ Jesus.[32]

Paul is calling us to give up our amateur prayer life. He wants us to push beyond our "bush league" attitudes and treat prayer as a necessary discipline. We can be "weekend warriors" when it comes to tennis or jogging but *not* with prayer. Paul is telling us to go beyond giving prayer a nominal place in our schedules. He is asking us to make prayer the atmosphere of our lives—to live within it and for prayer to become as natural and effortless to us as breathing. Prayer is to be an autonomic element of our spiritual lives, part of everything we do. So essential that it would be death for us to stop.

---

[28] S. Zodhiates, *The Complete Word Study Dictionary: New Testament*, electronic ed. (Chattanooga: AMG Publishers, 2000, c1992, c1993), S. G3973.

[29] Emphasis mine in bold.

[30] Eph 6:18, NIV, emphasis mine

[31] Phil 4:6–7, emphasis mine.

[32] 1 Thess 5:16–18, emphasis mine.

Paul wants prayer to burst the boundaries of Wednesday night prayer meeting. He is asking us, like Brother Lawrence, to "practice the presence of Christ." He calls us to live life in an attitude of prayer.

Where did Paul learn this radical attitude about prayer? I think he got it from Jesus. In Luke 18 Jesus told the parable of the persistent widow, encouraging us to be persistent in prayer. Don't stop, Jesus was saying. Keep it up! Stay in prayer. Persist in prayer.

It is significant that one of the very few situations that caused Jesus to lose His temper was when God's people demonstrated a low view of prayer. Luke tells us how after His triumphal entry Jesus

> went into the temple complex and began to throw out those who were selling, and He said, "It is written, My house will be a house of prayer, but you have made it a den of thieves!"[33]

Jesus gets angry when people sacrifice the practice of prayer in favor of the business of life. He wants us to treat prayer as seriously—and practice it as constantly—as He did. He wants us to do what Paul did, not just know what Paul said.

God's call to constant prayer extends to all of His children. It is especially important, however, for preachers to live in an atmosphere of prayer. Why? Consider the role of prayer in the preaching of the early church.

The Preacher's Prayer Life

In the early chapters of Acts we become privy to one of the most exciting eras in the history of the church. In these chapters we witness the apostles ministering with great power and enjoying huge response. The church was growing exponentially. Unbelievers were repenting and placing their trust in Jesus Christ by the thousands, while believers were taking large strides toward maturity in Christ. Why? A major reason for this accelerated spiritual growth was the apostles' powerful preaching.

You are probably familiar with Peter's unparalleled Pentecost sermon recorded in Acts 2. This sermon played an undeniably significant role in the birth of the New Testament church. While we are rightly impressed with the 3,000 who responded that day, we should not forget that Peter's sermon at Pentecost was not the only sermon preached during these early days.

In Acts 2:42 we read that the early believers "devoted themselves to the apostles' teaching, to fellowship, to the breaking of bread, and to prayers." Obviously preaching was taking place with regularity. This church enjoyed a consistent diet of good sermons.

In Acts 3 we read that Peter preached a sermon on Solomon's Colonnade that was so impactful that it frightened the religious leaders. We see in Acts 4

---

[33] Luke 19:45–46.

that they were so afraid of the power of Peter's words that the only way they thought they could limit his effectiveness was by putting him and John in jail.

> Now as they were speaking to the people, the priests, the commander of the temple guard, and the Sadducees confronted them, because they were provoked that they were teaching the people and proclaiming in the person of Jesus the resurrection from the dead. So they seized them and put them in custody until the next day, since it was already evening. But many of those who heard the message believed, and the number of the men came to about 5,000.[34]

This is powerful preaching! When was the last time that the authorities were afraid of your sermons? How long has it been since we have seen God use our words to transform our communities? Powerful preaching seemed to be almost commonplace when the apostles preached.

In Acts 4 we learn that the arrest strategy employed by the religious leaders backfired. The very next day Peter used his courtroom rights to preach another sermon. In this sermon, "filled with the Holy Spirit,"[35] Peter proclaimed, "There is salvation in no one else, for there is no other name under heaven given to people by which we must be saved."[36] And the people were amazed.

Day after day, the apostles were preaching "home run" sermons. They preached sermons so powerful that they deserved to be recorded in Holy Writ.

What was the secret of this powerful preaching? Part of the answer is prayer. Upon release from prison, Peter and John rejoined the believers and had a prayer meeting. "When they had prayed, the place where they were assembled was shaken, and they were all filled with the Holy Spirit and began to speak God's message with boldness."[37] "And with great power the apostles were giving testimony to the resurrection of the Lord Jesus, and great grace was on all of them."[38]

It is a mistake to underestimate the homiletical influence of prayer. John Piper is correct when he asserts,

> God has made the spread of His fame hang on the preaching of His Word, and He has made the preaching of His Word hang on the prayers of the saints . . . the triumph of the Word will not come without prayer.[39]

But prayer alone does not fully explain why the preaching of the apostles was so effective. Some of the greatest prayer warriors I have known cannot

---

[34] Acts 4:1–4.
[35] Acts 4:8.
[36] Acts 4:12.
[37] Acts 4:31.
[38] Acts 4:33.
[39] J. Piper, *The Pleasures of God* (Portland: Multnomah, 1991), 225.

lead a Bible study, let alone preach. So why was the apostolic preaching so deep? What was their secret? It certainly could not have been just "beginners luck."

By the end of Acts 5 and the beginning of Acts 6 some time had elapsed since Pentecost. The apostles were maintaining a grueling preaching ministry: "Every day in the temple complex, and in various homes, they continued teaching and proclaiming the good news that the Messiah is Jesus,"[40] while remaining powerful and effective: "In those days . . . the number of the disciples was multiplying."[41]

At this point the weariness of ministry would have hit the apostles. By this time they would have run out of whatever sermons they may have put "in the barrel" while listening to Jesus preach. Now they were on their own. And, as any senior pastor can tell you, it is much more difficult to preach grade "A" sermons week in and week out. If you only preach every six weeks you should be able to come up with a fairly decent sermon. But how do you hit "home runs" every week? How did the apostles do this? How did they preach both regularly *and* powerfully?

It's no secret. The apostles publically announced the modus operandi behind their preaching in Acts 6:2–4.

> "It would not be right for us to neglect the ministry of the word of God in order to wait on tables. Brothers, choose seven men from among you who are known to be full of the Spirit and wisdom. We will turn this responsibility over to them and *will give our attention to prayer and the ministry of the word.*"[42]

The key to the apostles' consistently deep and effective preaching is stated in Acts 6:4. Here the apostles plainly declare the ministry priorities that will preserve their powerful preaching. They will eliminate worthy but distracting tasks in order to free up their schedules for what is most important. They want to give their constant attention[43] to two primary tasks. Their first task is prayer. The second is the Word of God.

The meaning of "prayer" in verse 4 is plain, but take careful note of the phrase translated in the NIV "the ministry of the word." The Greek word behind this English phrase is *logos*. It literally means "word." What are the apostles, and Luke who recorded their words, saying here? What exactly is this ministry of the word in which the apostles were continually engaged?

Since the word *logos* is used elsewhere in the book of Acts to refer to the act of preaching,[44] it can, very legitimately, be understood here to be a reference

---

[40] Acts 5:42.

[41] Acts 6:1.

[42] Acts 6:2–4, NIV; emphasis mine.

[43] Again the word *proskarterō* is used in this verse.

[44] E.g. Acts 2:41; 4:4; 10:44; 13:15; 14:12; 17:11; 20:2, 7.

to preaching. But *logos* is not a word that is commonly used in Acts to refer to preaching.

In fact, when Luke wants to talk specifically about the act of speaking a sermon, he usually chooses a number of words that specifically refer to this task.[45] So why would he use a relatively rare word to talk about preaching here? *Especially* when the reader realizes that the word *logos* is usually used within the book of Acts to refer to Scripture.[46]

What is going on in this text? Are the apostles continually devoting themselves to prayer and Scripture, or to prayer and preaching? The answer is "yes."

I think that the word *logos* was specifically selected for use in Acts 6:4 because it was broad enough to embrace the priority that the apostles placed on spending time in the Scriptures and the priority that they gave to proclaiming the Scriptures. The word *logos* is broad enough to include both Scripture meditation *and* preaching.

While the apostles' first priority was to be in continual prayer, their second priority was to spend their lives immersed in the word—continually living within the Scriptures—saturating themselves with it, meditating on it—and then preaching out of this abundance.

When Luke tells us in Acts 6:4 that the apostles were spending their time unceasingly (*proskarterō*) in the word (*logos*), he is meshing the discipline of meditation with the task of preaching. The secret of the apostles' powerful preaching lay in their utilization of the classic spiritual disciplines of prayer and meditation.

The apostles did not come to the Scriptures as sermonizing "professionals" on Friday afternoons trying to pluck a sermon from the pages of Scripture. They were not eagles swooping down out of their natural element trying to get food for their brood by snagging a fish while trying not to get wet. Far from it. Their natural element was the Word of God.

In the same way that a planted seed slowly grows in the earth until it matures into a fruit-producing plant, so the apostles planted the Scriptures in their hearts, and allowed its truth to grow and mature in their hearts and minds until it matured into a sermon. They preached when the fruit was ripe.

The apostles insisted that the church allow them to devote their days to thinking and praying their way through Scripture. As they did, they combined the irresistible power of the Word of God with the illuminating work of the Holy Spirit, and the result was preaching. This potent combination led to extraordinary preaching. It resulted in "Deep Preaching."

---

[45] Words commonly used for preaching in the book of Acts are *kerussō*, which is used 8 times; *katangellō*, which is used 11 times; *euangelizō*, which is used 15 times; and *didaskō*, which is used 16 times.

[46] E.g. Acts 1:1; 4:29,31; 6:7; 8:4,14,25; 11:1; 12:24; 13:5,7,44,46,48,49; 14:3,25; 15:15,35,36; 16:6,32; 17:13; 18:11; 19:10,20; 20:32.

It now becomes clear why the apostles had to clear their calendars of other matters. No one can give themselves to continual prayer and fasting while still looking after all of the needs of a growing congregation.

Preaching was not a part of their ministry. It was the primary focus of their ministry. They devoted themselves to the Word of God. The apostles refused to divert their attention away from the main focus of their ministry—preaching—even to do the admirable work of feeding widows.

It is helpful to note, however, that the truth of Acts 6:4 is not orphaned in that text. In fact, *all* of the apostles employed the homiletical strategy contained in that passage. Even Paul, whose later conversion precluded him from the events of Acts 6:4, utilized its secret of homiletical success. In Acts 18:5 we read, "When Silas and Timothy came down from Macedonia, Paul was occupied with preaching the message and solemnly testified to the Jews that the Messiah is Jesus." Once again Luke gives us insight into the apostolic homiletical process.

The phrase translated in Acts 18:5 as "occupied" comes from a single Greek word *sunechō* that means to be seized by something. In Luke 22:63 *sunechō* is used to describe how Jesus was under constant guard while being blindfolded, mocked, and struck after his Gethsemane arrest. *Sunechō* is used to communicate to the reader that the attention of his captors was intensive and uninterrupted. In the context of Acts 18:5 the word means that "Paul is *dominated / occupied*—by his task as proclaimer of the word."[47]

Not only was Paul devoted, but he was devoted, devoted! He had a single-minded focus. What was Paul so obsessed about? Once again the apostolic preoccupation was the Word (*logos*). Since the inspired writer chooses to use the same word he used in Acts 6:4, we are drawn to the same conclusion. One of the reasons why the apostles were able consistently to preach such deep and powerful sermons was because of the devotion they gave to the Word of God. They studied and meditated on the Word. And they preached the Word.

The reason that all of the apostles were able to preach such consistently deep and effective sermons was because they lived immersed in prayer and the word of God. They mixed these complementary spiritual disciplines, and sermons erupted from their souls as a consequence.

In this they were following the example of their Savior. In Luke 4 Jesus refused to be diverted into a ministry of healing. Despite the pressing needs and demands of the crowds, Jesus established the parameters of His ministry: "'I must preach . . . because that is why I was sent.' And he kept on preaching."[48] I think Jesus turned away from the legitimate physical needs of the crowds because—like the disciples—He knew that the disciplines of meditation and prayer were so demanding that it was impossible to focus on both. The call to

---

[47] H. R. Balz and G. Schneider, *Exegetical Dictionary of the New Testament* (Grand Rapids: Eerdmans, 1990–c1993), S. 3:306.

[48] Luke 4:43–44, NIV.

preach is a call to study, and then to meditate and pray on the truth of Scripture.

For the preacher, prayer is a divine dialogue that flows out of exegesis. The discussion starts with meditation as we chew on the truth of Scripture. We meditate by muttering questions of the biblical text as we go through our day. And as we wonder, for example, what it means to our life, our ministry context, and the larger community, it is natural for us to ask the Holy Spirit what He thinks. As we meditate we enter into a seamless conversation between ourselves and the Holy Spirit. In the quietness of "the closet," prayer and meditation are welded together. They are fused by the intensity of our yearning to comprehend the passage we will be preaching.

Meditation and prayer are to be more like twin sisters than distant cousins. The Scriptures call us to meditate "day and night." They also insist that we "pray constantly." How can we fill our days with both of these activities? The answer is: by doing them simultaneously.

As the truth of Scripture sets the tempo, we are to sway between these disciplines like a dancer. During this spiritual dance we cling to the Holy Spirit like a bridegroom holding his bride during their wedding dance. We hold the Spirit tight to our chest, moving slowly across the dance floor, rhythmically shifting our weight from meditation to prayer and back again, patiently waiting for the Spirit to lean forward and whisper truth into our ear.

During this dance we edge away from the science of exegesis toward the mind of Christ. Here we seek spiritual wisdom rather than manuscript analysis. Here we weave the deep insights that will make up the fabric of our sermon. And we do so by working the loom of the spiritual disciplines back and forth between meditation and prayer. We live in the atmosphere of prayer by moving naturally and effortlessly from meditation to prayer and back again.

This is not new. I am not advocating a "new and improved" homiletical methodology that will lead you into dangerous and uncharted territory. The Puritans advocated the union of meditation and prayer.

> When you read Scriptures, think how God is speaking to me, and thereby furnishing me with matter to speak to him in Prayer; this passage suits my case, I will improve it in Confession, Petition, or Thanksgiving . . . , and thus you will arrive to an habit of free-conversing with God. Reading [Scripture] and Praying are near kin: the one is an help to the other: . . . . Be much employed in both.[49]

Unfortunately, the "habit of free-conversing with God" has largely been lost among preachers today. Most of us are content with a brief prayer before we start preparing a sermon—"God help me!"—and when we are finished—

---

[49] R. W. Williams, "The Puritan Concept and Practice of Prayer: Private, Family and Public" (Ph.D. diss.; University of London), 32, as quoted in S. A. Ratliff, "The Strategic Role of Prayer in Preaching," (unpublished D.Min. diss.; Trinity Evangelical Divinity School, 2000), 18.

"Please bless this mess!"—but not much more than this. The way we pray has a direct impact on the way we preach.

If we want to preach with the impact that Martyn Lloyd-Jones had, we would be wise to heed the advice he gave regarding the preacher's prayer life.

> Above all—and this I regard as most important of all—always respond to every impulse to pray. The impulse to pray may come when you are reading or when you are battling with a text. I would make an absolute law of this—always obey such an impulse. Where does it come from? It is the work of the Holy Spirit; it is a part of the meaning of, "Work out your own salvation with fear and trembling. For it is God which worketh in you both to will and to do his good pleasure" (Phil 2:12–13).[50]

Charles Spurgeon gave similar advice to the aspiring preachers of his day.

> Your prayers will be our ablest assistants while your discourses are yet upon the anvil. While other men, like Esau, are hunting for their portion, you, by the aid of prayer, will find the savory meat near at home, and may say in truth what Jacob said so falsely, "The Lord brought it to me." If you can dip your pens into your hearts, appealing in earnestness to the Lord, you will write well; and if you can gather your matter on your knees at the gate of heaven, you will not fail to speak well. Prayer, as a mental exercise, will bring many subjects before the mind, and so help in the selection of a topic, while as a high spiritual engagement it will cleanse your inner eye that you may see truth in the light of God. Texts will often refuse to reveal their treasures till you open them with the key of prayer.[51]

Sermons that have the strength to touch the deepest recesses of the human heart are forged in a furnace stoked with meditation and prayer. They arise out of what Eugene Peterson calls "contemplative exegesis" and explain why, as a preacher, Peterson came to see that "prayer [is] at the very heart of the vocation I had entered."[52]

A. W. Tozer said that "to get to the truth I recommend a plain text Bible and the diligent application of two knees to the floor . . . a few minutes of earnest prayer will often give more light than hours of reading commentaries."[53]

Have you longed to preach deep sermons? And wondered why you don't? Why you can't?

---

[50] D. M. Lloyd-Jones, *Preaching and Preachers* (Grand Rapids: Zondervan, 1971), 170–71.

[51] C. H. Spurgeon, *Lectures to My Students: Complete & Unabridged*, new ed. (Grand Rapids: Zondervan, 1954), 43.

[52] E. H. Peterson, *Working the Angles: The Shape of Pastoral Integrity* (Grand Rapids: Eerdmans, 1987), 64.

[53] A. W. Tozer and J. L. Snyder, *The Early Tozer: A Word in Season, Selected Articles and Quotations* (Camp Hill, PA: Christian Publications, 1998), 39.

The reason so many of us preach shallow sermons is that we write our sermons like term papers. That is what I did when I began as a full-time senior pastor. After deciding what book of the Bible I would preach, I would purchase every commentary available on the book.

The content of those commentaries became the fodder for my messages. I would lay them out on a huge table and sift through them to see what their authors knew about my passage. As I gleaned the best insights from the best commentaries ever written I thought I was guaranteed to end up with the greatest sermon ever preached. It didn't work. It was not long until I owned one of the largest theological libraries in my denomination—and some of its driest sermons.

I was spending my weeks scraping truths out of these books into my homiletical stew pot—warming them up with the anxiety that grew as Sunday approached—and serving my people an unpalatable mess of information. This food kept them spiritually alive, but it was not good eating.

Sermons are not academic essays. They are love notes that God pens and asks us to share with His bride. They cannot be preached until we have heard from God Himself. Significant sermons grow out of the soil of significant meditation and prayer.

With the aid of technology, more sermons are being heard this week than in any other week in human history and, arguably, making less of an impact than ever before in human history. Why? Why do our sermons lack the depth for which we long? James answers this age-old preacher question in principle when he says, "You do not have because you do not ask."[54]

God does not answer questions about His book to those who do not ask. Nor does He assist those who decide to preach in their own power. When preachers do not take prayerful meditation seriously their ministry from the pulpit is seriously diminished—and so are those who sit under their ministry.

I am not the first to call preachers to a life of prayer. E. M. Bounds wrote many years ago that

> The power of the preacher lies in the power of prayer, in his ability to pray so as to reach God and bring great results. The power of prayer is rarely tested, its possibilities seldom understood, never exhausted. The pulpit fixed and fired with holy desires that presses these desires on God with a tireless faith will be the pulpit of power. Nothing is so feeble, so insipid, so nonproductive as a little tedious praying. To pray over our sermons in the same way as we say grace over our meals does no good. Every part of the sermon should be born of the throes of prayer; its beginning and end should be vocal with the plea and song of prayer. Its delivery should be impassioned and driven by the love from the furnace of prayer. Prayer, on fire with intense desire and

---

urged by a faith that does not fold its wings till God is reached, is the mightiest of forces. Prayer that carries heaven by storm and moves God by a resistless advocacy makes the pulpit a throne and its deliverances like the decrees of destiny.[55]

Bounds is calling us to go beyond "saying our prayers." He is asking us to take prayer as seriously as God does. He is reminding us that "deep calls to deep." Deep sermons are an overflow of deep communion with the God who wrote the book we preach. Superficial sermons result when truth is spooned from shallow hearts. Ian Pitt-Watson agrees.

> What we say in preaching becomes a part of us only if we have given a lot to that special kind of thinking where thinking and praying become almost indistinguishable. Thoughts turn naturally into prayers and prayers into thought. Sometimes the devotional element in our sermon preparation can degenerate into little more than variations of the theme, "God give me a sermon." We would do better to pray with the Book of Hours of 1514:

> > God, be in my head and in my understanding.
> > God, be in my eyes and in my looking;
> > God, be in my mouth and in my speaking;
> > God, be in my heart and in my thinking.[56]

Deep preachers understand what Hannah was doing in the temple in 1 Samuel 1. Hannah, a godly woman who was beside herself with the anguish of an unbearable home life, came to the temple when Eli was Israel's High Priest. Hannah was crying out to God. She was asking, begging God to help her know what to do, how to cope with an impossible domestic situation. Eli thought that Hannah was drunk because her lips were moving but she was not speaking. Hannah had to explain to him that she was not intoxicated, just crying out to God in distress.

Those who want to preach deeply will learn to pray over their biblical idea like Hannah prayed over her difficult circumstances—mumbling and praying, meditating and interceding, boldly approaching the throne of grace, without concern about appearances. They are desperate to hear from God. This is the kind of desperation that leads to fasting.

Fasting

Fasting is not nearly as popular a subject as eating. It's far easier to get people to line up at the buffet table than it is to get them to join you for a day of fasting. Fasting is a tough sell today—even among preachers.

One of the reasons God's people don't fast today—besides the hunger—is because God does not require us to do so. The Bible does not force us to fast.

---

[55] E. M. Bounds, *Powerful and Prayerful Pulpits* (Grand Rapids: Baker, 1993), 19–20.
[56] I. Pitt-Watson, *A Primer for Preachers* (Grand Rapids: Baker, 1986), 73.

In the Old Testament, God only required Israel to fast one day a year—on the Day of Atonement. And the New Testament does not include one command to fast. Not one.

Despite the freedom God gives His people in regard to fasting, the Scriptures contain many examples of godly men and women who fasted. Why? What is fasting?

Fasting is not dieting. It's not a biblical Jenny Craig weight loss system. Nor is it a deliberately unpleasant form of Christian asceticism demanded by God. God takes no pleasure in the unnecessary suffering of His children.

ↄ Fasting is our reflexive response to overwhelming situations and involves both the cessation of eating and the seeking of someone who can help in the crisis. The situations that start us fasting are similar to a household electrical circuit that experiences a sudden spike of electricity. What happens when this happens in your house? The breaker in your electrical panel snaps, and the electricity is immediately shut down. The breaker gives you time to find an electrician to help you to fix your electrical problem.

In the same way, when you experience an overwhelming spike of stress in your life, the hunger "breaker" in your body trips and your desire for food shuts down. You can use the time you normally would spend making and eating food to spend time with the person who can help you with your problem. Has this ever happened to you? Probably. Fasting is a common human response to a "secular" life crisis.

Think for a moment what people—even atheists—do if their spouses are diagnosed with cancer; if it then turns terminal; if the doctor has to take them aside and say that the time is short, and they have to bring the ones they have loved home to die. At this point the stress of healthy atheists would spike into overload. They would obviously be distraught over the imminent loss of their spouses. They are overwhelmed by the stresses of life. So to whom do they turn? Who can best salve their wounded souls? Their dying spouses. They want to spend every moment with the lover who will soon be leaving them.

Every moment becomes precious. Minutes become diamonds and no one wants a single one to slip through their fingers. People spend every possible moment with their dying spouses because it hurts even worse when they leave their side. Everyone wants their lover's presence more than anything in life—even more than food. So, without realizing it, they fast. This is a secular fast.

It is common for caregivers to care for their loved ones with such intensity that they forget to eat. This is not wrong; it is human. Whenever people find themselves in a traumatic situation that exceeds their natural capacity and normal coping mechanisms, they fast. Fasting is a normal human response to overwhelming situations in life. But for the people of God, fasting can also be an intensely spiritual experience.

Spiritual fasting typically occurs when godly people face one of two types of crises: an overwhelming encounter with God, or being overwhelmed with the events of life. Let's look at some examples.

1. The Trauma of Being Overwhelmed by God

- When Moses faced the trauma of spending 40 days of intimacy with God receiving the law, he did not eat for 40 days.[57] Who thinks about ordering pizza when you are alone in the presence of God receiving the moral foundation of civilization?
- When Israel retrieved the Ark of the Covenant from the Philistines in 1 Samuel 6, they faced the trauma of God's presence. Some guys in the town of Beth Shemesh decided to have a peek under its lid, and God responded to their disobedience and disrespect by killing seventy of them. The people cried out, "Who is able to stand in the presence of this holy LORD God?"[58] They were so traumatized by the person of God that they sent the ark to the nearby town of Kiriath-jearim, where it sat for twenty years. Israel was paralyzed by the presence of God. It was not until Samuel led the people in a time of fasting and confession that the relationship was restored.
- When Paul's "threats and murder against the disciples of the Lord,"[59] were interrupted by the resurrected Christ who said, "I am Jesus, whom you are persecuting," he responded by not eating or drinking anything for three days.[60] Jesus' personal appearance so shattered Paul's spiritual worldview that food was the last thing on his mind.
- Anna was a godly prophetess who "did not leave the temple complex, serving God night and day with fastings and prayers."[61] Her experience with God was so intense that it led to fasting.

2. The Trauma of Being Overwhelmed by Life

- When Israel learned about the gross sexual sin of the tribe of Benjamin, they wept and fasted about whether they should take judicial military action against their brothers.[62]
- When the Moabites, Ammonites, and the Meunites combined their military might to launch an attack, and Jehoshaphat heard that "a vast multitude . . . has come to fight against you,"[63] he "proclaimed a fast

---

[57] Exod 34:28.
[58] 1 Sam 6:20.
[59] Acts 9:1.
[60] Acts 9:1–9.
[61] Luke 2:37.
[62] Judg 20:26.
[63] 2 Chr 20:2.

for all Judah, who gathered to seek the LORD. They even came from all the cities of Judah to seek Him."[64]

- When the Jewish community learned about Haman's plan to "destroy, kill, and annihilate all the Jewish people,"[65] they responded with fasting.

- When Nineveh heard from Jonah that God was going to destroy them in forty days they responded by declaring "a fast and dressed in sackcloth—from the greatest of them to the least."[66] There is something about the threat of divine annihilation that focuses a nation's attention upon the Lord.

- As Ezra prepared to lead about 5,000 Israelite exiles from Babylon back to Jerusalem, he called for a time of fasting.[67]

- When Saul fell on his sword on mount Gilboa, his kinfolk from Jabesh-gilead rescued his body from the humiliation of being fastened to the wall of a Philistine city and fasted seven days. These mighty men were so traumatized by the tragedy of Saul's death that fasting was the only appropriate response.[68]

- David fasted when the child of his illicit relationship with Bathsheba became sick. After God strikes your baby with illness,[69] to whom else do you go? David has no choice but to go to the source of his child's illness. He goes to God, begging for the life of his offspring. When the life of your child hangs in the balance, who cares about food?

- Before Jesus began His ministry the Holy Spirit led Him into the wilderness where He fasted for forty days.[70] Jesus knew that the spiritual destiny of all humanity rested on the ministry He was about to begin. He knew that He needed to do His ministry in total unity with, and dependence upon, His heavenly Father. So He began by fasting.

- When the Holy Spirit asked the early church to send Paul and Barnabas off on the very first Christian missionary assignment, to unknown places for an undetermined period of time, they fasted.[71] The overwhelming number of variables contained within this mystery assignment must have been unnerving. How could they possibly prepare for such a vague ministry project? The nature of the Holy Spirit's command drove them to fasting.

---

[64] 2 Chr 20:3–4.
[65] Esth 3:13; 4:3.
[66] Jonah 3:5.
[67] Ezra 8:21,23.
[68] 1 Sam 31:13.
[69] 2 Sam 12:15–17.
[70] Luke 4:1–2.
[71] Acts 13:2–3.

In and of itself, fasting is not *de facto* evidence of intimacy with God. In Luke 18 Jesus told the parable of the Pharisees and the tax collector. And in his now infamous self-righteous prayer, the Pharisee stood in the temple and bragged before God and humanity about his practice of fasting "twice a week."[72] And he left the temple a sinner. Paul warns in Colossians 2:23 about regulations that although they have "a reputation of wisdom by promoting ascetic practices, humility, and severe treatment of the body, they are not of any value against fleshly indulgence."[73] Yet it would be a tragic mistake for you to dismiss fasting as a relic of religious history.

Jesus fasted, and He clearly expected that His followers would practice the spiritual discipline. His comments on fasting are frequently prefaced with "when you fast" rather than "if you fast."[74] When Jesus was criticized by John the Baptists disciple for not fasting enough, he responded by saying that His disciples will fast more after His earthly ministry is over. And Jesus empha-sizes in response to John the Baptist's disciples that His disciples will fast more after His earthly ministry is over.[75]

Jesus assumed that His followers would fast. So why don't we? Why do so many of us view this discipline as the exclusive domain of ancient mystics dressed in hair shirts?

At its best, fasting is a spontaneous act spawned out of desperation. It is practiced during times of extreme crisis, when our need for God is so great that people forget to eat. Genuine fasting is a spontaneous reaction of the heart. It cannot be forced or faked. Fasting is the visceral response of our souls to a traumatic situation.

We fast when we face a spiritual situation so desperate that only God is good enough—when we need His presence more than anything else. Even food.

Preachers should not feel obligated to fast every week. Or even every month. We don't fast to gain God's favor. We fast to gain His presence.

We fast when we don't understand why God wrote what He did in His Word, when His truth does not seem to make sense to us, or when it will be misheard by those to whom God has asked us to preach it.

We fast when we are desperate to communicate God's Word faithfully and don't know how, when we are at our wits end, and when all of our skills, train-ing, and experience are not enough. We fast when failure is as certain as it is unacceptable, and when the unstoppable force of our obligation to preach well meets the immovable obstacles of our sinful selves, schedules, and ministries.

If the leader of your denomination passed an edict requiring ritual fasting, this discipline would lose its force. When social or calendar obligations require us to fast a set number of times a year, week, or month, the discipline degen-

---

[72] Luke 18:12.
[73] Col 2:23.
[74] Matt 6:16–17.
[75] Matt 9:15; Mark 2:18–20; Luke 5:33–35.

erates. Muslims are required to fast during the 29 or 30 days of the month of Ramadan. Christians are not. Our call to fast comes from our hearts, not a religious playbook. But this observation can be as damning as it is liberating.

What if I Don't Fast?

The good news is that as a Christian preacher you never have to skip lunch. The bad news is that if you don't fast there are, unfortunately, three implications that can be made of your preaching ministry. The first implication is that *you are not experiencing real intimacy with God*. Since fasting is an automatic response to the trauma of unbearable intimacy with God, the absence of fasting may indicate our remoteness from God.

How sad it is to have to admit that the God of Scripture never overwhelms us. What an indictment about our own relationship with Him. What a chilling influence this must be having on our preaching and on the lives of those who listen to us.

When the God who looms over all creation never overwhelms you as you study His Scriptures, then you are studying incorrectly. While your exegesis of the biblical text may be accurate, it is also coldly scientific. The time you spend in God's Word must resemble the efficient dissection of a medical examiner more than a bride reading a tear-stained letter from her husband.

If you don't find yourself fasting involuntarily during your sermon preparation then you are keeping God at a "safe" distance. You are not allowing the beauty of His holiness to invade your personal space. You are holding God at arms length. You have reduced God to a subject to be mastered rather than a God to be loved. God is not as wild and beautiful and unpredictable as a butterfly. You have captured Him in the grid of your theological system and pinned Him down to a display board in the museum of natural history. You know a lot about God, but He does not overwhelm you. When God overwhelms people, they fast.

Only those who stand in direct sunlight need to wear sunglasses. Those who choose to wear sunglasses at night are just making a fashion statement. In the same way, only those who stand in the presence of God have a legitimate need to fast. Those who fast for any other reason are just making a fashion statement. They want people to see them as spiritual.

The second implication that arises from an absence of fasting is *an ego* the size of the Milky Way. Think about it. Why do people fast? One of the reasons for fasting is the visceral response to the overwhelming challenges of life. Time and again the Bible shows us how God's people fasted when they came to the end of their rope.

So if you never fast as you prepare to preach, I can only assume that you always feel entirely adequate for the task. Week after week you consider yourself entirely capable of fully performing the homiletical challenges of your ministry. Your failure to fast is an accurate caloric indicator of your unshakable faith in your exegetical and homiletical competence.

I don't think you should fast every week. Preachers can and should learn the skills needed to accomplish the common demands of ministry. But should there not be occasions when we are overwhelmed by a particularly difficult text or bewildered regarding the best way to present the idea of the biblical text to your people? Has there ever been a time when you have thrown your hands up and said, "I give up! I don't know what to say in this difficult situation? Who is adequate for such a task?" If not, then may God save His people from such arrogant preachers!

If we take the task of preaching with the seriousness it deserves, and if we have a realistically humble assessment of our exegetical and homiletical prowess, then we will find ourselves fasting, and not because someone tells us to do so. Neither do we fast to gain a "spiritual" reputation.[76] We fast because it is unthinkable to fail to preach God's Word properly, but you don't know how to succeed. Fasting is a spontaneous recognition that you are "over your head," an acknowledgment that you can't pull this one off. So if you never fast, you must have never found yourself at the end of your spiritual rope. You are either God's ultimate gift to preaching, or you have an ego the size of the universe. I suspect the latter.

The third implication of an absence of fasting is that *you have never experienced God's power fully released in your ministry*. In almost every one of the examples cited earlier, God moved in dramatic and miraculous ways when His people's prayers intensified into fasting.

- When Jehoshaphat called out to God with prayer and fasting, the prophet told him, "Do not be afraid or discouraged because of this vast multitude, for the battle is not yours, but God's . . . for the LORD is with you."[77] And God was true to His word. The enemy armies began to fight each other, and by the time Jehoshaphat's army showed up for battle "there were corpses lying on the ground; nobody had escaped."[78] God responded to their prayer and fasting by supernaturally intervening in dramatic fashion.
- Haman's plan "to destroy, kill, and annihilate all the Jewish people"[79] did not unfold as Haman had hoped. God's people fasted, Esther acted, and "the Jews put all their enemies to the sword, killing and destroying them. They did what they pleased to those who hated them."[80] God responded to their prayer and fasting by supernaturally intervening in dramatic fashion.

---

[76] See Matt 6:16–18.
[77] 2 Chr 20:15–17.
[78] 2 Chr 20:24.
[79] Esth 3:13.
[80] Esth 9:5.

- When Nineveh responded to news of their imminent destruction, "they proclaimed a fast and dressed in sackcloth—from the greatest of them to the least."[81] When "God saw their actions . . . [He] relented from the disaster He had threatened to do to them."[82]
- As a result of the prayer and fasting, Ezra was able to safely lead the 5,000 Israelite exiles from Babylon back to Jerusalem because they "were strengthened by our God, and He protected us from the power of the enemy and from ambush along the way."[83] What is more, God used Ezra to accomplish a significant spiritual renewal among the entire nation.
- While the fasting of the men of Jabesh-gilead did not change Saul's plight, out of the devastation of that day arose the best king that Israel would ever know. David immediately began to assume his rightful position as leader. These brave men could not have seen the better future that was being birthed in their fasting.
- The ministry that Jesus began with fasting[84] was entirely successful. When He announced on the cross "It is finished!"[85] He had managed to accomplish with the power of God every single objective that the Godhead had for His ministry. Not bad.
- Paul and Barnabas also did pretty well on their missionary journey. The proconsul of Paphos was converted after a miracle,[86] "almost the whole town assembled to hear the message of the Lord" in Pisidian Antioch the week after Paul's first sermon,[87] and "the message of the Lord spread through the whole region."[88] In Iconium, Paul and Barnabas "spoke in such a way that a great number of both Jews and Greeks believed."[89] In Lystra, Paul performed an astounding miracle that attracted the attention of the entire city.[90] In Derbe they "evangelized that town and made many disciples."[91] Then Paul and Barnabas returned to Lystra, Iconium, and Antioch, and "when they had appointed elders in every church and prayed with fasting, they committed them to the Lord in whom they had believed."[92] By any measure, the first missionary journey of the Christian church was an overwhelming success. And it was bookended with fasting.

---

[81] Jonah 3:5.
[82] Jonah 3:10; insert mine.
[83] Ezra 8:31.
[84] Luke 4:1–2.
[85] John 19:30.
[86] Acts 13:12.
[87] Acts 13:44.
[88] Acts 13:49.
[89] Acts 14:1.
[90] Acts 14:8–18.
[91] Acts 14:21.
[92] Acts 14:23.

Fasting does not guarantee that God will always answer our prayers the way we want Him to do. God did not, for example, acquiesce to David's prayer that the child he conceived out of wedlock with Bathsheba would live, even though David begged God with earnest prayer and fasting.

There can be no doubt, however, that God frequently responds to prayers that are heightened through fasting. A survey of Scripture reveals that those who fast often experience a mighty moving of God. When God's people pray with fasting, God often responds with obvious supernatural power.

Fasting does for the people of God what a nitrous system can do for the car in your driveway. If you were to install a nitrous oxide system to your commuter car, you could increase its horsepower by 50, 75, or even a 100-hp.[93] Street racers have used this secret for years. They know that by opening a valve they allow the nitrous gas within the metal bottle installed in their trunk to enter the fuel system of their car. And the result is an instantaneous and breathtaking jolt of power. The nitrous "juice" enables them to win races they would normally lose. It gives them access to power that those who drive unmodified cars can never imagine and will never experience.

While street racers don't use their nitrous gas system all the time—like when they are commuting to work—when they are in high-pressure race situations they find it comforting to know they have a secret weapon in their trunk. They can "turn on the juice" and blast their way to victory. Fasting has the same impact on ministry.

When we fast we open the valve to God's unlimited resources. We ask God to give a supernatural jolt to our ministries and to intervene in breathtaking ways so that we will succeed when we would normally fail. We access power that those who don't fast cannot imagine and will never experience.

While preachers will not fast every week—when they find themselves in high-stakes, high-pressure situations, when they know that they don't have the power to win their race—they have a secret source of power. By fasting they can ask their God to "turn on the juice." They can ask God to give them a supernatural push to victory. And God often responds when His people fast and pray.

Fasting can help you succeed in the pulpit where you would otherwise fail.

Your Partner in Preaching

Sermon preparation is not supposed to be a lonely task. God does not ask us to "go it alone." He longs for us to involve Him in the homiletical process and to reach out to Him constantly in dialogical prayer as we meditate day and night on His Word. And, on those occasions when we hit the wall exegetically or homiletically, we can cry out in desperation as we fast. He makes all the difference in our preaching. How much difference does He make?

---

[93] *Chevy Rumble* (February 2006): 84; http://www.zex.com/ (accessed 10/27/08).

Imagine that a beautiful garden lay just behind your home. It is a masterful planting, filled with a wide variety of the most beautiful plants on the planet. It looks and smells so heavenly you spend hours walking through it, admiring the skill with which it was put together and basking in its beauty. You have spent so much time that you can easily find your way through the garden. Some would call you an expert on the garden. You even give tours.

But imagine that one day the naturalist who planted the garden (the Holy Spirit) comes to you and says:

> Take my hand and walk with me. I want to show you all the wonders of my garden. I want you to understand what I planted and why. Why I selected the plants that are here and why I arranged them the way that I did. And let me explain the unique characteristics of each of the plants.
>
> You understand my garden well enough to find your way around it, but let me help you fully comprehend it. Let me show you things that you have seen but never noticed. Allow me to present my garden to you in all of its intended glory.

This is what the Holy Spirit wants to do with us. He wants to show off His magnificent Scripture garden. He understands what He wrote better than anyone. All we need to do to keep stride with Him during the tour is to meditate, pray, and fast when we are in particular need of help. Go deep with God, and let Him take you deep into His garden so that you can show others what He reveals to you.

> The world doesn't need more busy people, maybe not even more intelligent people. It needs "deep people." People who know that they need solitude if they are going to find out where they are; silence, if their words are to mean anything; reflection if their actions are to have any significance; contemplation, if they are to see the world as it really is; prayer, if they are going to be conscious of God, if they are to "know him forever."[94]

---

[94] D. Postema, *Space for God: The Study and Practice of Prayer and Spirituality*, 3rd ed. (Bible Way; Grand Rapids: CRC Publications, 1997), 18.

Chapter 8

The "Closet Work" Begins

Where do you get your sermons? Far too many of us are homiletical fast-food junkies. Because of our hyper-scheduled lives we drop spiritual Pop Tarts onto the plates of our parishioners rather than take the time to prepare a gourmet meal. We prefer Internet wi-fi connections over our spiritual closets.

"Most of my wisdom comes from looking things up on the Internet."

Why not buy the "Purpose-Driven" series? Why not fire up your Logos software, slide down the Passage Guide, and make the easy click on the link to SermonCentral.com? Keep going down to PowerPoint. com, and you won't even have to create your own graphics! "You'd have to be an idiot to spend the time required to cook up a gourmet sermon." We say to ourselves, "All you have to do is log on. Think of the time I can save!"

But sermons are like meals: the quality ones take effort. How would you describe a mother who served her children nothing but Jiffy peanut butter and Kellogg's Pop Tarts? Negligent. You and I know that children require the nutrition contained in a proper home-cooked meal if they are to grow into their full potential.

How would you describe a pastor who served their congregation a continual diet of Internet wisdom? Negligent. Pop-Tart sermons are easy, but they stunt spiritual growth.

The spiritual junk food that you can pick up from the Internet is similar to what is available from the drive-through window of a fast-food joint. Junk food makes you feel full, without meeting your genuine nutritional needs. Junk-food sermons fill minds without nourishing souls.

Great sermons, like great food, are not strip mined in Texas, do not roll off an assembly line in China, or slide across fast-food counters. Gourmet meals are created by hours of Closet Work. And meditation, prayer, and fasting are the kitchen tools used by homiletical master chefs.

Starting Your Closet Work

But what exactly should we do in our closets? Knowing the importance of meditation, prayer, and fasting is not the same as knowing what to do with them. What do we pray and mediate about?

I suggest that you consider the idea of your biblical passage from five different perspectives, by asking five different questions. Each question will challenge you in a different way. Each question will take you deeper into the biblical passage and the idea it contains.

Please keep in mind that, at this point, you are *not* writing your sermon. The five questions are the content of your Closet Work. They are what you meditate on and pray about in your closet. The five questions give your time with God focus and purpose.

Don't think about homiletics yet. Don't worry about how many points you will have or what they will be. Don't lose your focus by fretting over your introduction or conclusion. Deliberately push those questions out of your mind. They will have to be answered eventually but not yet. The sole goal of your Closet Work is to allow the Holy Spirit to lead you into a fuller comprehension of your passage. Take your time. Enjoy the opportunity you have to be with Him. Meditate and pray. Listen and learn.

I recommend that you ask these five questions with a fresh pad of lined paper to help you keep track of what the Holy Spirit shows you. Be sure to write down every question that crosses your mind, every insight, as well as every insight/answer that the Holy Spirit shows you throughout the process. The more technologically adept among us may prefer a digital voice recorder for paper and pen. Whatever recording method you prefer, choose something. *Don't think that you will remember.* You won't. Our minds are like sieves at the beach, and insights are grains of sand that slide, all too easily, through the holes back into obscurity.

A summary of the five questions is included in the appendix, but let's start in this chapter by looking at question #1.

Look Backward

The first question to ask in your closet is "Why was this exegetical idea *necessary* for its original recipients?" Be sure that you have a clearly stated exegetical idea of the biblical text. Write it down at the top of the first page on your pad.

Like all ideas, this should be stated as a subject and complement, question and answer format. Since it is exegetical, it should be an accurate and concise description of what the inspired biblical author communicated to his original audience.

It is imperative that you start with a *written* exegetical idea. Writing clarifies thought. I am ashamed to admit how many times I have had an idea in my mind and invested hours thinking about it as I drove through traffic or endured a bad meeting. But when I got to my closet, what had previously seemed so clear fled from mind like a cat at a dog show. My motto now is: if it's not written, it's not real. Start with an exegetical idea that is derived from a grammatical-historical investigation of the biblical text. Closet Work augments the study of Scripture; it does not replace it.

Here are some subquestions you will want to ask of your text to confirm that you really do understand what the original author communicated in the passage you are preaching.

Question #1: Why was this exegetical idea necessary for its original recipients?

1. To whom did the biblical author deliver this message?
2. What problem did it address?
3. Why did they *need* to hear it? How urgent was it? Why?

   Your goal here is to determine what the problem "looked like" in the lives of the original recipients. Visualize the situation that required this biblical truth. See it in your mind. Be sure that the problem you see is tangible. If it is not real in your mind, ask why. What additional information do you need to make it concrete? Is it exegetical? Is it cultural? Go find what you need.

4. Does the antecedent history of the recipients help explain why this instruction was necessary for these people at this time?
5. Are there any cultural factors that would have incubated or accelerated the need for this instruction? Why were the hearts of the original recipients so prone to wander in this direction? Why did God think that *they* specifically needed to be given this idea?

6. What do you think the emotional response of the original recipients of this biblical truth would have been? What was their visceral reaction when they first heard it? Why do you think so?

7. What did the original recipients of this message do with it? Did they heed this word or ignore it? Do we know?

8. How *did* this truth transform, or how *could* it have transformed the recipient's life?

Haddon W. Robinson has said that "something is not true because it is in the Bible; it is in the Bible because it is true." In other words, the truth of Scripture is true to life. And our decision to obey or disobey it determines if our lives flourish or flounder. With this in mind, develop two scenarios.

a. What would life have been like for the original recipients if they *had* fully responded to the truth of this passage?

b. What would life have been like for the original recipients if they had ignored or disregarded this truth?

9. Is this the only time that this principle is mentioned in Scripture? Have others struggled with this issue throughout biblical history? Who? When? Why? With what outcome?

10. What metaphors best capture the meaning of this passage?

Get the Story

My goal for these opening questions is to get you deeper into the biblical text than you have ever been before. I want you to understand more than just the grammar of a biblical text. The software on your laptop can figure that out. As a person indwelt by the Holy Spirit you can and should go further into the text—much further. I want you to press the idea back into its original context, *to push beyond the abstract into the concrete*; in other words, to understand the real-world situation of the original audience that caused God to inspire the original author to develop and deliver the exegetical idea of your passage. Concretism is a critical element of effective preaching.

Shallow preachers speak the truths of Scripture so abstractly that they are essentially meaningless. They speak, for example, of "the importance of holiness" but never take the time to show us what holiness actually looks like. Their listeners hear the truth but have no idea what to do with it. It is irrelevant.

When we preach abstractions, our words skim off the lives of our listeners like skipping stones across a pond. To make the kind of splash God intends, the truth needs to plunge into the daily lives of our people. This is what Jesus did in His sermons.

I don't think many of those listening to the Sermon on the Mount would have been terribly offended when Jesus said that their righteousness needed to surpass "that of the scribes and Pharisees."[1] But imagine the shocked looks that would have formed when Jesus began giving specific, concrete examples about what this kind of righteousness actually looked like. When Jesus equated murder with being angry,[2] adultery with lustful looks,[3] and love for neighbor with love for enemies and prayer for those who were persecuting them.[4]

Don't launch God's ideas into orbit above the lives of your listeners. Bring that truth down to earth. Land it right in the middle of their lives.

Truth on Display

These questions I've suggested will help you understand your exegetical idea concretely by forcing you to understand the idea of the passage you will be preaching as part of a larger narrative. Every portion of Scripture has a story behind it, and stories are inherently specific. Stories don't discuss truth; they display truth. The apostle Paul knew this.

In Romans 3, for example, the apostle Paul discusses the abstract concept of justification by faith. But in Romans 4 he uses the story of Abraham to show us what justification by faith looks like.

> He considered his own body to be already dead (since he was about a hundred years old), and the deadness of Sarah's womb, without weakening in the faith. He did not waver in unbelief at God's promise, but was strengthened in his faith and gave glory to God, because he was fully convinced that what He had promised He was also able to perform. Therefore, "it was credited to him for righteousness." Now "it was credited to him" was not written for Abraham alone, but also for us. It will be credited to us who believe in Him who raised Jesus our Lord from the dead. He was delivered up for our trespasses and raised for our justification.[5]

By using story, Paul roots his abstract truth in real life. As we step into Abraham's narrative, we see the doctrine of justification by faith at work. Stories, by their very nature, are concrete. And concretism is realism.

I am not asking you to *create* a story for your exegetical idea. I am asking you to use these questions to recreate the story of the original audience to determine why it was necessary for them to receive this truth. As you unearth the ancient story of your text you will discover the importance of the idea. The story will show you *when* and *why* the truth is so critical to godly living.

A secondary benefit of discovering the narrative of the biblical idea is that the story will help you spot the similarities between the story of the ancient recipients and the story of the contemporary audience to whom you will be

---

[1] Matt 5:20.
[2] Matt 5:22.
[3] Matt 5:28.
[4] Matt 5:44.
[5] Rom 4:19–25.

speaking. When you know and show these similarities in your sermon you will be forging a connection between your audience and the biblical text. You will be preaching more effectively.

But I want you to go further than just discover the original story of your exegetical idea. To make *sure* that you understand your exegetical idea concretely, I want you to do something else with it. I want you to make it a metaphor.

Look and Learn

Metaphors are critical for deep preaching. You do not understand a passage well enough to preach it unless you can make it a metaphor. If you can't put the idea of a passage into a metaphor, you don't really understand it. And you are certainly not ready to preach it.

A noun is a word you use to refer to a person, place, or thing. You see and touch nouns every day of your life. You sit on a noun when you eat breakfast. You pour a noun into your cereal bowl. You drive a noun to work. Your husband and dog are nouns. So is the sandwich you're going to have for lunch. We understand nouns. They are the bumps on the landscape of life.

Metaphors use the concrete nouns that we already understand to help us grasp abstract concepts by suggesting a likeness or analogy between them. The word "metaphor" comes originally from the Greek word *metapherein* which means "to transfer."[6] Metaphors transfer what we know to what we don't know. They compare two unlike objects or ideas and emphasize the similarities that exist between them. "The essence of metaphor is understanding and experiencing one kind of thing in terms of another."[7] And "because they make use of everyday concrete things to illustrate intangible, complex and relational aspects of life, they are vivid and memorable."[8]

Consider the following:

> *To forget one's ancestors*
> *is to be a brook without a source,*
> *a tree without a root.*
>
> *Chinese Proverb*[9]

Here the value of one's family (an abstract concept) is equated to nouns that we know; brooks and roots. The author is saying, in a vivid and memorable way, that our ancestors are as foundational to our lives as the source of water is to a brook and as roots are to trees. To forget our ancestors is to forget that which makes our life possible. In addition to being interesting, however, metaphors are also valuable educationally.

---

[6] Merriam-Webster, Inc, *Merriam-Webster's Collegiate Dictionary*, 11th ed. (Springfield, MA: Merriam-Webster, Inc., 2003).

[7] G. Lakoff and M. Johnson, *Metaphors We Live By* (Chicago: University of Chicago Press, 2003), 5.

[8] J. Lawley and P. Tompkins, *Metaphors in Mind: Transformation through Symbolic Modelling* (London: Developing Company Press, 2000), 9.

[9] E. Sommer with D. Weiss, *Metaphors Dictionary* (Canton, MI: Visible Ink Press, 2001), 19.

Metaphors are highly effective teaching tools in the learning process because they fit perfectly with the way people learn. As Lawley and Tompkins point out, from birth to death we all create mental models of how the world works.[10] We create these mental models by examining what we find to be true in life. These "truths" become bedrock assumptions that we use to build our lives on. They are intellectually unassailable. Everything we learn in life is built upon these previous assumptions.

Berman and Brown point out that

> it is our ability to make metaphorical connections that allow us to learn anything at all. When something new is like something we've done before, we take what we know from the first situation and transfer our knowledge to the new situation.[11]

Do you remember how you learned addition in grade school? Your teacher probably asked you how many apples you had if you took three apples and your mother gave you another one. You learned that three apples plus one apple equals four apples. Why did you learn that lesson? You learned it because you already knew about apples, and that your mother gives you things. What your teacher did was to build upon what you already knew. Good teachers deliberately graft their new material into your existing mental models.

Building mental models is similar to building an apartment building. No contractor starts constructing a high rise by building the penthouse. That would be impossible. Even laughable. Why? Because penthouse apartments are located at the very top of the structure. And while a penthouse apartment may be considered somewhat independent from the apartments below, they cannot float in midair. They must be securely fastened to the apartments below. Every floor of an apartment rests on the one previously built. What is true of penthouse apart-

---

[10] Lawley and Tompkins, *Metaphors in Mind*, 21–22.
[11] M. Berman and D. Brown, *The Power of Metaphor: Story Telling and Guided Journeys for Teachers, Trainers and Therapists* (Williston, VT: Crown House Publishing, 2000), 3–4.

ments is also true of knowledge. This is why there are prerequisites for courses. Educators know that you cannot succeed in a course if you do not know the material that it rests upon.

Everything we learn is an extension of what we know. Learning new information is like using an extension ladder. You begin using a ladder by setting it on the solid ground you are currently standing upon. Then you slide the ladder onward and upward to where you would like to be. Metaphors work the same way. They stand with you in your knowledge and help you climb to the next level intellectually.

Did you notice the metaphors I just used? First grade arithmetic, penthouse apartments, and extension ladders. The only thing that ties these things together is that they are part of your life. You understand that children learn to add by using apples, that penthouse apartments cannot be suspended in midair, and how to use a ladder. We learn by taking elements of what we already know and extending them to what we are trying to learn. Good educators use metaphors. That's why God scattered them so liberally throughout the Bible.

The rise of modernity and systematic theology encouraged people to view Scripture as propositions and abstractions. Countless hours have been spent and gallons of ink spilled by theologians as they have amplified their theories and explored the implications of various systems of belief. But our modern penchant for abstraction stands in sharp contrast to the Bible itself.

The Bible speaks "largely in images . . . the stories, the parables, the sermons of the prophets, the reflections of the wise men, the pictures of the age to come, the interpretations of past events all tend to be expressed in images which arise out of experience. They do not often arise out of abstract technical language."[12] Just a glance at the massive—and magnificent—*Dictionary of Biblical Imagery*[13] will convince you of God's love of concrete communication.

Who is Jesus? Go to a theological library and you will find thousands of complicated tomes dedicated to answering this simple question. But Jesus used the stuff of life to tell people who He was.

I am living water.
I am the bread of life.
I am the light of the world.
I am the good shepherd.
I am the vine.[14]

Jesus used metaphors as descriptors because of their enormous educational value. He knew that metaphors would help people "get a handle" on who He

[12] J. A. Fischer, *How to Read the Bible* (Englewood Cliffs, NJ: Prentice-Hall, 1981), 39.

[13] L. Ryken, et al., *Dictionary of Biblical Imagery* (Downers Grove, IL: InterVarsity Press, 1998).

[14] Compare John 4:10; 7:38, and see John 6:35; 8:12; 10:11,14; 15:5.

was, but He didn't limit their use to self-disclosure. For Jesus, anytime was a good time for a metaphor. In fact, Jesus was so convinced of their value, that when He preached He scattered metaphors as freely as rice at a wedding.

Preach Like Jesus

The Sermon on the Mount in Matthew 5–7 opens a window into the way Jesus preached. Consider the prominence that metaphors enjoy in this homiletical masterpiece.

Jesus commended the "poor in spirit," and "those who hunger and thirst for righteousness."[15] He calls his followers "salt" and "light" and urges them to store up "treasures in heaven" instead of "treasures on earth."[16] He says that "the eye is the lamp of the body" and that money wants to be our "master."[17] Jesus tells us not to worry because if God can clothe the lilies of the field He can look after you. Jesus asks us, "Why do you look at the speck in your brother's eye but don't notice the log in your own eye?" and recommends that we do not toss "pearls before pigs."[18] On the subject of prayer He tells us to ask, seek, and knock because "What man among you, if his son asks him for bread, will give him a stone? Or if he asks for a fish, will give him a snake?"[19] And we all must be careful to "enter through the narrow gate. For the gate is wide and the road is broad that leads to destruction."[20] Speaking of caution, be sure to watch out for false prophets. They are ferocious wolves "in sheep's clothing."[21] And the only way you can identify them is by their fruit because "every good tree produces good fruit, but a bad tree produces bad fruit."[22] And whatever you do, do not dismiss Jesus teaching because "everyone who hears these words of Mine and acts on them will be like a sensible man who built his house on the rock. . . . But everyone who hears these words of Mine and doesn't act on them will be like a foolish man who built his house on the sand."[23]

The sermon ends with Matthew telling us that "the crowds were astonished at His teaching, because He was teaching them like one who had authority, and not like their scribes."[24] The Greek word translated here as "authority" is the Greek word *exousia*, a word that can also be translated as "freedom; ability; power; authority."[25] Yes, Jesus preached with authority. But in this sermon Jesus also demonstrates incredible rhetorical freedom, ability, and power. His

---

[15] Matt 5:3,6.

[16] Matt 5:13–14; 6:19–20.

[17] Matt 6:22,24.

[18] Matt 7:3,6.

[19] Matt 7:9–10.

[20] Matt 7:13.

[21] Matt 7:15.

[22] Matt 7:17.

[23] Matt 7:24,26.

[24] Matt 7:28,29.

[25] H. R. Balz and G. Schneider, *Exegetical Dictionary of the New Testament* (Grand Rapids: Eerdmans, 1990-c1993), S. 2:9.

ability to speak directly, decisively, and clearly was awesome. Why was Jesus such an effective preacher? A significant part of Jesus' homiletical success was due to His extravagant use of metaphor. Jesus' mastery of metaphor helped Him create sermons that have resonated for centuries.

Compare your use of metaphors with His. We may not ever be able to preach as deeply as our Savior, but we can learn from Him. We can be better.

Not as Easy as It Looks

Don't allow the ease with which our Master uses metaphors to fool you into thinking that metaphors are easy to master. They are not. What experts do often looks easy—until you try and do it. Tiger Woods makes playing golf look easy, but my friends who play tell me that it is harder to play the game than Tiger makes it look. They are not on the pro tour earning millions of dollars of prize money. Bob Villa makes furniture-making look easy on TV, but the bookcases I make aren't even square.

Good metaphors are simple, and simple looks easy. But it's not. Any idiot can be complicated. It takes genius to be simple. Reducing a complex abstract idea to a readily accessible metaphor is a significant challenge. Just ask Aristotle. He writes in *Poetics* that: "the greatest thing by far is to have a command of metaphor. This alone cannot be imparted by another; it is the mark of genius, for to make good metaphors implies an eye for resemblances."[26]

What makes metaphors effective is what also makes them difficult. Standing "midway between the unintelligible and the commonplace, it is metaphor which most produces knowledge."[27] Metaphors are more than just "figures of speech"; they are central to how we make sense out of reality. Metaphors are the mental scaffolding that people need in order to reach the next intellectual level. They are a critical component of communication and teaching.

You *must* learn to use metaphors well in order to preach Scripture effectively. You cannot be a deep preacher without developing competency in the development and use of metaphors. Deep preachers have always known this.

What the Masters Mastered

Marcel Danesi, professor of Semiotics and Communication Theory at the University of Toronto, points out that "St. Thomas Aquinas . . . said that the writers of Holy Scripture presented 'spiritual truths' under the 'likeness of material things' because that was the only way in which humans could grasp such truths. For him, metaphor was a tool of cognition . . . (Aquinas himself said that)

It is befitting Holy Scripture to put forward divine and spiritual truths by means of comparisons with material things. For God provides for

---

[26] Aristotle, *Poetics* 9.4.

[27] Aristotle as quoted in M. Danesi, *Poetic Logic: The Role of Metaphor in Thought, Language, and Culture* (Madison, WI: Atwood Publications, 2004), 9.

everything according to the capacity of its nature. Now it is natural to man to attain to intellectual truths through sensible things, because all our knowledge originates from sense. Hence in Holy Scripture spiritual truths are fittingly taught under the likeness of material things."[28]

Charles Haddon Spurgeon, one of the greatest preachers of all time, was a master of metaphors. As Richard Lischer points out, "Spurgeon uses his own gift of metaphor-making—the image of a window—to explain the function of illustrations in the sermon. He suggests a limit of eight metaphors per sermon, a rule he broke with great exuberance."[29] If you have read many of Spurgeon's sermons you will know that metaphors dripped from his tongue like water from a faulty faucet. One of the reasons for Spurgeon's success as a preacher was the way that he used metaphors to help his hearers see what he said.

The most famous sermon ever preached in America, Jonathan Edwards' "Sinners in the Hands of an Angry God," is replete with metaphors. One of the reasons it made such a tremendous impact on those who heard it was because of Edwards' powerful use of metaphors. Consider the following excerpt:

> There is no want of power in God to cast wicked men into hell at any moment. Men's hands cannot be strong when God rises up. The strongest have no power to resist him, nor can any deliver out of his hands.—He is not only able to cast wicked men into hell, but he can most easily do it. Sometimes an earthly prince meets with a great deal of difficulty to subdue a rebel, who has found means to fortify himself, and has made himself strong by the numbers of his followers. But it is not so with God. There is no fortress that is any defence from the power of God. Though hand join in hand, and vast multitudes of God's enemies combine and associate themselves, they are easily broken in pieces. They are as great heaps of light chaff before the whirlwind; or large quantities of dry stubble before devouring flames. We find it easy to tread on and crush a worm that we see crawling on the earth; so it is easy for us to cut or singe a slender thread that any thing hangs by: thus easy is it for God, when he pleases, to cast his enemies down to hell. What are we, that we should think to stand before him, at whose rebuke the earth trembles, and before whom the rocks are thrown down?[30]

In this message, Edwards wedded sound theology with powerful metaphors. This powerful combination helped it burrow deeply into people's hearts. It helped bring a wayward nation back to God.

---

[28] Ibid., 14.

[29] R. Lischer, *The Company of Preachers: Wisdom on Preaching, Augustine to the Present* (Grand Rapids: Eerdmans, 2002), 316.

[30] http://www.ccel.org/ccel/edwards/sermons.sinners.html (accessed 11/10/08).

Deep preachers have always recognized the power of metaphors. They still do.

Making Metaphors

A common question students ask about metaphors is "Where can I buy the book?" The answer, of course, is that there is no book. And if there was, you should not buy it.

Using prepackaged metaphors in your pulpit makes as much sense as mailing a potato from Mexico to Idaho. Your prepackaged metaphor will arrive to your listeners the same way the potato would arrive at a restaurant in Idaho—stale and irrelevant. The best metaphors are always grown locally, out of the lives of your listeners. And they are always picked fresh, for the precise occasion to which you are speaking.

At the risk of sounding like Martha Stewart, the best is always homemade. Let me show you how you can create your own metaphors. There are three tasks that you need to keep in mind to create an effective metaphor.

1. Find the similitude.
2. Select the emotion.
3. Decide on the length.

1. Find the Similitude

The most basic element of a metaphor is, as we have seen, that it communicates a similarity between the concrete and the abstract, between what you know and what you do not yet know, between the lives of our listeners and the idea of your biblical passage. To create a metaphor for a sermon you can start at one of two places. You can start with the idea in your biblical text and then look for a metaphor in the world, or you can start with an idea you saw in the world and then find its idea in the biblical text.

Metaphors work because "something is not true because it is in the Bible, it is in the Bible because it is true." Since the Bible is true to reality, you can expect that reality will correspond to the truth of the Bible.

When it comes to metaphors, I go both ways. Many times I see a truth in the world—on a billboard, a bumper sticker, the nytimes.com or reuters.com Web sites, anywhere—which I find really interesting. When that happens, I will first capture the moment. Web pages are easy to save on the laptop, and I will often take a picture with my cell phone of a billboard or bumper sticker. If this is not possible, I will immediately jot a note on my iPhone. I will not try and remember the metaphor until a later time because I invariably forget.

Once I have captured the truth in the world, I go looking for a biblical passage that contains the same subject and complement. Sometimes a passage just springs to mind; other times I have to rack my brain and scour my Bible software. But when the match is made, I have found similitude.

When I am working on a sermon, however, I start with the idea of a biblical text and then begin looking for that same idea in the world. Because of the way our minds work, finding images from this direction works best if you give yourself some time. Let me explain.

Have you ever gone through the process of buying a car? I have. Last summer my old F150 pickup met an untimely end, and I had to start looking for a new vehicle. As I started the car shopping process, I first considered buying another F150. At that point, the strangest thing happened. I suddenly began noticing scads of F150s. They seemed to be everywhere I went! I wasn't consciously looking for them—they just seemed to appear. I noticed what I was thinking about.

Then I began thinking about downsizing from an F150 to a Ford Mustang. The same thing happened again. Once I had Mustangs on my brain, it seemed like I was seeing Mustangs at every stoplight. I noticed what I was thinking about.

As gas prices in California climbed towards the $5-per-gallon mark, however, I changed my focus. Who could afford to keep filling up the gas tank of such a thirsty car? How about a Mini Cooper? You guessed it; as I drove around, Mini Coopers grabbed my attention everywhere I went. As you consider an idea, you begin to see that idea all around you. You notice in life what you are thinking about.

After you have discovered the big idea of your passage you will begin seeing that idea "pop up" as you go through life. Just make sure that you pay attention to what is going on around you.

Some people take a cruise around the world and see almost nothing. Other people walk to the local grocery store and see the world. Pay attention to the commonplace. Think about what is happening and why. I read the news regularly online. I read *Time* magazine and *National Geographic*. I stop at my local bookstore and pick up a book just because it is interesting. If you do this—and give yourself time between when you discover your idea and when you preach your sermon—you will have no problems finding metaphors for your sermon.

By the way, metaphor-hunting takes place best when you are practicing the spiritual disciplines. Meditate and pray constantly over question #1: Why was this exegetical idea *necessary* for its original recipients?

I find myself constantly talking to God and myself—for days—about the idea I am going to preach. "God, what did You say here? Why was it so critical? What does this idea *look like?* Where do I see it in life?" It is in the process of this divine dialogue that God gives me my best metaphors. If nothing happens, then it is time to cry out to God in fasting!

Once is rarely enough. Keep in mind that when it comes to metaphors, one will not be enough. You need a number of metaphors to help you make your point properly. It takes time for truth to penetrate deeply into our heads and hearts. When you layer different metaphors on a single idea, you force people to ponder your point. The longer you linger on an idea, the deeper that idea can burrow into their lives and the deeper your sermon can impact them.

The technique of layering metaphors is not something I invented. It was what Jesus did. When you layer your metaphors to make a single point, you step into Jesus' homiletical sandals.

In Luke 15 Jesus' goal is to explain to the Pharisees and the teachers of the law why He welcomes and eats with sinners as reprehensible as tax collectors. Not an easy task! For this reason, Jesus is not content to use just one metaphor with His point.

- Jesus begins by telling the parable of the lost sheep. He explains how a shepherd would leave the ninety-nine who were OK in order to rescue the one who went missing. Everyone was so happy to see the lost sheep come home that a party broke out when the sheep came home.
- Then Jesus tells the story about the woman who lost one of her ten precious silver coins. Her anxiety over its loss—even though she had many others—was so great that she tore the house apart to find it. Her friends and neighbors entered into the joy of finding it by celebrating its recovery.
- Then Jesus tells the story of the man who had two sons who were estranged from him. The youngest son came home after choosing foolishly for a season. His father's joy was so great when he returned home that the father threw a huge extravagant party.

All of these stories have the same point. In each one something precious was lost and recovered. And in each case the appropriate response was to celebrate with wild abandon. What Jesus was saying to the Pharisees was that their response to the return of these lost people should not be anger and disapproval. How could they react to the unexpected recovery of these wayward people with anything but ecstatic joy? Their disapproval was as shameful as that of the older brother, who publically embarrassed his father by refusing to join the party.

In this passage Jesus gives three of the best pictures of reconciliation the world has ever seen. Three images stacked on top of each other to make a single point. Multiple metaphors result in maximum impact.

To find multiple metaphors you cannot discover your exegetical idea on Friday afternoon. You have to move your preaching schedule forward. Plan in advance. Get organized. Set priorities. Allow the Holy Spirit to help you with your preaching as you meditate, pray, and fast. Stop trying to do it at the last moment and all on your own.

To be effective, however, metaphors need more than a cognitive similitude with the idea of your passage. They also need to share the same emotion as the passage you are preaching.

2. Select the Proper Emotion

It has often been said that preachers can do only three things with the ideas of Scripture: explain, prove, or apply. The three functional questions are: What does the idea mean? How do I know the idea is true? What difference does it make? While every biblical sermon must, to some degree, touch upon all three of these functional questions, effective sermons focus primarily on just one of these three questions.

As helpful as these questions are, however, I suggest a fourth functional question: *"How should the passage make me feel?"* In addition to explaining, proving, and applying a biblical idea, biblical preachers need to ensure that their hearers emotionally resonate with the biblical text. Occasionally, a preacher's primary focus should be to change the way that their listeners feel about a biblical idea. Feelings matter.

The accusation "the church is twenty years behind the times" is frequently made. But when it comes to appreciating and harnessing the role of emotion, homiletics lags even further behind.

It has been more than three decades since Benjamin Bloom published his *Taxonomy of Educational Objectives* in which the outlined three learning domains: cognitive, psychomotor, and affective. According to Bloom, effective teachers develop their lesson plans knowing that to be understood, the subject matter needs to be dealt with on an intellectual level, skill level, and emotional level. For effective learning to occur, all three elements need to be addressed. Think how this would play out for a high school basketball coach trying to teach his freshman team how to win.

To be effective, the coach will first deal with cognitive learning. He will use a blackboard to explain the theory of the game of basketball. Each player will learn what each of the positions is and what their positional objectives are when they enter the game. They will learn game theory and why zone defense is so effective. Good coaching involves teaching content, but it does not stop there.

Good coaches will also get the players on the court to develop their psychomotor skills. They understand that it's not enough for the basketball players to know in their heads what they should do; they also must develop their skills necessary to execute the game plan. Good coaches will run endless skill drills because without the psychomotor element of the game, the team will not win any games.

But the third learning domain that good coaches tap into is the affective. Great coaches do more than just give theory and skill. They instill a *love* of the game in their players. They develop a sense of *pride* in the way that they play. To do this they make the players wear ties on game day. They teach them to gather at center court, get in a circle, join hands, and shout the team cheer. They give emotional "rah-rah" speeches that end with the players wanting to go and "win one for the Gipper." What is the point of all this? Great coaches know that to win, a team needs more than knowledge and skill. They need to run out on the court with emotions running high. He needs them to "play their hearts out." Most preachers could learn a few things from their old high school basketball coaches.

The people to whom we preach are not cognitive machines. Researchers have recognized for some time that what people learn from your teaching is related to how they feel about what you are teaching. A person's previous emotional experiences regarding your subject will have a profound impact on whether they learn what you are teaching.[31] If, for example a teenager in your congregation has had a great time acting out sexually, your exegesis of 1 Thessalonians 4 is not going to make him stop sleeping with his girlfriend. I'm not saying that you should not preach against premarital sex, but if you want your sermon to change his behavior you will have to change how he *feels* about his sin, not just tell him its wrong.[32] He is not a computer. Data alone will not change his behavior. If, however, you can also change his feelings about the subject, he will be far more likely to choose holiness.[33]

Our goal as preachers cannot be simply to download biblical data, as valuable as that data is. Information alone is not enough to transform. In this case, Joe Friday of *Dragnet* fame had it wrong. When we preach we need to present more than "just the facts." We also have to communicate the appropriate emotion because to teach with a sterile attitude is ineffective, and it does a tremendous disservice to the God we serve.

Our goal as preachers is not just to communicate information about God, but also to entice people into love with God. A cognitive response to God is inadequate. We cannot know God properly without fully engaging our emotions. As Alice Mathews points out:

> "Knowing" is not an abstract knowledge of a doctrine of God; it is a personal relationship with the personal God. It is the difference between the French verb *savoir*, meaning knowing a fact, and *connaître*, meaning knowing a person. Spirituality is not less than cognitive, it is more than cognitive. It is growth in a relationship with the living God.[34]

---

[31] A. Bandura, "Human Agency in Social Cognitive Theory," *American Psychologist,* 44.9 (1989): 1,175–84.

[32] A. R. Damasio, *Descartes' Error: Emotion, Reason, and the Human Brain* (New York: Penguin Books, 2005).

[33] "Cognitive Assonance" is a term commonly used to refer to the role of emotion in decision-making.

[34] A. Mathews, *Preaching that Speaks to Women* (Grand Rapids: Baker, 2003), 95.

What attitude does the passage call for? Every biblical passage has a mood. Some, like Psalm 150, are overflowing with praise. Other passages, like Matthew 23 where Jesus castigates the Pharisees, are filled with anger and condemnation. Still others, like 1 Samuel 31 where King Saul commits suicide, are just downright depressing.

To fulfill your responsibility as a biblical preacher, make sure that you preserve both the meaning and mood of the original author. While explaining, proving, and applying are obviously important, each can be frustrated unless the proper emotional note is struck. The fourth functional question: *"How should I feel about this passage?"* cannot be ignored.

There are many ways to influence how people feel about your sermon. Your tone of voice, for example, or the way that you gesture will help establish the emotion of your sermon. But so also will the metaphors you choose. Metaphors are powerful because they communicate mood and meaning simultaneously. And, they do it so forcefully that sometimes they can even turn your orthodox explanation of a text into heresy. Let me show you how.

When metaphors hurt. Suppose I was preaching on the doctrine of election from Romans 9, and I centered on the text:

> (for though they had not been born yet or done anything good or bad, so that God's purpose according to election might stand, not from works but from the One who calls) she was told: "The older will serve the younger." As it is written: "Jacob I have loved, but Esau I have hated."

> What should we say then? Is there injustice with God? Absolutely not! For He tells Moses: "I will show mercy to whom I show mercy, and I will have compassion on whom I have compassion."[35]

The meaning of this text is clear. Paul is saying that our salvation is a matter of God's divine choice; that none of us did anything to earn or deserve God's sovereign favor. We are entirely indebted to God's grace. But what if the mood of my metaphor undermined the meaning of my passage? Could I sabotage a beautiful idea with an ugly metaphor? Yes! Suppose I suggested that

> Election is like finding a lottery ticket on the ground and discovering that, far from being trash, this ticket had the numbers required for you to win your state's Powerball Lottery. It was worth $296 million dollars! Now you are wealthier than you could ever have imagined.

> See, you didn't purchase the ticket; you did nothing to earn or deserve it! But God provided you with the ticket you needed to live like a spiritual king! Now, as you are chauffeured by those people still

---

[35] Rom 9:11–15.

stuck in their sinful squalor, remember to thank God that you don't have to live there! You won the spiritual jackpot!

The doctrine of election is a beautiful, mind-stretching, and humbling truth of Scripture. But my metaphor stained it with an attitude of pharisaic self-righteousness. My exegesis may have been correct, but my metaphor would have led God's people astray.

Be sure only to select those metaphors that will amplify the mood of your biblical passage. Too many preachers labor over their messages like new mothers wanting to serve their children nothing but 100-percent pure organic foods. These preachers spend hours cooking up sermons from the scratch of the original languages and then end up polluting the entire meal by stirring in the wrong emotion.

When metaphors help. I was recently preaching a series of sermons on the seven churches in Revelation 2–3. When I came to the memo to the church in Thyatira, I found a very sober passage. Here Jesus is not portrayed as "gentle Jesus, meek and mild"! Here Jesus is portrayed as being "One whose eyes are like a fiery flame, and whose feet are like fine bronze"![36] Why is Jesus so upset? Because unlike previous churches that have battled heresy, Thyatira chose to "tolerate the woman Jezebel, who calls herself a prophetess."[37] What separates Thyatira from the other churches is that this church chose to *tolerate* false teaching and the sin that it spawned. They were willing to live with it. They decided that sin was not that serious. They chose to overlook it.

Jesus is clear that toleration is a mistake. He states,

> Look! I will throw her into a sickbed, and those who commit adultery with her into great tribulation, unless they repent of her practices. I will kill her children with the plague. Then all the churches will know that I am the One who examines minds and hearts, and I will give to each of you according to your works.[38]

This is not a happy passage. It is a clear statement that choosing to ignore heresy will result in death. How do you find metaphors that will show this?

I first showed that toleration of wrong behavior always results in an increase of wrong behavior. Toleration is not an effective strategy for reducing the sin of heresy.

- What would happen if traffic cops decided to tolerate speeding?
  - ➤ There would be more speeding, not less.

- What would happen if border officials decided to tolerate illegal immigration?
  - ➤ There would be more illegal immigration, not less.

---

[36] Rev 2:18.
[37] Rev 2:20.
[38] Rev 2:22–23.

- What would happen if schoolteachers decided to tolerate cheating?
  ➤ There would be more cheating, not less.

- And what will happen if you and I decide to tolerate sin?
  ➤ There will be more sin, not less.

All of these metaphors had the negative mood for which I was looking. The repetition of these short metaphors kept driving the idea deeper into the minds of my listeners. Then I transitioned to an extended metaphor that heightened the emotion of the text. I wanted the people to feel the mood of the words "I will kill her children." To communicate this mood as well as the idea that tolerated sin results in death, I used this metaphor.

> Suppose you went to your doctor for a physical on your thirtieth birthday and your doctor asked you about your diet. You acknowledged that you know it is wrong, but confessed to him that you love junk food. Value menu, double cheeseburgers, and French fries drenched with gravy are your favorite and most frequent meal.
>
> Your doctor tells you that this is a problem. He explains that these foods contain cholesterol and are clogging your arteries. "You need to deal with this," your doctor tells you. "You need to stop eating junk food."
>
> But suppose you ignored your doctor's instruction. Suppose you decided to tolerate your cheeseburgers and gravy and fries. Suppose you decided you were willing to live with it. Suppose you decided that it was not that serious. Suppose you decided to overlook your diet.
>
> What do you think would happen? You don't have to suppose because you know for sure. One day you will collapse on the floor of a McDonald's clutching your heart in intolerable agony. Tolerating a stratospheric cholesterol level is a death sentence.
>
> Tolerating sin will do the same thing. The wages of sin is not $32 an hour with a 401K. Sin never pays. Never. And if you choose to tolerate it, it will keep building up until it kills you. Those who tolerate sin will be killed by it.

Creating appropriate metaphors requires that you find a similitude between your biblical passage and the "real world" in which your people live. It also requires that you carefully match the mood that is created by your metaphor with that of the text. But there is still a final decision to make.

3. Decide on the Length

As you may have already noticed, metaphors can enormously vary in length. They can range from just a few words such as "you are the salt of the earth" to extended similitudes like Jesus' Prodigal Son or the story of sheep stealing that Nathan told David after he murdered Uriah. Even full-blown stories can be considered metaphors. Berman and Brown point out,

> Story telling is . . . where the "ahas" of metaphor take place. . . . A story can be called a metaphor if the listeners can relate to it and draw a parallel between the action in it and their own lives. It has been suggested that if a picture is worth a thousand words, then perhaps we can regard a metaphor as being worth 1000 pictures.[39]

"Concrete and narrative exemplifications are, by their very nature, *metaphorical* strategies. They are effective explanatory strategies because they allow us to make the world 'visible.'"[40]

Metaphors begin by creating pictures in people's minds but go beyond by allowing people to visualize themselves in the picture—to experience it.

Stories that help people to understand themselves can be considered metaphors. These extended metaphors can be used as powerful instruments of learning. This is evident in our children's books. We read our children Dr. Seuss' *Green Eggs and Ham* to teach our children to try new foods. When they get older we have them read C. S. Lewis' *The Lion, the Witch and the Wardrobe* to grasp the significance of the death and resurrection of Jesus Christ.

How do you decide how long your metaphor should be? There are two factors you need to keep in mind.

a. The longer a metaphor is, the greater its emphasis will be. If you spend 10 minutes developing a metaphor you better be sure that the point of the metaphor is the main point of your message. If not, the extended metaphor will pull you away from the central idea of your passage.

   Think of a solar system. The reason planets circle their sun is because the sun is larger than they are. The huge mass of the sun creates a gravitational pull so strong that the planets cannot escape its pull. When metaphors grow in size, they exert a similar influence on your sermon. The larger they grow, the greater their influence.

b. The longer the metaphor is, the greater its emotional impact has to be. Remember the three metaphors that Jesus used in Luke 15? The lost sheep, the lost coin, and the lost son. The last metaphor is the longest by far. Its size dwarfs the others—four or five times as long! But notice as well that it is also the most emotional. Any parent will tell you that the loss of a child is *far* worse than an animal or a coin.

   If you decide to make a significant point by growing your metaphor to a more significant size, be sure that you also increase its

---

[39] Berman and Brown, *The Power of Metaphor*, 4.
[40] Danesi, *Poetic Logic*, 9.

emotional power. Without significant passion, a very big metaphor can become very boring. Big metaphors can easily go bad.

Remember the solar system? The sun dominates its universe because of its huge mass. But it also burns with incredible intensity. And all of the planets in its orbit benefit from the light and heat that it generates. Jesus' largest metaphor—of the lost son— also burns with great intensity. And its passion provides helpful illumination of the surrounding passages.

Deep preachers don't just think about the truth of Scripture; they see it. After analyzing and summarizing the meaning of a text, they visualize it. They place the truth in a metaphor.[41]

We begin our "Closet Work" by looking backward. We ask exegetically and prayerfully: what did God communicate in this passage? Why was this exegetical idea *necessary* for its original recipients? This critical question has not been answered until:

- you know the story of the truth.
- you can convey the truth in a metaphor.

Only when this is done can we move on to the second question.

---

[41] Two examples of extended metaphors are included in the appendixes.

Chapter 9

The "Closet Work" Continues

All the world's a stage,
And all the men and women merely players;
They have their exits and their entrances;
And one man in his time plays many parts.[1]

If Shakespeare was right, you and I do not enjoy star billing in the story of Scripture. God does. He is the protagonist. He drives the action. He determines its outcome. God is the unrivaled star of the greatest show on earth—which is not surprising since He also created the theater!

The Bible is about God. God wrote it to reveal Himself and how we should live in response to Him. As we study the truths of Scripture we see different aspects of His character from a variety of perspectives, but we always see Him. Scripture was written by and about God.

In 2 Timothy 3:16 we learn that all Scripture is "God-breathed" (NIV). The phrase "God-breathed" is an adjective that comes from the Greek word *theopneustos.* God exhaled the book you will preach. By using this very rare word, Paul is saying that the Bible is very different from every other book. Other authors wrote their books by scratching on paper or pounding a keyboard. But the Bible is not an external document written by hand; it came out of God. It was birthed out of the womb of His personhood. The words of Scripture, and the ideas it contains, flow from the essence of His being.

One of the implications of the "God-breathed" origin of Scripture is that the ideas it contains come out of God's person. Inspiration roots the truth of the

---

[1] W. Shakespeare, *As You Like It*, Act 2, Scene 7.

Bible in God's character. Its content is necessitated by and grounded in God's essence, His personhood. Every natural unit of Scripture contains God's moral DNA.

The "God-breathed" nature of Scripture means that preachers can launch an investigation similar to that carried out on the *CSI* crime shows so popular on TV. We can take the ideas of Scripture and trace their moral DNA back to the God who birthed them. We can match each truth of Scripture with the specific aspect of God's character that caused God to breath it into existence. Did God's holiness require this idea? Or His mercy? Perhaps His love? Some element of God's character *required* the truth of the passage you exegete to be written. Which one? Why?

After looking backward at the idea you identified in your Scripture passage, you can examine it from an entirely different perspective. After looking backward, look upward.

Look Upward

The second question to meditate and pray about in your closet is "What is God revealing about *Himself* in this text?" Write this question down at the top of a fresh sheet of paper on your pad.

Question #2: What is God revealing about Himself in this text?

God's commands are never artificial or arbitrary. They are the inevitable and logical outflow of His moral character into the situation of the original recipients of the idea you have discovered.

As you look at the idea you have discovered as a result of your exegesis, you are looking at how God's personhood responded to the specific situation that was faced by the original audience. Exegetical ideas are God's natural response to their particular circumstances; His moral character necessitated them.

1. What does this text reveal about God's character? From which of God's attributes does its idea emanate?

   No one acts without a reason. What you choose to do in a day comes from deep within you. Your actions are an expression of your values. Everyone's are. Only the legally insane act absolutely irrationally. For the rest of us, there is a causal link between who we are and how we act.

   If you are married, you have learned to understand the link that exists between character and behavior—between who someone is and how they act. It is this congruence that allows us to predict reliably the behavior of the people we know best.

If your wife quotes "cleanliness is next to godliness" as if she could find its biblical reference, you just know that Saturdays are—now and forever—the days you will vacuum and dust the house. Her edict will not (and cannot) ever change because it is rooted in who she is.

If your husband's bedrock conviction is that his most important task is to provide for his family, you know that he will spend an ungodly number of hours at the office, even over the holidays. No amount of begging or pleading will change his schedule because his behavior is rooted in his core values.

Everyone's actions are rooted in his or her character—even God's. Your task here, therefore, is to establish a causal link between God's person and His revelation. What is it about God's character that necessitated Him to breath out this truth? Why is the truth of your passage the only way that God could have responded to the situation of the original audience that received this communication? How is this truth anchored in the person of God?

Sometimes the relationship between God's character and the biblical text is made clear within the text itself. In the second commandment, for example, we see the words "Do not make an idol for yourself. . . . You must not bow down to them or worship them." Why? "For I, the LORD your God, am a jealous God."[2] Here God's command is linked to His jealousy. What is jealousy? It is the legitimate response of love to unfaithfulness. Jealousy is the logical outflow of the passionate covenantal devotion that God has extended to Israel. Jealousy cannot burn unless it is fueled by love. The greater the love, the stronger the jealousy. It is obvious in this commandment that God loves His people a great deal. No husband who genuinely loves his wife wants to share her affections with another.

Usually, however, the relationship between God's character and God's truth is implicit. Not every diamond lies on the surface. Most are buried and require that we dig into the text and context to find them. Take the first commandment as an example.

"Do not have other gods besides Me."[3] Looked at in isolation, this commandment seems rude and intolerant. "Doesn't God know

---

[2] Exod 20:4–5.
[3] Exod 20:3.

that you cannot force love?" What kind of God would try and coerce our affections?

Ask yourself the following.

2. Why is the truth of this text theologically necessary? Why would God ask this of His people or do this to His people? Is God being unreasonable or unfair? Does He have your best interests at heart? How do you know that?

It is very important that you are honest here. Don't succumb to the temptation to use clichés. Don't let yourself use "god talk." You can be—and must be—honest with God here. Don't worry about theological orthodoxy as you wrestle with hard passages and the God whose character necessitated the idea you will be preaching.

There is nothing you can say that will shock or surprise God. He knows you and all you have been thinking. Besides, you are not the only person who has asked such serious questions.

If David can say, "God, hear my voice when I complain,"[4] why can't you speak what is on your mind? Asaph wrote in Psalm 73, "Look at them—the wicked! They are always at ease, and they increase their wealth. Did I purify my heart and wash my hands in innocence for nothing?"[5] The psalmist does not end his psalm mired deeply in doubt, but he has to walk down the path of skepticism in order to say with full conviction "But as for me, God's presence is my good. I have made the Lord GOD my refuge, so I can tell about all You do."[6]

Honest questions that challenge orthodoxy are not sinful and do not cause sin. In fact, you will not be able to combat or correct sinful behavior—in yourself or others—until you understand its theological core.

This is *not* the place to say, "God said it, I believe it, and that settles it!" Deep preachers need to know why. They try their best to see God's character in His words and actions. Whereas God is clear when He says,

> "My thoughts are not your thoughts,
> and your ways are not My ways."

---

[4] Ps 64:1.
[5] Ps 73:12–13.
[6] Ps 73:28.

This is the LORD's declaration.
"For as heaven is higher than earth,
so My ways are higher than your ways,
and My thoughts than your thoughts,[7]

deep preachers do their best to comprehend the God who, from a human perspective, is sometimes inexplicable. No person has ever fully understood God, and many, like Job, have wrestled intently with how to reconcile God's actions and God's character. But God welcomes our hard questions. On two occasions God said to Job,

Get ready to answer Me like a man;
when I question you, you will inform Me.[8]

God welcomes, encourages, and participates in healthy debate and honest theological inquiry. C. S. Lewis also encourages us to ask hard questions about God when he points out,

If our religion is something objective, then we must never avert our eyes from those elements in it which seem puzzling or repellent; for it will be precisely the puzzling or the repellent which conceals what we do not yet know and need to know.[9]

Spend time in God's presence here. Cry out to Him for insight. Ask God to reveal Himself to you more fully. Ask Him to sweep away all of your lesser ideas of who He is. Your goal here is to see God as He truly is, not necessarily as He has traditionally been portrayed in church and in the lives and words of fellow Christians. God is holy. He stands apart and separate from everyone and every institution.

Be encouraged by the fact that this question will become easier to answer as you grow in your relationship with God. The better you know someone—even your spouse—the easier it is to predict and explain his or her behavior. I know it is tough to look upward, but the only way that we can grow in our knowledge of God is to look at Him.

By the way, why do you know why God gave His first commandment? The command was prefaced by the statement that "I am the

---

[7] Isa 55:8–9.
[8] Job 38:3; 40:7.
[9] C. S. Lewis, *The Weight of Glory and Other Addresses*, 1st HarperCollins ed. (San Francisco: HarperSanFrancisco, 2001), 34.

LORD your God, who brought you out of the land of Egypt, out of the place of slavery."[10] God was not coercing love from a reluctant Israel. On the contrary, He reminds them that He was the one who had miraculously redeemed them from generations of horrific slavery. Then God tells Israel that he is not a "cut and run lover." If Israel responds to God's special grace to them by giving special status to Him, God will continue to be their God. This commandment is not coercion. It is the best deal in the universe. Why would anyone *not* want to follow a God who is so good?

Look Inward

We began our Closet Work by looking backward and asking "What did God communicate in this passage?" Then we look upward at what our text tells us about God. Now we need to look inward and ask: "What is God saying to *me* in this text?"

Question #3: What is God saying to me in this text?

Whether I like it or not, if I do not make a significant attempt to practice what I preach, I am a hypocrite. No amount of homiletical competency can compensate for my own refusal to listen to what God is saying.

It was John Calvin who said that "true and sound wisdom, consists of two parts: the knowledge of God and of ourselves."[11] But "it is certain that man never achieves a clear knowledge of himself unless he has first looked upon God's face, and then descends from contemplating him to scrutinize himself."[12]

If Calvin is correct that true self-knowledge is only possible through the knowledge of God, and knowledge of God can only come through the Bible, then preachers should be more self-aware than anyone. After all, our job descriptions require us to know God and we are paid to study the Bible.

But do you know the true state of your heart? I am not asking if you have assurance of salvation, but if you know how close each area of your life is to God. It is all too easy for us to preach to others but not to ourselves. It is tempting to scratch our heads thinking about how our text can apply to our listeners, but not ask how it should touch our own lives. But "the preacher's first, and most important task is to prepare himself, not his sermon."[13]

A leading cause of shallow preaching is professionalism. When homiletics is viewed primarily as an occupational responsibility, and when we see our job as locating and disseminating biblical truth for others, we sentence ourselves to a lifetime of superficial ministry.

Philips Brooks famously defined preaching as "truth through personality;" not *around* our personality. The path that leads to deep sermons leads through

---

[10] Exod 20:2.

[11] J. Calvin, *Institutes*, Book One, chapter 1:1 (p. 3).

[12] Ibid., Book One, chapter 1:2 (p. 37).

[13] D. M. Lloyd-Jones, *Preaching and Preachers* (Grand Rapids: Zondervan, 1971), 166.

our own hearts. Unless we purposefully place our own lives under the weight of the Word of God that we preach to our people, our sermons will be inauthentic and irrelevant.

Before you think about how the idea you discovered should impact other people's lives, *first* ask how it should impact yours. Here are a series of questions that can help you do that.

In what ways am I similar to/does my life parallel the original recipients of this book?

1. Are my weaknesses their weaknesses?
2. Are my temptations theirs? Have I succumbed as they did?
3. Has my life been warped as a result?
4. In what ways? With what consequences?
5. When was I more likely to fall into this sin?
6. What habits / practices exist in my life that contribute to this problem?
7. What is it about me that made me vulnerable to this particular attack by the enemy (i.e. what is the root problem that manifests itself in this sin)?
8. How has my life and ministry suffered as a result of this sin?
9. How have others been affected by this?
10. How could my life and ministry have been enhanced by withstanding this temptation?
11. How will the idea of this text force your life spiritually forward?
12. Picture the different reality that you and your people could be experiencing right now, if you had made different choices.

Walk in this for a time. Allow these questions to penetrate into your soul. Practice the presence of Christ. Allow the Holy Spirit to illuminate your mind with the knowledge of who you really are behind the role you occupy and the image that you portray. Our public personas can be deceptive. Our public reputations can distort our private understanding of who we really are. We can begin to believe our own press releases.

Cry out to God with the psalmist: "Search me, God, and know my heart; test me and know my concerns. See if there is any offensive way in me; lead me in the everlasting way."[14] These are perhaps some of the most poignant words in the entire Bible. In these two verses there is so much. We see the psalmist asking God to search him, to look to the deepest part of who he is, his own heart. Why would the psalmist ask this? And, why would any of us ask it? The reason is simple. We cannot know our own hearts as well as God can. He indwells us, knows every thought, is aware of every feeling, and He understands us better

---

[14] Ps 139:23–24.

than we do. If we ever needed anyone to reach down in the depths of our hearts to find out what is unholy so that it can be removed, it is God.

How to Apply

A tool that has proven helpful in my life has been the book *My Heart, Christ's Home*.[15] In this simple book, Robert Boyd Munger uses the metaphor of a house to help us gain insight into our heart. The story begins when the author invited Jesus into his heart. "Lord, I want this heart of mine to be yours." Munger says to his new Savior, "I want you to settle down here and be fully at home. . . . Let me show you around and point out some of the features of the home so that you may be more comfortable."[16]

As Munger takes his Lord on a tour of his heart they begin by entering his study, a room that represents his mind. As they walk in, Jesus

> looked around at the books in the bookcase, the magazines on the table, the pictures on the walls. As I followed his gaze I became uncomfortable. Strangely enough, I had not felt bad about this room before, but now that he was there with me looking at these things, I was embarrassed. There were some books on the shelves that his eyes were too pure to look at.[17]

From there they go to:

- the dining room—the room of appetites and desires
- the living room—a quiet and secluded spot for good talks and fellowship with Jesus
- the workroom—where things are produced for the kingdom of God
- the recreation room—where I go to relax and have fun
- the bedroom—where my marriage is celebrated
- the family room—where relationships with the family of God are developed and enriched
- the kitchen—where I come together with others to serve the family of God
- the hall closet—where we try and hide our secret sins

As Munger walks with Jesus from room to room, he is forced to view his lifestyle choices through the eyes of his Savior. The tour forces him into a comprehensive review of the choices he has made in light of his commitment to the lordship of Christ.

This simple book, with its simple metaphor, provides me with a straightforward methodology to apply the idea of the passage to my life. What rooms of my life are affected by this truth? Would I be embarrassed if Jesus peeked

---

[15] R. B. Munger, *My Heart, Christ's Home*, 2nd rev. ed. (Downers Grove, IL: InterVarsity Press, 1992).
[16] Ibid., 10, 11.
[17] Ibid., 11.

into this corner of my life and saw what I was doing? *My Heart, Christ's Home* may help you apply to your own life the truth you intend to apply to others.

But why try and do it all alone? We all have blind spots, areas of our life that, for our own sinful reasons, we prefer to ignore or gloss over. But the benefit of being part of a small group of caring believers is that we can help each other on our sanctification journey. You will be well served to find or create a group of likeminded people who share your commitment to radiate Christ. They can help you see yourself in light of the idea you are going to preach.

Alone or with the help of others, the key question you need to ask yourself is *"What is stopping me from radically applying this truth to my life?"* Why do I refuse to act on it, as I know I should? Why does it have such a hold on my life?

Spend time crying out to God in confession and repentance. Ask God for the insight to spot the enemy's strategies in this area. Then beg Him for the strength to withstand the devil's attacks.

According to Scripture, the goal of biblical knowledge is *always* the renovation of our lives. The purpose of biblical information is ethical transformation. This is why Paul wrote to the Colossians,

> We haven't stopped praying for you. We are asking that you may be filled with the knowledge of His will in all wisdom and spiritual understanding, so that you may walk worthy of the Lord, fully pleasing to Him, bearing fruit in every good work and growing in the knowledge of God.[18]

Whatever you do, *don't preach holiness to others without practicing it yourself.* It is so easy to stand above our sermons rather than in them. Our old nature wants us to lecture others on godliness, while standing in the stench of our own iniquity. It encourages us to spot the speck in our brother's eye while overlooking the log in our own, to minister hypocritically. We can avoid this ministry pitfall by first taking the truth we are going to preach for a tour of our own heart.

What the Bible Should Do to Preachers

Can we know if we are properly applying the truths we preach to our own lives? Yes. I am pleased to be able to tell you that there is a test that is as simple as it is reliable—a test that can reveal—with 100 percent reliability—if you practice what you preach.

You can accurately assess how intently you look in the mirror after you look into God's Word, by listening to the way you describe your spiritual life to others. When you are in a small group, what do you admit? Do you admit to any spiritual flaws? Many people don't. Many deflect attention from their own

---

[18] Col 1:9–10.

spiritual state by constantly asking for prayers for others or only for physical ailments.

But what does that look like when you do address the state of your own soul? Do you confess with tears things that are really dark and personal? Or do you specialize in "confessing" your strengths as weaknesses? Do you play it safe by saying things like "my problem is that I pray too much; please pray for me," or "I can't stop thinking about the deep things of God after my three hours of quiet time every day." This is not true confession; it is badly disguised bragging.

Here is the rule: *the more spiritual you think you are, the further from God you really are.*

Think about it. The people with the best spiritual reputation in the New Testament were the Pharisees. They honestly saw themselves as the spiritual elite, as spiritually superior to everyone. Their unshakable confidence in their own righteousness and moral superiority gave them the confidence to preach judgment to everyone else. But Jesus declared that the Pharisees' self-assured, spiritual self-assessment was horribly wrong. They were completely out of touch with their hearts. God was not pleased with their holiness. Their pious-looking lives were whitewashed tombs. Their hearts were rotten to the core.

Now consider the apostle Paul. Near the end of his life he wrote to Timothy, a young preacher he was training in ministry, and confessed: "This saying is trustworthy and deserving of full acceptance: 'Christ Jesus came into the world to save sinners'—and I am the worst of them."[19] Paul was the *worst* of all sinners? I read that statement with disbelief. How could that be true? What about Judas? What about Hitler? How could Paul, who is the world's premier church planter, preacher extraordinaire, and esteemed apostle, make such an outrageous confession? But he did. And not just once. He confessed to the entire church of Rome that

> I am made out of flesh, sold into sin's power. For I do not understand what I am doing, because I do not practice what I want to do, but I do what I hate. And if I do what I do not want to do, I agree with the law that it is good. So now I am no longer the one doing it, but it is sin living in me. For I know that nothing good lives in me, that is, in my flesh. For the desire to do what is good is with me, but there is no ability to do it. For I do not do the good that I want to do, but I practice the evil that I do not want to do. Now if I do what I do not want, I am no longer the one doing it, but it is the sin that lives in me. So I discover this principle: when I want to do good, evil is with me. For in my inner self I joyfully agree with God's law. But I see a different law in the parts of my body, waging war against the law of my mind and taking

---

[19] 1 Tim 1:15.

me prisoner to the law of sin in the parts of my body. What a wretched man I am! Who will rescue me from this body of death?[20]

I do not know a single pastor who would tell his congregation what Paul said here. He calls himself unspiritual and sold into the power of sin!

Yet, there is no question that the apostle Paul enjoyed a close relationship with God. Not only was Paul given his ministry by personal appointment of the resurrected Christ, but his own experiences with God were quite literally out of this world. Paul arguably described such an experience in 2 Corinthians 12 when he admits that he was

> caught up to the third heaven. Whether it was in the body or out of the body I do not know—God knows. And I know that this man—whether in the body or apart from the body I do not know, but God knows—was caught up to paradise. He heard inexpressible things, things that man is not permitted to tell.[21]

It is no accident, however, that in the very next verse Paul says that he will not boast about himself "except of my weaknesses."[22] If anyone could have projected an image of impressive super spirituality, it was Paul. But he didn't. He preferred to boast in his weaknesses! Why is Paul so preoccupied with his sin? Because he is so close to God.

Since God is light, the closer we come to the light of His holiness, the more evident our sin becomes to us. The closer we come to God, the more aware we become of our own iniquity. This is why *the more spiritual you think you are, the further from God you really are.* Only those who are far from God's light think they are spiritually presentable. You have to approach the light of God's holiness to realize that your righteousness is as filthy rags.

Know Thyself

Preaching that does not lead us to a greater awareness of our own depravity and total dependence upon the grace of God is not deep preaching.

Every week, as we study God's holy Word, we should be driven into a greater awareness of our own sin. If this does not occur we, like the Pharisees, are developing a perilous overconfidence in our own righteousness. We are walking away from the God we are preaching. We are walking toward hypocrisy, and even worse, we are taking our congregations with us on our terrible journey—just as the first-century Pharisees did. Jesus said to them, "Woe to you, teachers of the law and Pharisees, you hypocrites! You travel over land and sea to win a single convert, and when he becomes one, you make him twice as much a son of hell as you are."[23]

---

[20] Rom 7:14–24.
[21] 2 Cor 12:2–4, NIV.
[22] 2 Cor 12:5.
[23] Matt 23:15, NIV.

Whether we like it or not, we *will* reproduce after our own kind. The people who sit under our ministry will carry our spiritual DNA. Ilion Jones writes that "sermons cannot be detached from the person who preaches them. They are conditioned by what he is, what he does, what he thinks, and what he feels."[24] Richard Baxter begged pastors in his landmark book *The Reformed Pastor* to

> preach to yourselves the sermons that you study, before you preach them to others. . . . When your minds are in a heavenly, holy frame, your people are like to partake of the fruits of it. . . . They will likely feel when you have been much with God; that which is on your hearts most is like to be most in their ears. . . . I confess . . . that I publish to my flock the distempers of my soul. When I let my heart grow cold, my preaching is cold; and when it is confused, my preaching will be so; and so I observe too oft in the best of my hearers, than when I have a while grown cold in preaching, they have cooled accordingly, and the next prayers which I have heard from them have been too like my preaching.[25]

The only way that we can ensure that the harvest of our ministry is Christlike is by radically applying God's Word to our lives—every single week. We need to commit ourselves to God and our congregations to practice what we preach. We should beg God to work His holiness in our lives. To do otherwise is to choose sin. And you and I both know the ministry consequences of that horrible choice.

Isaiah tells us, "Indeed, the LORD's hand is not too short to save, and His ear is not too deaf to hear. But your iniquities have built barriers between you and your God, and your sins have made Him hide His face from you so that He does not listen."[26] Sin sabotages our ministries by alienating us from the very God we are trying to serve.

When we handle the truths of God's Word but are not cut to the quick by them, we should be afraid. Be very afraid. Proverbs 28:9 reads, *"Anyone* who turns his ear away from hearing the law—even his prayer is detestable."[27] God will not use unholy vessels. If we choose to say no to God's revealed will, God will use someone else. We cannot stop God's eternal purposes, but we can choose to sit on the sidelines.

It is tragic that the maxim "know thyself" may be better known outside of the pulpit than within it. Deep preaching requires that we look deep into the Scriptures and also look deep into the state of our own souls. Then we apply the Word of God to our lives with ruthless rigorousness. Robert Murray

---

[24] I. T. Jones, *Principles and Practice of Preaching* (New York: Abingdon, 1956), 49.
[25] R. Baxter, *The Reformed Pastor* (Richmond: John Knox Press, 1956), 33.
[26] Isa 59:1–2.
[27] Prov 28:9, emphasis mine.

McCheyne, the great Scottish preacher of the nineteenth century, declared, "My people's greatest need is my personal holiness."[28] It still is.

No amount of homiletical competency can compensate for our refusal to listen to God and act upon what He is saying to us.

Look Outward

After investing Closet Time looking backward, upward, and inward at the idea of the passage that we are going to preach, it is time to look outward and ask: "What does God want to *accomplish* through this text?"

Question #4: What does God want to accomplish through this text?

After first examining how God wants the idea of your passage to impact your own life, now you begin to think about how your idea should impact other people's lives.

My assumption here is that you agree that sermons should actually *do* something in the lives of your listeners. Only those sermons that accomplish a specific purpose in the lives of those who hear them are successful. There should be visible results in the lives of our listeners after we have faithfully preached God's Word. But I realize, however, that not everyone agrees with me. All too often sermons come across as stained glass versions of the History Channel.

I have some friends who really enjoy watching the History Channel on television. As they tune in to the various segments they are fascinated by the tidbits of information they learn on these shows. The ratings of episodes such as "How the Titanic really sank," "Why the Challenger space shuttle tragedy was inevitable," "How Hitler sabotaged the efforts of his own army during WW 2," indicate that many people enjoy learning the fascinating and oft forgotten facts of history. Humanity seems to have a fascination for trivia, especially when it involves learning about the mistakes that other people have made. It is fun to point fingers at the mistakes of others.

But this is not preaching. Our goal as preachers is not to simply gloat over the heroism of Daniel or David or rail against the stupidity of Naboth, the pride of Saul, and the materialism of the Rich Young Ruler. Our goal is not to communicate sacred history but to use sacred history to communicate life-changing truth. We preachers need to push beyond the trivia to the transformational. When we do, we follow in the footsteps of the greatest preachers in history.

Every sermon recorded in Scripture calls for a specific behavioral response. Not once does someone preach a message just so that the listeners will increase their cognitive understanding of a biblical doctrine. Every single sermon recorded in Scripture was preached for transformational reasons. They were preached in order to accomplish specific behavioral objectives. The question

---

[28] T. Sargent, *The Sacred Anointing: The Preaching of Dr. Martyn Lloyd-Jones*, 1st U.S. ed. (Wheaton, IL: Crossway, 1994), 128.

that you now need to ask is, "What would you like God to do in the lives of your listeners as a result of your sermon?"

You need to ask what you want the truth of your passage to accomplish in the lives of your listeners and the world in which they live. This enormous power is at your disposal. As a preacher, you will hold the Bible in one hand and the tiller of people's lives in the other. Your words will help plot the direction of people's lives. So in which direction should their lives turn?

This is the place to dream dreams and envision a better and brighter tomorrow. What would it look like if the people you preach to were to implement *fully* the idea of your passage? What difference would it make in the lives of your listeners next Tuesday morning if this idea were to become fully operational? What would it look like if God's agenda in your passage were to be realized fully?

A good place to start is by looking at how the original author applied the truth initially. If you know how this truth was originally applied to the people in the original context, and you can identify the similarities that exist between the original audience and those who will be listening to you, you will have a starting place for your application.

Here are some questions that may help focus your thoughts on the similarities and dissimilarities between yours and the original audience.

1. In what ways are the people you lead similar to the original audience? Consider the similarities that may exist. Consider factors such as

   a. Socio-economically—poor or affluent?
   b. Socially—comfortable family units or widows/orphans?
   c. Morally—living surrounded by licentiousness? Affluence? Hedonism? Secularism?
   d. Politically—is your country being led by someone trying to follow God's direction or by a pagan?
   e. Spiritually (length of time they have walked with God, the spiritual heritage you may enjoy, the temperature of their spiritual passion—i.e. cool, lukewarm, or boiling hot?)

Now spend some time thinking about the receptivity that your listeners are likely to have to the idea of your passage.

1. Do you think that your people want to live in harmony with the teaching of this text? Why or why not? What would their objections be?
2. What is keeping you and your people from living out this text? Are there any structural/organizational barriers?

I recommend that you get a group of people from your congregation and get some "feedback in advance." We usually think of getting feedback after we have preached, but the obvious problem with that is its timing. The good news is that you learned how to preach your passage more effectively. The bad news is that the sermon is over. The information arrived too late for you to use it. For this reason I recommend that you get feedback *before* you preach.

Ask a group of people if they would be willing to help you with your sermon. Five or six is a good number. Just make sure that your group is a cross section of your congregation. If you do not have significant groups within your congregation represented in your group, you will not hear from them. If, for example, you have a significant number of women in your pews, then make sure they are proportionally represented in your feedback group. If you have single, recently divorced people in your church, invite them to the discussion. The rule here is to be inclusive rather than exclusive. It will be easier for you to speak to the diversity of your audience if you listen to them.

As you gather, tell them that you are interested in their unique perspective on what you will be preaching. Then take the time to show them the passage with which you will be dealing. Explain what the idea of the passage is and why, exegetically, you think so. This is important because the purpose of this meeting is not for people to say "what this passage means to me." I am *not* trying to facilitate pooled ignorance. Every natural unit of Scripture has a single fixed meaning intended by the original author. This is determined by exegesis not consensus.

After you have briefly outlined the exegetical idea of your passage, invite your guests to speak regarding how this truth specifically impacts their lives. You want to know how middle-aged unemployed autoworkers hear tithing taught from Malachi 3 or how young bored affluent housewives respond to the Great Commission or how a visible minority rape victim interacts with the Parable of the Unforgiving Servant in Matthew 18. You need to learn how people of different ages, races, cultures, worldviews, genders, professions, income and education levels, family situations, and levels of spiritual commitment and maturity interact with the idea of your passage. You need these people to help you see God's idea from the perspective of the pew.

Here are some questions that may be useful as you meet with your group.

- Does this idea attract or repel you? Excite or scare you? Why?
- Does this idea seem like nonsense or common sense? Imminently practical or hopelessly idealistic? Why?
- If you could tell God to His face what you thought of this idea, what would you say? What would you be afraid to say?
- If you could talk to people in the pew about this idea, what would you say? To whom would you say it? Why?
- Who in the secular community desperately needs to hear this truth? Why?
- Who in the secular community would react violently either for or against this idea? Why?

- If you made a decision today to take this truth very seriously, what difference would it make in your life? Why?

I guarantee that both you and those in your group will enjoy the experience! Everyone likes to be listened to. Everyone enjoys being heard and valued. And while you may think that those who participate in the discussion would not want to hear your sermon on the passage they discussed, the opposite is the case. Your "feedback in advance" group will be eager to hear your message and then find out how what was said in the group impacted what you preached.

I recommend that you change the makeup of your group regularly. This will ensure that you gain meaningful input from a wide variety of people. It will also indirectly teach a greater number of people how to see into the heart of a biblical passage.

Changing the make-up of a group is also important to prevent strong-willed people from trying to co-opt your pulpit. You want to listen to these people, not surrender your ministry to them!

1. What people in your congregation have lived in obedience to this text? (Think of specific people.)
2. What people in your congregation have lived in violation of this text? (Again, think of specific people.)

The point of these two questions is *not* to mention names from the pulpit. It is helpful, however, to think about why some people struggle with the implementation of a particular truth while others do not. Is this a phase of life issue? Is there a genetic predisposition to the behavior in question? Can the difference in behavior be "chalked up" to self-discipline? Education? The support of their spouse?

Answering these two questions can make a significant contribution to your understanding of your passage and its idea. They are worth some time.

3) How could this truth transform your people and/or the community where you and your people live and minister? What are the ripple effects that could result from embracing the truth of this text?

This is where you get to dream big! What would happen if this idea were to be adopted outside of your community of faith? What difference would this idea make if it were adopted on mass in your community, county, state, and country? How would individual and corporate destinies be changed for the better?

Missiologists refer to the difference that God's truth makes in the lives of secular people as *redemptive lift*. Since "something is not true because it is in the Bible, it is in the Bible because it is true," the biblical truth you exegeted and are dwelling on in your Closet Work will improve the lives of everyone. It will improve the lot of those outside the family of God as well as within it.

For example, Paul says in Ephesians 5:18, "And don't get drunk with wine, which leads to reckless actions"[29] The command not to get drunk was clearly written to Christians who attended church. But could non-Christians benefit by heeding these words? Of course! If they don't get drunk, they will be far less likely to engage in stupid, dangerous, or harmful actions—actions that could cost them their money, their jobs, their families, and even their lives. Everyone who applies the ideas contained in Scripture benefits from it. Everyone.

Since this is true, how would the secular community that you live in be transformed by this truth? Can you imagine it? If you were to film a documentary showing the world the wonderful benefits of living this truth, what would the plot of your movie be? Who would it star? How would it end?

Look Forward

After investing Closet Time looking backward, upward, inward, and outward at the idea you are going to preach, it is time to look forward and ask: "What could *negate* the progress I have just made through this text?"

Question #5: What could negate the progress I have just made through this text?

In *The Lost Art of War* one of the greatest military strategists of all time, Sun Wu, said, "Warfare is a path of subterfuge." His descendant Sun Wu elaborated on this when he urged commanders to

> let them think you lack resolve, feign lack of ability, and appear to have a defeatist attitude, so as to seduce them into arrogance and laziness, making sure that they do not recognize the real facts. Then, on this basis, strike when they are unprepared, attack where they are not defending, pressure those who have slacked off, and attack those who are uncertain or confused.[30]

For centuries, wise warriors have allowed their opponents to think that they are further ahead and have accomplished more than they really have. They encourage their adversaries to underestimate the fierceness of their resolve and, in the process, "seduce them into arrogance and laziness."

We would be wise to remember that even though you and I may not have laced up combat boots, we are still warriors in a fierce spiritual battle. Paul reminds us, "Our battle is not against flesh and blood, but against the rulers, against the authorities, against the world powers of this darkness, against the spiritual forces of evil in the heavens."[31] Our ministry is taking place on a spiritual battlefield, and our enemy is not stupid. If we can read *The Art of War,*

---

[29] Eph 5:18.
[30] B. Sun and T. F. Cleary, *The Lost Art of War*, 1st ed. (San Francisco: HarperSanFrancisco, 1996), 143.
[31] Eph 6:12.

Satan can too. Satan can use subterfuge to get us to let our guard down. He can fool us into slacking off so that we are not prepared for his next attack.

Do you really think that if you preached a sermon that accomplished all of your objectives that Satan would stand idly by? Do you think he will sit idly by allowing you to enjoy the spiritual ground that you may have just taken unchallenged? I don't think so. Prepare for a counterattack.

A counterattack is a battlefield tactic used by a defending force against their attackers. The purpose for launching a counterattack is to reverse the gains of the enemy. Don't let Satan fool you. As surely as tomorrow morning will come early, Satan will launch a vicious counteroffensive to take back whatever ground he may lose as a result of your sermon. Satan will try and negate any godliness that may result from your message.

To be forewarned is to be forearmed. So ask yourself, if *you* were the archenemy of the Lord of love, how would *you* counterattack? To defeat a battlefield enemy, you need to outthink your opposing general. I am not asking you to be as evil as Satan, but I am telling you that you need to be more cunning. And this is not easy.

Lucifer has many attributes, but stupidity is not one of them. Hell is generously populated with people who thought they were smarter than Satan. Even Paul sounds impressed with Satan's cleverness when he points out that "the serpent deceived Eve by his cunning."[32] Yet, in spite of the challenge posed by Satan's intellectual prowess, Jesus wants us to rise to the intellectual challenge of the evil one. Jesus tells His disciples, "I'm sending you out like sheep among wolves. Therefore be as shrewd as serpents and as harmless as doves."[33]

How can we do this? How can we figure out Satan's next steps? How do we scoop his strategic plans? By straining the brain God gave us, and crying out to God for insight and answers during your Closet Work. Fast if you need to, but you should not be caught off guard by how Satan decides to push back against the light you shed as you preach God's Word.

Here are some questions that may help get you started.

1. What method is Satan likely to use to counterattack?

   a. Will he tell lies? (He is the father of lies—John 8:44)
   b. Will he use discouragement?
   c. Will he try and cause division to advance his cause?
   d. Will he try and exploit some preexisting circumstance or condition?

2. What circumstances could make continued obedience to this truth difficult? (e.g. sudden singleness [divorce/death], economic recession/ job loss, loss of health)

---

[32] 2 Cor 11:3.
[33] Matt 10:16.

3. What age group (e.g. children, youth, college student, young married, middle aged, recently retired, elderly) will find the application of this truth most difficult? Why? How could those who won't struggle as much with this truth help those who will?

Why Bother?

Closet Work is hard work. It requires that you invest an enormous amount of time and energy to examine the big idea of a passage of Scripture from every possible angle. Mentally, spiritually, intellectually, and personally, Closet Work is one of the most challenging tasks you can undertake. But, if your desire is to preach deep sermons consistently, then you will be constantly bearing this burden. Why bother? Answer: because as we meditate and pray in our closet the Holy Spirit comes alongside us. He becomes our counselor, our teacher. And what a teacher He is!

It is "the Spirit [who] searches everything, even the deep things of God. . . . no one knows the concerns of God except the Spirit of God."[34] No one knows God as intimately as He does. Not me or you. Only the Holy Spirit is privy to the deep things of God. The Holy Spirit is the secret of deep preaching. Only with His assistance do we have a hope of preaching sermons that will impact lives for eternity. Unless He illuminates our minds, our time in the pulpit will be spent stumbling in the shadows of superficiality and irrelevance. We will be guilty of playing marbles with the diamonds of God's words.

I challenge you to move beyond the resources of your seminary training, academic books, and cool software programs. I dare you to set them aside after your exegesis is complete and look for inspiration beyond your Starbucks coffee. Enter the solitude of your closet and meditate and pray over what God is saying. Beg the Holy Spirit to illuminate your heart and mind. Ask for the mind of Christ, that you might be filled with all spiritual wisdom. Ask that the Spirit would allow you to grasp the grandeur of God's Word so powerfully and personally that when you preach, people would hear the words of God, see the face of God, feel the presence of God, and gladly surrender their wills to God. Ask Him to help you preach deep sermons.

The first time God answers this prayer you will know that the hours you spent doing Closet Work were well spent. There is nothing on earth as sweet as being used by God's Holy Spirit to communicate God's Word to reshape the lives of God's people into the image of Christ. Nothing.

---

[34] 1 Cor 2:10–11, insert mine.

Chapter 10

Preaching Deep Sermons

I t's early Thanksgiving morning, and I'm seated at my kitchen table surrounded by food. In anticipation of today's traditional feast I spent yesterday grocery shopping with my wife at Costco, Safeway, and a specialty food store. We have turkey, ham, Gold Coast Starbucks coffee, garlic stuffed olives, yellow potatoes, antipasto, baby spinach, shrimp, pine nuts, whipping cream, mandarin orange slices, Philadelphia Creamed Cheese, balsamic vinaigrette, Coca-Cola, Tellicherry black pepper (whatever that is), and much, much more. I have no shortage of ingredients. What I lack is the knowledge of how to put them together into a meal that my family will enjoy! What do I do with all this stuff?

You may feel the same way right now about "Deep Preaching." You have strong theological and personal motivation for preaching. You also have discovered—through hard exegetical work—the big idea of the passage you intend to preach. And you have spent hours of Closet Work with that idea: praying, meditating, and perhaps fasting as you've walked with the Holy Spirit and asked Him to open your mind and allow you to comprehend its meaning fully. Now what do you do? How do you take the mountain of material you have gathered and put it together into a sermon that will make a deep impact in people's lives?

You have now arrived at the final stage of Deep Preaching. Now is the time that you have to put it all together. Now you begin to think about how all the ingredients of your exegesis and Closet Work should come together for your listeners. So how do you do this? What does a Deep Sermon look like?

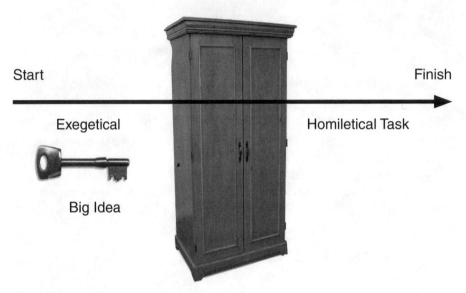

Start   Finish

Exegetical   Homiletical Task

Big Idea

How to Spot a Deep Sermon

Deep Sermons are not as easy to identify as you may think. Deep sermons are like deep people; they come in all shapes, sizes, colors, and genders.

What makes a person spiritually deep is who they are on the inside, not the outside. It is impossible to identify spiritual people by focusing on externals like hair, height, eye color, or clothing styles. No correlation exists between what we see on the outside and what is going on in the inside. The same can be said for sermon forms.

A "traditional" deductive three-point sermon in which you "tell them what you are going to tell them, tell them, and then tell them what you told them"— and then end with a poem is not necessarily deep. Likewise, a clever and engaging narrative sermon that is delivered with enormous dramatic skill is not automatically deep. Or shallow! Deep sermons, like deep people, come in all shapes and sizes. Externals are irrelevant. It is what's inside that counts.[1]

---

[1] Since deep sermons can be found in many different sermon types, I cannot teach you *the* way homiletically to construct a deep sermon. But let me suggest a few resources that will help you increase your homiletical proficiency. Spend time reading, marking, and inwardly digesting H. W. Robinson's *Biblical Preaching: the Development and Delivery of Expository Messages*, 2nd ed. (Grand Rapids: Baker Academic, 2001). This book is a contemporary classic in the evangelical preaching world—and for good reason! I also strongly endorse D. R. Sunukjian's *Invitation to Biblical Preaching: Proclaiming Truth with Clarity and Relevance* (Grand Rapids: Kregel, 2007). I don't know *anyone* who understands the mechanics of an effective sermon better than Donald Sunukjian. Wherever you are on your homiletical journey, Robinson and Sunukjian will help you move forward. They understand preaching and practice it at a very high level! If you are particularly interested in the unique challenges of narrative literature, you may find help in my book, *Effective First-Person Biblical Preaching: The Steps from Text to Narrative Sermon* (Grand Rapids: Zondervan, 2005). While the book focuses on first-person style sermons, you will find this book helpful with all types of narrative preaching.

This does not mean, however, that your commitment to Deep Preaching will not influence your homiletics. On the contrary, the commitments that undergird this kind of preaching will manifest themselves homiletically in a number of ways.

Deep sermons contain unique content and are delivered by unique people.

1. The Content of a Deep Sermon

Deep sermons are biblical. To qualify as a sermon, the truth of the passage you are preaching must be featured. A temptation faced by deep preachers is to abuse the lyrics of the old children's chorus and go "deep and wide": wide of the exegetical mark. Some "deep" preachers seem to value the perception of profundity over Scriptural fidelity and audience impact over authorial intent. When preachers "go wide" of biblical truth they tend to do so in one of two ways.

One way that the content of our sermon can go "wide" of the mark is when Scripture passages are used as springboards for preachers to bounce off into a "hot topic." Preachers who enjoy appearing deep often want to address current and emotionally charged issues. Unfortunately, however, they often don't know where—or perhaps if—the issue of their month is addressed in the Bible. So they force a passage to serve as the starting point rather than the destination of their sermon.

It is very easy to succumb to the "this passage reminds me of . . ." approach to sermon preparation. These sermons often create a buzz and draw crowds. But preachers who bounce off Scripture into tangential "hot button" subjects are not long viewed as deep. They begin looking like radio talk show wannabes and enjoy a similar notoriety.

A second way that "would-be" deep preachers go "wide of the mark" is by spending their Closet Time asking the Holy Spirit to give a "fresh word" (read: inspire new revelation) rather than illuminating the canon of Scripture He has already given us. The Holy Spirit, of course, does not acquiesce to these prayers for additional revelation—the Bible is complete—but some people are adept at convincing themselves and others that He does. These "Bible-plus" preachers use their special knowledge to make their sermons appear more spiritual than biblically orthodox preachers.

The practice of claiming unique direct revelation always engenders spiritual pride and is a clear rejection of Paul's assertion that the Scriptures we have are sufficient to make "the man of God . . . complete, equipped for every good work."[2] But those who choose to "go wide of the mark" this way often develop reputations of "super spirituality" and attract significant crowds, and frequently, significant sums of money.

Both of these paths take preachers wide of God's Word. Those who walk them will miss the mark with their sermons. They will sin when they preach

---

[2] 2 Tim 3:17.

by saying in God's name what God did not say. That is the mark of a false prophet. And false prophets have always been as popular as they are dangerous. The market is always ripe for nonbiblical preaching!

Jesus warned His disciples in the Sermon on the Mount to "Beware of false prophets who come to you in sheep's clothing but inwardly are ravaging wolves."[3] And the disciples took their Savior's warning very seriously. It is fascinating to see the number of times that the apostles warn the early church about the dangers of these counterfeit communicators. It is just as interesting to note the strong language that they employ. It seems that when preachers go "deep and wide" of Scripture they become a significant threat to the church.

Peter warned of the inherent attractiveness and danger of these purveyors of untruth when he said that

> there will be false teachers among you. They will secretly bring in destructive heresies, even denying the Master who bought them, and will bring swift destruction on themselves. Many will follow their unrestrained ways, and because of them the way of truth will be blasphemed. In their greed they will exploit you with deceptive words. Their condemnation, pronounced long ago, is not idle, and their destruction does not sleep.[4]

Likewise, the apostle Paul urged the elders of the church in Ephesus to

> be on guard for yourselves and for all the flock, among whom the Holy Spirit has appointed you as overseers, to shepherd the church of God, which He purchased with His own blood. I know that after my departure savage wolves will come in among you, not sparing the flock. And men from among yourselves will rise up with deviant doctrines to lure the disciples into following them.[5]

And to the church in Galatia, Paul, in no uncertain terms, writes,

> I am amazed that you are so quickly turning away from Him who called you by the grace of Christ, and are turning to a different gospel—not that there is another gospel, but there are some who are troubling you and want to change the gospel of Christ. But even if we or an angel from heaven should preach to you a gospel other than what we have preached to you, a curse be on him! As we have said before, I now say again: if anyone preaches to you a gospel contrary to what you received, a curse be on him![6]

---

[3] Matt 7:15.
[4] 2 Pet 2:1–3.
[5] Acts 20:28–30.
[6] Gal 1:6–9.

The church in Colossae received a similar warning to

> Let no one disqualify you, insisting on ascetic practices and the worship of angels, claiming access to a visionary realm and inflated without cause by his fleshly mind. He doesn't hold on to the head, from whom the whole body, nourished and held together by its ligaments and tendons, develops with growth from God.[7]

Paul also encouraged young Timothy to preach well,

> For the time will come when they will not tolerate sound doctrine, but according to their own desires, will accumulate teachers for themselves because they have an itch to hear something new. They will turn away from hearing the truth and will turn aside to myths.[8]

Whenever preachers say what God did not say or pretend that God gave them additional direct revelation, they are not going deep. They are going astray—and taking others with them.

Whenever we go wide of the mark in the content of our messages, we miss God's purposes. We are guilty of forging God's signature during our sermon preparation and then fraudulently cashing the check when we preach the sermon.

Truly deep preaching will always contain exegetically valid truth, illuminated by the Holy Spirit through the classic spiritual disciplines. Truly deep preachers will always take their listeners deep into the legitimate meaning of a biblical passage—never away from it.

Deep sermons are interesting. Not only is it a sin to bore people with the Word of God; it is also counterproductive. If the people to whom you are speaking have no interest in listening to you, the communication process has failed. You cannot impact people who are not paying attention to you.

Audience interest is especially important in a culture like ours that is facing information overload. All of us are overwhelmed with data. As our information age generates an ever-increasing amount of data, it threatens to bury us beneath its bulk. The only way people can defend themselves from it is by developing the skill of filtering out irrelevant information and only processing meaningful data. Like laptops, people in the information age have installed "spam filters" onto their consciousness. If they detect some irrelevant information, they automatically consider it as "junk mail" and delete it from their memories.

In order for our sermons to make a deep impact in the lives of our listeners, we have to find a way around these spam filters. Deep sermons have to be so riveting that people want to give us one of the rarest gifts of our generation: their undivided attention. If we are not riveting, some of our listeners will put their minds on pause. The others will fire up their BlackBerrys and iPhones and

---

[7] Col 2:18–19.
[8] 2 Tim 4:3–4.

start catching up on their e-mail. Either way, you have lost your listeners and wasted a wonderful opportunity to touch their lives with God's Word. What can you do to be more interesting? Organize your material like a funnel.

Start by speaking broadly. Speak to your listeners about the issues and concerns that impacted their lives last week, and will again next week. You want to begin your sermon in the secular environment in which your listeners live. Begin inclusively by entering into their anxieties, questions, and concerns rather than your own. Their "spam filters" will be asking: "Why should I listen to this sermon? Does this matter? Who cares?" so you better have answers.

You want your sermon to have a sense of urgency and importance. People should be thinking, *I need to hear this!* You cannot expect people to listen to you if you are not talking to them.

Second, proceed down the funnel and identify the core question or issue that is the cornerstone of their anxiety. What is the impetus behind what they are feeling right now? Clarify it. Name it. Define it. Your goal is for your listeners to nod their heads in agreement when you state the core issue behind their concern. You want them to know that you understand their issue.

Third, introduce the biblical passage that you will be preaching and explain to your audience why this text is uniquely appropriate to speak to the need you have just identified. You understand their issue, and the Bible speaks to their issue. The answer to their angst needs to be clearly rooted in the biblical text.

I am not saying here that sermon *preparation* should start with the listener. In fact, I have consistently suggested that sermon preparation begin with the biblical text. But I am saying that as you *arrange your material,* do so with your listener in mind.

When you begin to speak to your congregation about the Scriptures, start with them. Everyone is interested in—and gives their attention to—that which affects their lives. Show your listeners how the passage you are preaching will alter their reality, and they will listen to what you have to say. They will want to listen to what God is saying in His Word. You will be interesting.

Deep sermons are lean. If your goal is to preach deeply, serve lean meat; don't try and communicate everything you know about your passage and its idea. That would be like me taking everything on my Thanksgiving kitchen counter, dumping it into a single pot, and calling it dinner.

The consequence of dumping everything into a single sermon is that you end up with a message—like the aforementioned meal in a pot—that is at best unappetizing and at worst unpalatable. If you put too much in, you will end up creating a mess. Your sermon will be running in every direction and going nowhere.

Go lean. Be ruthlessly selective about what you include in your message. The best meals include only the finest of ingredients. Say what needs to be said and no more.

The length of time you preach will vary depending upon the idea you are communicating and the passage it comes from. Some extended narrative passages, for example, cannot be contained in a 20-minute sermon. There is just too much material to cover! But the temptation is for preachers to take more time than is needed.

Don't pad. Don't inflate your content in a vain attempt to appear spiritual. That is like the butcher injecting water into a chicken so that the "heavier" bird can be sold for more money—and is just as tasteless. Take the time you need to communicate the deep truth of your passage and not a minute more.

Have you ever watched the "bonus features" at the end of a DVD movie you just watched? They often include deleted scenes. These are scenes that seemed to make sense when they were shooting the movie but never made it into the final version of the movie. As painful as it must have been, the director left them on the cutting room floor. What impresses me as I watch these deleted movie scenes is, in retrospect, how much stronger the movie was without these scenes. With the deleted scenes gone, the movie was tighter and better focused. Sometimes less is more.

Take a tip from Hollywood. After your sermon is finished, go through it like a director going through a movie in the unforgiving atmosphere of the editing room. What scenes should be removed? Which content muddies the focus? Which ones are "rabbit trails"?

God is eternal, but our sermons don't need to be. Deep sermons are not necessarily longer sermons—just spiritually significant.

Cut out the fat. Good sermons are lean.

Deep sermons are clear. Do not confuse muddy with deep. Far too many preachers make this mistake. An example of this was, until his death in 2005, a TV preacher well known to California viewers. After his telling his audience that he had earned a PhD from a prestigious university, this preacher would proceed to fill numerous chalkboards or dry-erase boards with factoids. He made much of the original Greek, Hebrew, and Aramaic as he preached, discussing the nuances of biblical languages and their interpretations. I have no idea what this TV preacher was trying to say through the mess of information he presented, but those white boards and $20 words sure looked impressive! He may have raised millions of dollars with his routine, but he was not a deep preacher—just muddy.

Deep preaching is clear and direct. It is profound in its simplicity. Deep preaching does not shed a diffused light on the preacher; it opens a window in the Word of God to allow people to see—without distortion—the face of God.

The best example of preaching that is both clear and deep comes from Jesus Himself. Jesus' sermons did not include extensive footnotes citing the leading rabbis of His day. Nor did He use His messages as showcases for His encyclopedic knowledge of the Old Testament. Jesus did not tell everything He knew; He said what He knew would make His meaning clear. And He did so using the language and the common knowledge of His day. Jesus was breathtakingly straightforward. He was clear because He was simple.

When we finish our sermons people should not be amazed at how smart we are. They should say, "Of course! That's obvious!"

Any idiot can be complicated, but it takes genius to be simple.

Deep sermons are highly visual. People don't understand what you are talking about unless they "can see what you mean." You need to image the truth that you are preaching.

An image in a sermon is like an icon on the desktop of your computer. Your computer icons are a simple graphic that visually represent a highly complex and abstract computer code that lies below the surface. If you and I were to see the code of the programs below the surface, we would be totally lost. But we don't need to. All we need to remember is the visual icon. Just click and go!

In the same way, you need to summarize the complex exegetical information of the passage you are preaching into a simple-to-understand image. You need to present to your listeners a visual representation that they can use to access the truth of your passage.

This does not mean that you have to use a PowerPoint presentation or a movie clip in every sermon. I very rarely use either! As mentioned in chapter 8, metaphors are one of the most effective ways to show people the meaning of a biblical text. Metaphors make abstract truth concrete. They make the complex clear. They help people understand what we are talking about.

When amateur communicators see lost looks on the faces of their listeners they say, "Let me repeat myself." Effective preachers respond to those lost looks with the words, "Let me illustrate." Deep preachers show and tell the ideas of Scripture.

Deep sermons have a clear purpose. When the Spirit is leading, your sermons will not wander in the wilderness of irrelevance. Deep sermons have a destination, a clear behavioral objective that they intend to accomplish in the lives of their listeners.

Look back at the Closet Work you did when you looked outward and asked the question: "What does God want to accomplish in this text?" Also, go over your notes from the "feedback-in-advance" discussions in which you were involved. After all the work you have already invested in this area, you should be able to identify the most important change that God wants to accomplish in the lives of your listeners as a result of this sermon. What is it? State it clearly, and then arrange your material to ensure that everything leads your audience to a clear point of decision and ultimate transformation.

Deep preachers refuse to let biblical truth lying unapplied on the surface of people's minds. Deep sermons change the way people live.

Deep sermons mirror the genre of the text. Communication not only involves speaking words but arranging those words in a literary form. The way that we arrange our words is called genre. Poetry is a genre. A newspaper obituary is a genre. So is narrative. So is a PhD dissertation.

Each literary genre has its own unique strengths and weaknesses. I do not, for example, know of many people who have chosen to express their love for their girlfriend in the form of a PhD dissertation. Poetry seems to be a preferred genre for expressing romantic love.

Wise communicators recognize the relative strengths and weaknesses of each genre and match the idea they want to communicate with the genre whose inherent strengths will best help them accomplish their purposes. They don't, for example, try to say "I love you" by writing an obituary!

As an expert communicator, God combined the best words and the best genre possible to communicate His meaning effectively in your biblical text. God's combination of word and genre cannot be improved upon. Together, the Bible's inspired words and genres accurately communicate God's ideas. Recognizing how words and genre work together in the communication process has huge implications for the preacher.

It means that, in order to retransmit accurately the meaning of a biblical passage, preachers must preserve both the words and genre of the biblical text in their sermons. If preachers tamper with either the words or the genre of a Bible passage, they are tampering with the meaning of that Bible passage. Only if both are acknowledged and preserved will authorial intent be correctly communicated. Sadly, a large number of evangelical preachers do not do this.

Many preachers are content to take the one "acceptable" sermon form they learned in seminary and try and shoehorn every genre of Scripture into it. They confuse traditional homiletical methodology for theological orthodoxy. What a mistake! When you try to preach the dramatic stories of Scripture in the form of a PhD dissertation, the result is both hideous and tedious.

The genres of Scripture need to be preserved homiletically in custom-crafted sermon forms. Preachers who do so will do more than preserve authorial intent. They will also provide their listeners with the same rich and refreshing communication experiences that Bible readers have enjoyed for centuries!

Deep sermons mirror the form of the passage from which they come.

Deep sermons have an emotional crescendo. A deep sermon should not be emotionally vacuous. They are not dry lectures delivered by impassionate scholars who focus entirely on the cerebral. God's Word did not come in the form of a phonebook; it was given by men who cared passionately about those to whom they ministered. They carried God's Word on their lips and His emotions on their shirtsleeves.

Why should Jeremiah be the only weeping prophet? Certainly Paul was not afraid of emotions. In his farewell address to the church of Ephesus, Paul reminded the elders that he served "the Lord with all humility, with tears"[9] and "that night and day for three years I did not stop warning each one of you with tears."[10] I am not suggesting that we should dissolve into a puddle of tears every week, but I do think that the mood of the biblical text should be evident in our sermons. And, our sermons should not end with a whimper.

All too often I hear people conclude their sermons with statements like, "We will pick up again next week at verse 11." How uninspiring is that?

When God writes a book (the Bible) it ends with Jesus returning to earth as conquering king on a white stallion.

> His eyes were like a fiery flame, and on His head were many crowns. He had a name written that no one knows except Himself. He wore a robe stained with blood, and His name is called the Word of God. The armies that were in heaven followed Him on white horses, wearing pure white linen. From His mouth came a sharp sword, so that with it He might strike the nations. . . . And on His robe and on His thigh He has a name written: KING OF KINGS AND LORD OF LORDS.[11]

Now that is an emotional climactic ending! And when Jesus wrapped up His masterful Sermon on the Mount, He did so with a storm so wild and rain so fierce that a sturdy-looking house "fell with a great crash."[12] When God wraps up His communication, it has the emotional excitement of a James Bond movie or a *Die Hard* flick. Why don't our sermons end with similar emotion?

More of our sermons need to culminate with the emotion expressed by a volley of cannon fire at the end of Tchaikovsky's *1812 Overture*—rather than the excitement of a C-SPAN rerun. Our sermons need to do more than end; they need to climax.

Deep sermons stir our emotions as they rouse our souls.

2. The Look of a Deep Preacher

Deep preachers come in a wide variety of sizes, ages, educational backgrounds, denominations, cultures, genders, cultures, and rhetorical preferences. But the characteristic which best distinguishes deep preachers from others is the way that they view themselves. A critical element in the formation of a deep preacher is a biblical self-image.

Deep preachers know who they really are. Preaching has some obvious performance elements to it. You cannot preach without standing in front of people and speaking. As you stand alone under the glare of the spotlights, with your words being amplified and recorded, the pressure begins to mount. There is no place to hide and no one else to blame. Every eye is on you and the stakes are high for you personally! You know that if your words touch people's hearts,

---

[9] Acts 20:19.
[10] Acts 20:31.
[11] Rev 19:12–16.
[12] Matt 7:27, NIV.

they will speak highly of you, and your life and ministry can go much better. But you also know that if your words are not well received, they will speak badly about you. A negative reputation will begin to spread, and the path of your life and ministry will get steeper.

Being a preacher can feel a bit like being a contestant on the *American Idol* TV show. Contestants on this popular show know how high the stakes are. If they do well, they will be launched into a life of wealth and musical fame. If they don't, Simon Cowell may make a laughing stock out of them. Everything depends on how well they look and perform. Does their hair look right? Will they hit that last note?

It takes a considerable amount of courage for an *American Idol* contestant, and a preacher, just to walk out on stage. Performing on stage requires a confidence—a moxie—that many don't have. But under the relentless pressure to perform, moxie is frequently transformed into arrogance and egocentricity. It is no surprise that some of our best-known entertainers (and preachers) have well-earned reputations for being difficult to work with! Their egos have grown haughty in the entertainment atmosphere of performance or perish.

The evangelical church in America makes celebrities of its preachers. Compared to other pastoral staff, preachers enjoy considerably higher pay, visibility, and influence. Preachers at Bible conferences are pursued for autographs and photographs. People vie for the opportunity to take them to dinner. Conferences begin to resemble rock concerts.

Preacher pride is as common, but when moxie bloats into pride, effective ministry becomes impossible. Pride destroys deep preaching.

While deep preachers may speak to large crowds at "A-list" events, they have a sober view of what they bring to the pulpit. Rather than viewing themselves as "God's gift to the church," deep preachers downplay the importance they play in the preaching event. They take their cue from the apostle Paul who said,

> We are not proclaiming ourselves but Jesus Christ as Lord, and ourselves as your slaves because of Jesus. For God, who said, "Light shall shine out of darkness"—He has shone in our hearts to give the light of the knowledge of God's glory in the face of Jesus Christ. Now we have this treasure in clay jars, so that this extraordinary power may be from God and not from us.[13]

Did you notice how Paul views himself? He describes himself as a "clay jar." What an image! I am told that this is a reference to the commonly used household containers of the first century. So common in fact, that even when they are unearthed today they are set aside as archaeologically irrelevant. Paul is saying that he is the ministerial equivalent of an ordinary kitchen container.

---

[13] 2 Cor 4:5–7.

He views himself as an ignoble container that would be considered totally inappropriate for special occasion use. We have a container like that in our house. It is a used Tupperware container that my mother gave us when my wife and I were married 27 years ago. It is a small ugly brown bowl. The only lid we have for it is orange. And the lid is cracked so that it doesn't even make an airtight seal. Quite frankly, it is an embarrassment.

We consider this old Tupperware container as acceptable to hold a bit of left-over rice in the refrigerator for a day or two but not to put on our kitchen table before a family meal. And it certainly would never be placed on the dining room table with fancy china dishes for a special holiday meal! No, this bowl does not qualify for that honor. It is virtually worthless, almost trash. It is the twenty-first-century equivalent of a Corinthian clay jar.

This is how Paul views himself as a preacher. Yes, his preaching has changed countless lives and been instrumental in the planting of many churches. Yes, even today, centuries after his death, the influence of Paul's preaching ministry remains. And, yes, Paul's preaching is considered to have been unusually powerful and effective. But Paul discounts his role in his preaching ministry. He knows that the power of his preaching does not come from him.

Paul wants everyone to know that his great messages do not come from his great abilities. No, Paul is nothing special. He is just a brown Tupperware bowl with a cracked orange lid. He knows that he is an embarrassment best kept hidden in the kitchen. So if his ministry touches you, it can't be because of the plastic container in which you find it. The power of his preaching must come from a great God who condescended to put something so wonderful into a container so unimpressive.

Why would God put such a treasure into such pedestrian containers? Why didn't God get some of His nice dishes out of His china cabinet for the assignment? God chooses to use castoff Tupperware preachers "so that this extraordinary power may be from God and not from us."[14]

Paul is not using the words "clay jars" lightly; he really believes them. His humility is as deep as it is genuine.

Paul knew that the real power behind a deep sermon is not the preacher. As important as human ability and homiletical aptitude may be, Paul knew that the true power of preaching lay beyond his purview. This is why he said, "I am not ashamed of the gospel, because it is God's power for salvation to everyone who believes."[15]

The word translated as "power" (*dunamis*) in Romans 1:16 means the ability to produce a strong effect; to accomplish something. The term is from where the English word "dynamite" comes. When Paul admits that the *gospel* is "God's power" in his ministry, he is confessing that he is not. Paul is personally

---

[14] 2 Cor 4:7.
[15] Rom 1:16.

powerless; his strength rests in the message he preaches. Paul may throw the stick of dynamite when he preaches, but it is the dynamite that changes the world. All the preacher does is bring the dynamite to the worksite.

Paul knew he was not the source of the power behind his preaching. He couldn't be. He was just an old Tupperware container with a cracked orange lid.

Those preachers who insist on putting themselves forward, thinking that they are pivotal to God's work in the world, will not enjoy God's blessing. God makes this very clear when He says in Isaiah 42:

> I am Yahweh,
> that is My name;
> I will not give My glory to another,
> or my praise to idols.[16]

And for those who may have missed it, God repeats Himself a few chapters later, saying:

> I will act for My own sake, indeed, My own,
> for how can I be defiled?
> I will not give My glory to another.[17]

If we try and step into God's limelight, He will take us off the stage. If our moxie grows into preacher pride, God will set us aside. Deep preachers know that God does not need them. They realize that they are Tupperware containers that God chooses to use because their obvious deficiencies will help set off His magnificent "extraordinary power."

The shorter catechism is right when it says, "Man's chief end is to glorify God, and to enjoy him forever."[18] Our life and ministry is not about us; it is about God. It always was and always will be. Deep preachers know this.

Deep preachers read with delight the story of Gideon, a sad-sack man so afraid of the Midianites that when he is introduced he is threshing wheat while hiding in a winepress. And to make sure that no one would think that this kind of man was capable of destroying the combined army of the Midianites, Amalakites, and other eastern peoples, God refused to allow Gideon to attack with his original army of 32,000. In fact, to make sure no one gave credit for the forthcoming victory to Gideon, God whittled the size of Gideon's army down to just 300. 300?! It was impossible for a small group of men like this to win a decisive victory against an overwhelming enemy. But they did.

Why did God use such an improbable warrior as Gideon and a tiny handful of men to win such a tremendous victory? He did this so that the credit for

---

[16] Isa 42:8.

[17] Isa 48:11.

[18] R. Steel, *The Shorter Catechism with Proofs, Analyses and Illustrative Anecdotes* (London: T. Nelson and Sons, 1885), 9.

this battlefield success would be given to the person obviously responsible for Israel's success: God Himself.

God *used* Gideon to win that battle, but He did not *need* Gideon to win that battle. Gideon's contribution was his uselessness. God used him because no one who looked at Gideon could possibly think that *he* had routed the enemy armies. God used Gideon so that the world would know that it was God's power—not Gideon's skill—that made the difference in this battle.

While God chooses to use you and me as preachers, He does not need us. God uses you and me in the pulpit because no one who looks at us could possibly think that *we* were responsible for the deep sermons we preach. It is obvious to the world that the power of our preaching must come from God, not us. We are old Tupperware. He is God.

There are two ways to learn this lesson: the easy way or the hard way. The easy way is by believing 2 Corinthians 4. The hard way is when God forces us, through the circumstances of life, to rely entirely on Him and His power to do ministry. This is what the apostle Paul, in 2 Corinthians 12, confessed that God had done to him:

> . . . so that I would not exalt myself, a thorn in the flesh was given to me, a messenger of Satan to torment me so I would not exalt myself. Concerning this, I pleaded with the Lord three times to take it away from me. But He said to me, "My grace is sufficient for you, for power is perfected in weakness." Therefore, I will most gladly boast all the more about my weaknesses, so that Christ's power may reside in me. So because of Christ, I am pleased in weaknesses, in insults, in catastrophes, in persecutions, and in pressures. For when I am weak, then I am strong.[19]

The secret of Paul's power was his realization that he didn't have any. The more he stopped trying to do ministry in his own strength the more he was able to enjoy the limitless and overwhelming power of Christ. This counterintuitive approach to ministry was so successful that, in time, Paul started delighting in his own weaknesses because he knew that it was then that God would act with power.

Deep preachers know that they are Tupperware. They realize that anything and everything they accomplish in the pulpit is due to God's power and not theirs. God uses deep preachers because they do not try and take God's glory for themselves.

Deep preachers are publicly vulnerable. Have you ever asked yourself why such a disconnection exists between who the people in our pews are and who they say they are? Why do so many of them pretend to live in spiritual victory, when they are really morally adrift? How did they come to value image over

---

[19] 2 Cor 12:7–10.

substance? Why do they prize a reputation for godliness instead of its reality? In too many cases the answer is us. People become like their leaders.

Far too many preachers are concerned about how they look more than who they are. We look into our mirrors far more often than we look into our hearts. The clothes we wear, the cars we drive, the houses we live in, the movies and TV shows we admit to watching are all calculated to project the right pastoral "image." We act more like politicians while our spouses function as political advisors. Do you want proof?

Why is it that after a decade of ministry in a church, our parishioners can know so much about us: what our favorite baseball and football teams are, what music we like, what our favorite foods are, our preferred vacation spots, and even what our dream car is. So why is it that, in so many cases, those parishioners do not know when and where we have wrestled with God? Or, how we are doing in our practice of the classic spiritual disciplines? Or, where we have made strategic spiritual advances and retreats, and where we have utterly failed morally? Why doesn't anyone in our church really know who we are spiritually?

This condition exists because we are not honest with our people when we preach. We work hard at erecting and maintaining a socially acceptable spiritual façade that everyone knows is faked. It must be! Aren't we all sinners who still struggle with sin?

This kind of spirituality makes us look like a bald man wearing a cheap toupee, fooling no one, and looking stupid in the process. When we paste a cheap spiritual veneer on our lives, nobody wants to buy what we are selling. We look cheesy and disingenuous.

Preachers who know who they really are do not find it difficult to be publicly vulnerable. While they take no pleasure in the sin they see in themselves, they hate hypocrisy with a passion. They want to be honest with God and His people more than they want an impossibly perfect reputation. For this reason, deep preachers are not afraid to admit their frailties, failures, and insecurities.

Like the apostle Paul, deep preachers eschew pretense. They have long since stopped trying to be "a perfect pastor," pretending that they are adequate for the ministry in which they find themselves. Deep preachers know the truth about themselves and freely admit their weaknesses and limitations. They know that the doctrine of sin is the best-proved doctrine of the Christian faith and take responsibility for their part in it.

Deep preachers refuse to use vulnerability as a communication gimmick. They genuinely and passionately want to push their lives into God, and they only approach their congregation after this has taken place. Deep preaching is the rich cream that rises to the surface of lives of those who have met God in a significant way. Deep preaching leaks from the lips of people whose passion is to know God in the fullness of his glory. Deep preachers take the third question of their Closet Work very seriously. They are not afraid to look inward and ask, "What is God saying to *me* in this text?" Like Paul in Romans 7, deep preachers approach the passage they are preaching with an almost frightening fearlessness. They are ruthlessly honest in their self-assessment and ask the Holy Spirit to show them what they do not see. Deep preachers want to be transparent with both God and humanity.

Deep preachers examine their hearts with confidence because they know that regardless of what sin they may find hidden in the dark crevices of their hearts, God will not reject them. God will not turn His back on them, no matter how badly they may have messed up. As David said about God after his sin with Bathsheba,

> You do not want a sacrifice, or I would give it;
> You are not pleased with a burnt offering.
> The sacrifice pleasing to God is a broken spirit.
> God, You will not despise a broken and humbled heart.[20]

God wants us to bring sacrifices of broken spirits and bruised hearts. He wants us to come to Him and say, "Father, forgive me for I have sinned!" God delights in honesty as much as He hates hypocrisy. For this reason we preachers would be wise to hear and heed the challenge of D. A. Carson:

> Has the smoothness of the performance become more important to us than the fear of the Lord? Has polish . . . displaced substance? Have professional competence and smooth showmanship become more valuable than sober reckoning over what it means to focus on Christ crucified?

> Do not fear weakness, illness, or a sense of being overwhelmed. The truth of the matter is that such experiences are often the occasions when God most greatly displays his power. As long as people are impressed by your powerful personality and impressive gifts, there is very little room for you to impress them with a crucified Savior.[21]

Don't pretend that you are perfect to God or His people. Everyone knows you're not perfect—because no one is—and trying to look perfect just makes you look silly.

Deep preachers root their public ministries in personal honesty. They remove their evangelical makeup and let people see them as they really are. And as they do so, they model for their parishioners what true righteousness looks like.

Deep preachers are risk-takers. When you know who you really are and choose public integrity over image management, you will be willing to take risks in the pulpit.

---

[20] Ps 51:16–17.
[21] D. A. Carson, *The Cross and Christian Ministry: An Exposition of Passages from 1 Corinthians* (Grand Rapids: Baker, 1993), 38.

Jeremiah bought a new designer belt, wore it publicly for a while, and then buried it under some rocks. Many days later he dug it up and discovered that "it was ruined—of no use whatsoever."[22] He then used the decayed belt as an object lesson in his sermon to Judah to tell them how God would ruin their pride, and how those who refused to listen to his sermon are as useless as the belt.

Wow! That is strong stuff. And the radical way the message was delivered helped drive the point home. I'm pretty sure that moldy clothing was not common practice in the rabbinic preaching of the day. This is preaching on the wild side. It is proclamation of the Word that goes way outside of the lines of what was considered "normal."

Then Jeremiah really goes off the rails. The prophet tells them "Every jar should be filled with wine."[23] This is the ancient equivalent of you telling your church members from the pulpit to go to the liquor store and buy a case of beer. Not what you would normally expect to hear from a true prophet of God! So why does Jeremiah say this? To make the point that Israel is stumbling in a drunken stupor toward divine judgment.

As we reel in horror at Jeremiah's homiletical excesses, we need to remind ourselves that God not only allowed this culturally inappropriate preaching to occur, but it was His idea! God commanded it.

God's homiletics are not limited by the cultural niceties of His day. You get the idea here that God wants His prophet to do whatever it takes to communicate God's word to God's people. God doesn't care about the reputation of His preacher any more than the sensitivities of the congregation. All God cares about is the effective communication of His message. Everything else is secondary.

If you want to be as faithful a spokesperson for God as Jeremiah was, you must be willing to do anything but sin to accomplish your task as a preacher. You have to be willing to sacrifice your pride as well as your reputation. You have to be a homiletical risk-taker.

Since when did church ministry become a haven for the status quo? Why is the pulpit so often a refuge of yesteryear? Too many of our churches have the look and feel of the set of the old *Happy Days* TV show, and too many pastors look and sound like Richie Cunningham.

But yesterday is gone, and we have been called by God to communicate His word as effectively as possible to our generation. Are you willing to move forward? Are you willing to stand on the bleeding edge of homiletics?

When you know who you really are, and don't care about your reputation, you will be far more likely to step away from the trappings of traditionalism.

---

[22] Jer 13:7.
[23] Jer 13:12.

Who cares if we wear jeans? Or don't? Or if we wear ties? Or don't? Or if we preach a narrative sermon rather than a three-point one? Or if we go longer than normal? Or shorter? Or if we used a video montage similar to the "Jay Walking" segment on the *Tonight Show* to set up our sermon? What if a sermon was dominated by a huge metaphor like refusing to turn on the auditorium lights to emphasize the spiritual darkness of our world? Or, giving everyone a Starbucks gift card with $5 on it, with the caveat that they can only use it when they are sharing the gospel with someone?

What if Sundays were not predictable? And if the only criterion we used to judge the effectiveness of our preaching was whether God's Word was accurately communicated the most effective way possible?

Are you willing to say that you will do anything—no matter how professionally embarrassing or personally humiliating—to communicate God's Word more effectively? Anything?

What does it say about us when we hesitate to answer that question with less than an immediate "yes"? Jesus was willing to humiliate Himself by becoming flesh. John the Baptist was willing to eat bugs. Paul was willing to make himself

> a slave to all, in order to win more people. To the Jews I became like a Jew, to win Jews; to those under the law, like one under the law . . . to win those under the law. To those who are outside the law, like one outside the law . . . to win those outside the law. To the weak I became weak, in order to win the weak. I have become all things to all people, so that I may by all means save some. Now I do all this because of the gospel.[24]

Deep preachers have always been willing to step out of their comfort zones to communicate the Word of God effectively. Are you?

Deep preachers embrace community. Why do we consider preaching a competition sport? Doesn't it seem strange to you that so little genuine community exists among preachers, especially when we have so much in common?

I have spent my entire pastoral ministry as part of a denomination, but it was only during some of the very early days that I felt emotionally and spiritually connected to other denominational pastors. Everyone seems absorbed in their own churches and careers. Pastors view other pastors as a pride's male lion on the savannah would view a younger bachelor lion—as threats trying to take away their pride.

Deep preachers refuse to view other preachers as rivals. They know who they are before God and have no ego to protect; all they want is for God to be glorified. Deep preachers genuinely resonate with John the Baptist that "it is okay if my ministry decreases, as long as Jesus' ministry increases." They view other preachers as fellow laborers in the kingdom and understand that our

---

[24] 1 Cor 9:19–23.

joint goal is to bring in the harvest for the God we jointly serve. And, they are willing to hold the ladder while their colleague picks the fruit.

So why do our sermon preparation alone? Why not try and find other deep preachers in your area and get together with them on a regular basis? This could be like one of John Wesley's "Holy Clubs" as you combine a vigorous time of sermon discussion with relentlessly vigorous application of God's Word to your own lives.

If you are interested in starting a contemporary "holy club," I recommend that you establish that the primary purpose of these groups is to do spiritual life together. The secondary purpose of these groups should be sermon assistance. In order to preserve intimacy and allow everyone to participate, I would restrict the size of a group to about a half dozen people.

Since this group will be working through the five questions of Closet Work, you will be practicing the spiritual disciplines together and holding each other accountable for holy living as you work through biblical passages. Membership in this group will, therefore, require absolute transparency, honesty, and confidentiality. Those who won't commit to this should be politely excused from the group.

These "holy clubs" could meet as often as every other week, but I suspect that most pastors will find that monthly meetings work best. I would put on a pot of coffee and set aside an entire morning (8:00 a.m.—12:00 noon) for the meeting. You have a lot of work to do!

When you meet, begin by sharing the exegesis that group members have done in advance on your preassigned passages. Depending on how often your group meets, you may have two or four passages to talk about. Regardless of how many passages you plan on working through, be sure that everyone comes with their homework done. I would be very firm here and refuse to allow people to attend or participate unless their exegesis is complete. By "complete" I mean that the big idea of every passage scheduled for that morning is written down and ready to be defended exegetically and discussed. This group is not a place where people can avoid hard work in the biblical text. "What does this passage mean to you?" should not be allowed. The world has enough "pooled ignorance"; we don't need to contribute to it. Ideally, the participants would all work with and through the same biblical texts at the same time. This would mean that the preachers, and their churches, would be preaching the same biblical passages at the same time. I've never heard of this happening, before, but why not? Why couldn't preachers and churches work together to proclaim God's word to a region?

Start your "holy club" meeting by having people take turns presenting one of the assigned exegetical ideas. Spend some time trying to reach group consensus on your ideas in the context of the give and take of group discussion. If agreement on an idea is not possible, don't get stuck. Just move on. If a member of the group is constantly lost or way off the mark with their ideas, then your group has a problem. This may not be the right group for that person. Don't allow one person's exegetical struggles to sabotage the work of the entire group. As the group agrees on exegetical ideas, write those ideas on a white board. Now you are ready to start your Closet Work.

Use the summary of the five questions of Closet Work included in the appendix of the book to guide your discussion. When you look backward, be sure to place your idea in its original historical story. Then be sure you take time to make a metaphor of that idea. Having the group make metaphors can be very helpful. The process of deciding what metaphors work best and why will really sharpen people's understanding of the biblical idea.

My hunch is that your group will find the second question, where you look upward at God, to be the easiest. Not because the question is simple, or because God is, but because it feels safe to look away from our own hearts. For this reason it is important not to let the group spend all of its time here. Deal with it and move on.

The third question is the hardest. Looking inward is not a preacher's preference. We would rather examine other people's lives than our own. But the discussion around "What is God saying to me in this text?" is critical. It is here, and perhaps only here, where the biblical text and our group members will make sure that they are not just "playing preacher." This is where we are "honest to God" and with His people. This is where genuine intimacy can forge 14-carat quality relationships. This is where strangers are transformed into friends, where threatening lions become friendly allies. Pray, weep, and laugh together—just don't lie. And never, ever break a confidence. This is where Dietrich Bonheoffer's idea of community can become a living reality.[25]

The fourth question, where we ask what God wants to accomplish through this text in the lives of others will also be helpful for your discussion, but if you have already received feedback in advance, you will not have to spend too much time here. And be sure that you do not confess other people's sins or allow your time together to degenerate into a gripe session. Yes, ministry is tough and our congregants are all sinners; now let's move on.

The fifth question will be very helpful for you to discuss in your "holy club." You will find that those members of your group who have walked with God and led His people the longest will have some important insights to share. They have been around long enough to see how Satan operates; they've learned his *modus operandi*. Some significant teaching and learning can take place here!

End your discussion of the idea of a particular text by talking, in general terms, about how this idea could be preached. The idea is not for all of you to emerge from your "holy club" meeting with identical sermons. You are all different people preaching in different situations to different people; so your

---

[25] D. Bonhoeffer, *Life Together*, 1st ed. (New York: Harper, 1954).

sermons should all be unique. But it is helpful to bandy around ideas for every-one to consider. You can help each other become more homiletically creative. Together you can encourage the cautious preachers to take necessary risks and caution the impulsive preachers not to be stupid. Everyone will remain respon-sible for the sermons that they choose to preach, but wouldn't it be wonderful to have a group of trusted preacher friends off whom you might bounce your ideas?

Deep preachers understand the importance of getting alone with God to do serious Closet Work. But they also value community.

We are to work and pray for God's kingdom to come, not our own. And we are willing to work together for the glory of God.

Deep preachers live their priorities. One of the biggest problems with Deep Preaching is the time that it takes. Most pastors would prefer to spend only an hour or two in sermon preparation. They spend thousands of dollars on preaching tools to reduce the time required to create a sermon. They need another item on their schedule like they need another bill in the mail, which partially explains why so many pastors are scouring the Internet right now trying to find sermons to steal.

I know that you have more items on your "to do" list than you can hope to accomplish this week. Or even this month! So how can you hope also to squeeze the demands of Closet Work and deep preaching into your calendar? You can't. It is impossible for you to add the contents of this book to what you are doing now. I'm not asking you to do more things. I am asking you to do things differently.

Go back and read chapters 2 and 3 again. Remind yourself of the compelling theological, historical, and pragmatic reasons for preaching. Remind yourself of your calling. You are not just a pastor. According to Ephesians 4 you are a pastor-teacher. Preaching is embedded into your pastoral calling, and the health and future of the church depend on you fulfilling your God-given responsibili-ties. It is not good enough to toss pop-tart sermons at your spiritually hungry parishioners—that is what hirelings do. Good shepherds go further. Like our Lord, they lead their sheep into green pastures. Good shepherds feed their sheep well. And that takes time.

Do not add Deep Preaching to your existing schedule. Rearrange your sched-ule and remove items from your schedule to give yourself the time you need for Deep Preaching. Deep preachers have the same number of hours in their days and days in their weeks as the rest of us. The difference is that deep preachers don't try to do everything. They recognize the priority that Scripture places on preaching and respond to that priority by altering their schedules accordingly. They live their priorities, just like Jesus did.

In Luke 4:31–33 there is an amazing story about Jesus at the start of His min-istry. As He begins teaching the people, "They were astonished at His teaching because His message had authority."[26] Jesus was, not surprisingly, preaching amazing sermons at local synagogues. What is surprising, however, is that Satan interrupted one of Jesus' sermons with an unusual message. Rather than just heckling, we read that

> In the synagogue there was a man with an unclean demonic spirit who cried out with a loud voice, "Leave us alone! What do You have to do with us, Jesus—Nazarene? Have You come to destroy us? I know who You are—the Holy One of God!"[27]

And Satan does it again in Luke 4:41 when "demons were coming out of many, shouting and saying, 'You are the Son of God!'"

This is a strange message indeed. Why would Satan advertise Jesus' true identity? What was the point? After all, Jesus was not afraid of letting people know who He was. When He was baptized, God the Father announced to the world, "You are My beloved Son. I take delight in You!"[28] And in the sermon Jesus preached in Nazareth Jesus quoted the messianic passage Isaiah 61:1–2 and said, "Today as you listen, this Scripture has been fulfilled."[29] So why is Satan giving Jesus free advertising? And, even more bizarrely, why does Jesus keep telling Satan to stop revealing His identity? What is going on here?

The key to understanding this passage is to notice the reaction of the crowds when they hear Satan's messianic announcements. The people respond to the satanic announcements—and subsequent exorcisms—by being very impressed with Jesus' power. In fact the people started coming in huge numbers to experience Jesus' power themselves, in the form of physical healing. First, Simon's mother-in-law was healed. Then, "When the sun was setting, all those who had anyone sick with various diseases brought them to Him. As He laid His hands on each one of them, He would heal them."[30]

Did you notice the shift that just took place in this story? It started with Jesus doing some amazing and authoritative preaching in Capernaum's synagogue, but now, thanks to Satan's advertising campaign, Jesus is spending the majority of His time demonstrating His power by healing people.

Now, there is nothing wrong with healing people. Healing is a great thing to do. But now Jesus is so busy doing the good work of healing that He no longer has time to preach. Satan has succeeded in redirecting Jesus' ministry. *Jesus' calendar is now too full to fulfill God's primary objective intended for His ministry.*

It is not that Jesus didn't know what His primary mission was. He had stated it clearly in His Nazareth sermon when he quoted Isaiah 61:1–2,

---

[26] Luke 4:32.
[27] Luke 4:33–34.
[28] Luke 3:22.
[29] Luke 4:21.
[30] Luke 4:40.

> The Spirit of the Lord is on Me,
> because He has anointed Me
> to preach good news to the poor.
> He has sent Me
> to proclaim freedom to the captives,
> and recovery of sight to the blind,
> to set free the oppressed,
> to proclaim the year of the Lord's favor.[31]

Jesus knew that He would make His maximum impact in ministry by preaching. And so did Satan. That is why Satan sent all those helpless hurting people Jesus' way. Satan wanted Jesus to get so busy doing good things that He would not have time to do the best things. Satan was trying to blunt the effectiveness of Jesus' ministry by keeping Him too busy to make His maximum impact.

The lesson that this passage has for us is clear: *God does not send every ministry opportunity.* Some legitimate and worthwhile ministry opportunities are sent by Satan to keep us from our primary calling. Satan sends us good work to keep us from making our maximum impact for God.

This was a hard lesson for me to learn. Every weekend I would complain to my wife that my week of pastoring had been too busy to allow me to spend the time I wanted on my sermon. I would explain to her about how many people I had visited in the hospital that week and how many hours I had spent doing marital counseling and how still others had required premarital counseling. Then there were the committee meetings I had to attend and the elders' retreat that I had to plan. I was swamped!

Week after week, my wife would look at me and say, "But isn't preaching your primary gift? Why are you not giving your best time to your preaching?"

"You don't understand," I would respond, "I am the pastor, I can't say no to anyone who has a legitimate need that I can help them with!"

What a fool I was. If only I had noticed how Christ responded to the people who tried to keep Him too busy to preach.

> When it was day, He went out and made His way to a deserted place. But the crowds were searching for Him. They came to Him and tried to keep Him from leaving them. But He said to them, "I must proclaim the good news about the kingdom of God to the other towns also, because I was sent for this purpose." And He was preaching in the synagogues of Galilee.[32]

If only I had listened to my wife. If only I had looked at how Jesus handled Satan's subtle strategy to deflect Him away from His primary calling.

---

[31] Luke 4:18–19.
[32] Luke 4:42–44.

Satan's strategy to marginalize Jesus' ministry was brilliant. And it almost worked. We read in Luke 4:42 that Jesus needed a special time of prayer to regain His balance after the onslaught of human need that had come His way. He needed some closet time to recalibrate His priorities.

While Jesus would never totally stop helping and healing people, He would never again allow good activities to prevent Him from His primary task of preaching. First and foremost Jesus knew He was a preacher and that everything else was a distant second.

We need to learn the critical lesson of this passage. We need to know that it is OK to say no. We need to know that our ministries will only be fully effective if our ministries fully reflect our priorities. We need to know when to say no to people, even when they have needs we can meet. This is what the disciples did.

The disciples looked at how Jesus organized his calendar and applied that lesson to their ministries. This is why they were able to say,

> "It would not be right for us to give up preaching about God to wait on tables. Therefore, brothers, select from among you seven men of good reputation, full of the Spirit and wisdom, whom we can appoint to this duty. But we will devote ourselves to prayer and to the preaching ministry."[33]

Think about how radical this was. The disciples said no to feeding widows! Widows! Isn't that committing ministerial suicide? You and I can only imagine how much grief we would endure from some members of our congregation for behaving in such a "cold" and "uncaring" manner.

We are so fearful of the e-mail campaign that would result from our decision that we try and do it all. We feed the widows on the way to the hospital, attend every committee meeting we can, and then hit SermonCentral.com Saturday night looking for something to preach, while praying, "God help me!" But He won't. He wants you to change the way that you do ministry. He wants you to rearrange your ministry calendar to reflect your ministerial priorities.

It may be time for you to have some discussions with your church leadership to help them understand your true calling. It may be time for you to help people in your church discover their spiritual gifts so that they can help feed the widows and chair the committee meetings. God wants the work of the ministry to get done. He just doesn't want you to do it all.

If you try to do too much, you will spread yourself so thin that deep sermons will become impossible. Deep sermons come from deep preachers, and it takes serious time doing Closet Work to go deep.

If you want to preach deep sermons, you have to live your priorities. You must be willing to say "no" to people's legitimate needs and give your best

---

[33] Acts 6:2–4.

time to the preaching that God has called you to do. This is God's high calling on your life. It is time to step up to the challenge.

The deep preacher's reward. False prophets preach for paychecks. Deep preachers preach because they must. Preaching is part of the spiritual DNA of deep preachers. They preach God's Word for the same reason that fish swim; it is how God made them. They will die if they stop.

Deep preachers resonate with Jeremiah when he complained to God that

> You deceived me, LORD, and I was deceived.
> You seized me and prevailed.
> I am a laughingstock all the time;
> everyone ridicules me.
> For whenever I speak, I cry out—
> I proclaim: Violence and destruction!
> because the word of the LORD has become for me
> constant disgrace and derision.
> If I say: I won't mention Him
> or speak any longer in His name,
> His message becomes a fire burning in my heart,
> shut up in my bones.
> I become tired of holding it in,
> and I cannot prevail.[34]

Deep preachers know that their calling to preach comes from the throne of God Himself, and God is the one we must please.

When we open the Word of God we are not just fulfilling our contractual obligation to the church that employs us, as tough as they may be. As we preach that we also have a higher and more terrifying obligation to honor the God who commissioned us as preachers.

It is not enough, therefore, to measure success by the accolades of earth. "Good job, pastor!" one person says to us after a service. "An inspiring word, brother," another parishioner chimes in. As helpful and encouraging as those words may be, they should never be enough for us. Deep preachers want more.

A deep preacher's reward begins in those golden moments when God's Holy Spirit suddenly and powerfully begins coursing through our words as we preach, deeply impacting the lives of our listeners. It begins when we are gripped by the realization that what God is doing at that moment is beyond anything we could have engineered; the natural has been eclipsed by the supernatural.

We realize in that moment that God is using us to wield His Word "living and effective and sharper than any two-edged sword"[35] like a scalpel to perform spiritual surgery. As we stand on the edge of the platform we see God's word cutting

---

[34] Jer 20:7-9.
[35] Heb 4:12.

and reshaping the lives of our listeners into the image of Christ. This is truly a sweet moment! But as wonderful as this is, it is not our ultimate reward.

Beyond what happens here on earth, we yearn for the approval of the One who called and gifted us. We are listening for the applause of heaven. The ultimate goal of our preaching is to please the God who loves us as His bride. We want to be a source of delight to the God we love more than life itself.

There will come a day when we appear before His throne to give an account for the deeds that we have done. At that moment when we are lying prostrate on the ground overwhelmed by His holiness, the deep preacher longs to feel God's hand lifting him up. And to hear God whisper in his ear, "Well done, good and faithful slave!"[36]

Let us run the race of ministry well. Let us run to please the lover of our soul.

Deep preaching is a labor of love.

---

[36] Matt 25:21

Appendix 1

Closet Questions

I suggest that you spend Closet Time meditating, praying, and fasting if necessary over the idea you discovered during your exegesis. To guide you during this time I suggest that you focus on the idea of your passage from five different perspectives, by asking five different questions. Each question will challenge you in a different way. Each question will take you deeper into the biblical passage and the idea it contains.

Please keep in mind that as you work through these questions you are *not* writing your sermon. The five questions are the content of your Closet Work. They are what you meditate on, pray about, and fast when necessary while in your closet. These five questions are intended to give your time with God focus and purpose. The homiletics should not begin until your Closet Work is complete.

Look Backward

The first question to meditate and pray about in your closet is "Why was this exegetical idea *necessary* for its original audience?"

> *Question #1: Why was this exegetical idea* **necessary** *for its original recipients?*

1. To whom did the biblical author deliver this message?
2. What problem did it address?
3. Why did they *need* to hear it? How urgent was it? Why?

   Your goal here is to determine what the problem "looked like" in the story of the original recipients. Visualize the situation that required this biblical truth. See it in your mind. Be sure that the problem you see is tangible. If it is not real in your mind, ask why.

4. Does the antecedent history of the recipients help explain why this instruction was necessary for these people at this time?
5. Are there any cultural factors that would have incubated or accelerated the need for this instruction? Why were the hearts of the original recipients so prone to wander in this direction? Why did God think that *they* specifically needed to be given this idea?
6. What do you think the emotional response of the original recipients of this biblical truth would have been? What was their visceral reaction when they first heard it? Why do you think so?
7. What did the original recipients of this message do with it? Did they heed this word or ignore it? Do we know?
8. How *did* this truth transform, or how *could* it have transformed the recipient's life?

   Something is not true because it is in the Bible; it is in the Bible because it is true. Our decision to obey or disobey it determines whether our lives flourish or flounder. With this in mind, develop two scenarios.

   a. What would life have been like for the original recipients if they *had* fully responded to the truth of this passage?
   b. What would life have been like for the original recipients if they had ignored or disregarded this truth?

9. Is this the only time that this principle is mentioned in Scripture? Have others struggled with this issue throughout biblical history? Who? When? Why? With what outcome?
10. What metaphors best capture the meaning of this passage?

Look Upward

The second question to meditate and pray about in your closet is "What is God revealing about *Himself* in this text?"

Question #2: What is God revealing about **Himself** in this text?

1. What does this text reveal about God's character? From which of God's attributes does its idea emanate?

   Here you want to link actions and character. You want to understand why God's character necessitated that this truth be given to its original recipients at the time it was given.
2. Why is the truth of this text theologically necessary? Why would God ask this of His people or do this to His people? Is God being

unreasonable or unfair? Does He have your best interests at heart? How do you know that?

Look Inward

We began our Closet Work by looking backward and asking, "What did God communicate in this passage?" Then we look upward at what our text tells us about God. Now we need to look inward and ask, "What is God saying to *me* in this text?"

Question #3: What is God saying to me *in this text?*

Before you think about how the idea you discovered should impact other people's lives, *first* ask how it should impact yours. Here are a series of questions that can help you do that.

In what ways am I similar to/does my life parallel the original recipients of this book?

1. Are my weaknesses their weaknesses?
2. Are my temptations theirs? Have I succumbed as they did?
3. Has my life been warped as a result?
4. In what ways? With what consequences?
5. When was I more likely to fall into this sin?
6. What habits/practices exist in my life that contribute to this problem?
7. What is it about me that made me vulnerable to this particular attack by the enemy (i.e. what is the root problem that manifests itself in this sin)?
8. How has my life and ministry suffered as a result of this sin?
9. How have others been affected by this?
10. How could my life and ministry have been enhanced by withstanding this temptation?
11. How will the idea of this text force your life spiritually forward?
12. Picture the different reality that you and your people could be experiencing right now if you had made different choices.

Walk in this for a time. Allow these questions to penetrate into your soul. Practice the presence of Christ. Allow the Holy Spirit to illuminate your mind with the knowledge of who you really are behind the role you occupy and the image that you project.

My Heart Christ's Home.[1] In this simple book, Robert Boyd Munger uses the metaphor of a house to help us gain insight into our heart. Like Munger, take Christ for a tour of your life in light of the idea you discovered in your text.

- study—your mind
- the dining room—the room of appetites and desires

---

[1] R. B. Munger, *My Heart, Christ's Home,* 2nd rev. ed. (Downers Grove, IL: InterVarsity Press, 1992).

- the living room—a quiet and secluded spot for good talks and fellowship with Jesus
- the workroom—where things are produced for the kingdom of God
- the recreation room—where I go to relax and have fun
- the bedroom—where my marriage is celebrated
- the family room—where relationships with the family of God are developed and enriched
- the kitchen—where I come together with others to serve the family of God
- the hall closet—where we try and hide our secret sins

Are you pleased with what you discovered on your tour? Are there areas of incongruity between your actual life and what God is asking for in the idea of your text?

Alone or with the help of others, the key question you need to ask yourself is *"What is stopping me from radically applying this truth to my life?"* Why do I refuse to act on it, as I know I should? Why does it have such a hold on my life?

Remember the rule: *the more spiritual you think you are, the further from God you really are.* The people who think that they have "arrived" in their relationship with God are the furthest from Him.

Look Outward

After investing Closet Time looking backward, upward, and inward at the idea of the passage that we are going to preach, it is time to look outward and ask: "What does God want to *accomplish* in this text?"

Question #4: What does God want to accomplish through this text?

A good place to begin is by seeing what the original writer wanted to accomplish in the lives of the original recipients of this truth. Does it apply to your listeners in the same way? Here are some questions that may help focus your thoughts on the similarities and dissimilarities between yours and the original audience.

1. In what ways are the people you lead similar to the original audience? Consider the similarities that may exist. Consider factors such as

    a. Socio-economically—poor or affluent?
    b. Socially—comfortable family units or widows/orphans?
    c. Morally—living surrounded by licentiousness? Affluence? Hedonism? Secularism?
    d. Politically—is your country being led by someone trying to follow God's direction or by a pagan?

e. Spiritually (length of time they have walked with God, the spiritual heritage you may enjoy, the temperature of their spiritual passion—i.e. cool, lukewarm, or boiling hot?)

Now spend some time thinking about the receptivity that your listeners are likely to have to the idea of your passage.

1. Do you think that your people want to live in harmony with the teaching of this text? Why or why not? What would their objections be?
2. What is keeping you and your people from living out this text? Are there any structural/organizational barriers?

Ask a group of people if they would be willing to help you with your sermon. After you have briefly outlined the exegetical idea of your passage, invite your guests to speak regarding how this truth specifically impacts their lives.

Here are some questions that may be useful as you meet with your group.

- Does this idea attract or repel you? Excite or scare you? Why?
- Does this idea seem like nonsense or common sense? Imminently practical or hopelessly idealistic? Why?
- If you could tell God to His face what you thought of this idea, what would you say? What would you be afraid to say?
- If you could talk to people in the pew about this idea, what would you say? To whom would you say it? Why?
- Who in the secular community desperately needs to hear this truth? Why?
- Who in the secular community would react violently either for or against this idea? Why?
- If you made a decision today to take this truth very seriously, what difference would it make in your life? Why?

1. What people in your congregation have lived in obedience to this text? (Think of specific people.)
2. What people in your congregation have lived in violation of this text? (Again, think of specific people.)
3. How could this truth transform your people and/or the community in which you and your people live and minister? What are the ripple effects that could result from embracing the truth of this text?

These questions help determine if the application of your biblical passage is significantly influenced by a person's phase of life, genetic predisposition, self-discipline, education, spousal support, or some other factor. And the enormous benefits that will result from obeying it!

Look Forward

After investing Closet Time looking backward, upward, inward, and outward at the idea you are going to preach, it is time to look forward and ask: "What could *negate* the progress I have just made through this text?"

Question #5: What could negate *the progress I have just made through this text?*

Do you really think that if you preached a sermon that accomplished all of your objectives that Satan would stand idly by? Do you think he will sit idly by allowing you to enjoy the spiritual ground that you may have just taken unchallenged? I don't think so. Prepare for a counterattack. In what ways will he try and take back the spiritual ground that you just took for Christ and His kingdom?

Here are some questions that may help get you started.

1. What method is Satan likely to use to counterattack?
   a. Will he tell lies? (He is the father of lies—John 8:44.)
   b. Will he use discouragement?
   c. Will he try and cause division to advance his cause?
   d. Will he try and exploit some preexisting circumstance or condition?

2. What circumstances could make continued obedience to this truth difficult (e.g. sudden singleness [divorce/death], economic recession/job loss, loss of health)?

3. What age group (e.g. children, youth, college student, young married, middle aged, recently retired, elderly) will find the application of this truth most difficult? Why? How could those who won't struggle as much with this truth help those who will?

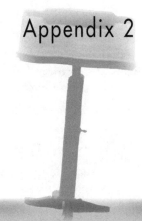

Appendix 2

Improving Perfection
(Extended Metaphor)

How do you improve perfection?[1] Would you have the audacity to add a brush stroke or two to a Rembrandt? Or renovate a house built by Frank Lloyd Wright? Or give putting pointers to Tiger Woods? Or how about adding a few bars to Handel's *Messiah?* Some things are so good, that the best thing we can do is keep our hands off them. They are better off left alone. Unspoiled. Untouched.

If this principle of "look but don't touch" were true of anything, it would seem to be true of a fine crystal bowl I recently discovered. This bowl stands 4.25" high and 13.25" wide and costs a breathtaking $6,100. Why so expensive? Because it was designed by Michele Oka Doner and produced by the Steuben Glass Company. It is a joint masterpiece.

Michele Oka Doner is an internationally acclaimed artist and designer whose career spans four decades. Her art can be found in the collections of the Metropolitan Museum of Art and Cooper-Hewitt National Design Museum in New York and the Chicago Art Institute. Her numerous public art commissions include New York's Herald Square Subway Station and the Miami International Airport. Ms. Donner is so respected in her field that she has even had two books written about her![2] So when Ms. Doner decides to create a crystal bowl, you just know that the results are going to be spectacular!

---

[1] This article first appeared in *The Voice* (Summer 2008), a publication of Woodland Hills Church, Woodland Hills, California. J. Kent Edwards is the pastor.

[2] See http://www.micheleokadoner.com/back.html.

What makes this $6,100 bowl even more impressive, however, is that Ms. Doner's concept was brought to life by the famed Steuben Glass Company of New York.

Steuben's New York City Flagship Store was built in 2000 on Madison Avenue at 61st Street. But don't let the modern magnificence of its 6,100-square-foot, three-level facility deceive you. This company has a long history of commitment to the highest quality.

Founded in 1903, Steuben Glass has always been made at their Corning, New York, factory. Steuben's unique glass is made by hand from an outstanding optical formula. The state-of-the-art melting process ensures that the glass is exceptionally pure and free of even the tiniest visual imperfections. Skilled artisans work in teams around reheating ovens called glory holes, as directed by a master "gaffer." Each gather of molten glass is carried from tank to glory hole, where it is formed "at the fire" with blowpipes, pontil rods, shears, calipers, and other tools little changed over centuries. Finished pieces are slowly cooled in annealing ovens, then cut, polished, and engraved by hand. Each example is minutely inspected before it is signed with a diamond-tipped pen. Imperfect items are destroyed. There are no seconds at Steuben. They only sell perfect product![3]

Michele Oka Doner and the Steuben Glass Company are the best of the best. They worked hand in hand, combining their formidable expertise, to create a crystal bowl that is a true work of art.

If you were to lay down $6,100 for this pedigreed crystal bowl, you could be forgiven for believing that there was nothing you could add to their impressive handiwork but your admiration. After all, how do you improve upon perfection? Yet, in this case you can. And Doner and Steuben ask you to do so.

Those who purchase this bowl discover that it comes with a diamond tipped Sterling Silver scribe. And the instructions that accompany it do not say: "don't touch" or "hands off." On the contrary, purchasers are encouraged to do exactly the opposite.

The creators of this beautiful work of art suggest:

> For memories that never fade, invite your guests to record their presence at an important gathering by signing their names on the voluminous Grand Signature Bowl with its accompanying Sterling Silver Scribe. The scribe has a special diamond tip that writes on glass, and comes with a card demonstrating how to hold the pen.

Rather than signing a standard guestbook on the way out the door, the joint creators of the bowl ask you to have your dinner guests pick up the scribe and etch their names—make their unique mark—on their beautiful crystal bowl. Michele Oka Doner and the Steuben Glass Company know that the only way

---

[3] See http://steuben.com/acb/article.cfm?section=9&subsection=62&subsubsection=70&aid=328.

you can make their beautiful bowl even better is by allowing others to place their unique and indelible mark on it.

God says the same thing with His masterpiece creation. Like Michele Oka Doner did with her crystal bowl, God the Father designed His people perfectly. In Genesis 1 and 2 we learn how God not only made a beautiful universe but also stooped down and got His hands dirty when making the crown jewel of His creation: humanity. We were formed by the fingers of God into the image of God. And when God the Father saw what He had made, He declared us good. God doesn't make junk!

As Christians, however, we benefit from the hands of a second master designer: the Holy Spirit. We were not only born, we were also born again. "Whatever is born of the flesh is flesh, and whatever is born of the Spirit is spirit" (John 3:6). And, like the Steuben Glass Company, the Holy Spirit does not do shabby work! The fruit of the Spirit is love, joy, peace, patience, kindness, goodness, faithfulness, gentleness, and self-control. The Holy Spirit makes truly beautiful people! How could we ever improve on such exquisite handiwork?

Surely God will provide us, His doubly-designed creations, with little instruction cards that read: "Don't touch. Hands off. Leave alone." Who would dare to dabble with what God, the ultimate designer, has created? It seems inappropriate to meddle with the work of His hands. It feels sacrilegious. But it's not.

In the same way that Michele Oka Doner and the Steuben Glass Company place a sterling silver scribe in the hands of ordinary dinner guests and invite those guests to etch into their beautiful bowl, so God places a spiritual scribe in our hands and invites us to etch into the lives of fellow Christians who are God's precious and beautiful creation. When God gave us our spiritual gift He handed us a supernatural ability, a diamond tipped tool capable of etching into the lives of others.

Our gifts are not all the same. "Now there are different gifts,"[4] but God intends every gift to be used for the same purpose: for the spiritual benefit of others. "A manifestation of the Spirit is given to each person," Paul says, "to produce what is beneficial."[5] God's gifts are for the common good—the good of others—not just for our own enjoyment.

Like Doner and the Steuben Glass Company, the Father and Spirit have made each of us beautifully. We are spiritually flawless. But God also distributed spiritual gifts—spiritual scribes—that He wants us to use to etch into the lives of others. We are to do more than admire God's handiwork in the people around us. God wants us to place our spiritual signature on His precious—and beautiful—creations. To improve upon His perfection.

Pick up your scribe. Start making your mark.

---

[4] 1 Cor 12:4a.
[5] 1 Cor 12:7.

Frozen Solid
(Extended Metaphor)

Five hundred years ago a beautiful 15-year-old Incan girl got dressed in her finest clothes and went on a hike up snowcapped Mount Llullaillaco in Argentina.[1] She made it to the 22,000-foot summit. And never came back.

She was one of hundreds of Incan children who were sacrificed as part of a religious ritual, known as *capacocha*. Only beautiful, healthy, physically perfect children were selected for this ritual, and it was an honor to be chosen. The chosen ones were taken to the mountain summit, given *chichi* (maize beer) and, when they fell asleep, left to freeze to death. The cold and the dry thin mountain air did the rest.

In 1999, the frozen body of this young woman, dubbed *La Doncella*, was discovered on top of this bleak and frigid mountain incredibly well preserved. Her clothes look brand new. Her internal organs are intact. There is still blood in her heart and lungs. Her hair is still combed. Even her skin looks good. Five hundred years after her hike, and she looks like a sleeping child, not a mummy. The cold, thin, high-altitude mountain air helped her look as if alive.

La Doncella was relocated to a new home within Argentina's Museum of High Altitude Archaeology. Here, within a triple-paned glass box that is ensconced within an acrylic cylinder, a computerized climate control system ensures that the oxygen levels, humidity, and temperature are identical to what she has experienced for the past five centuries.

---

[1] This article first appeared in *The Voice* (Winter 2007), a publication of Woodland Hills Church, Woodland Hills, California. J. Kent Edwards is the pastor.

Visitors to the museum display enter a room that has been darkened out of respect. With the push of a button, however, lights begin to glow, and La Doncella emerges out of the darkness.

Sitting cross-legged in her brown dress and striped sandals, bits of coca leaf still clinging to her upper lip, her long hair woven into many fine braids, a crease in one cheek where it leaned against her shawl as she slept. The sight is eerie and unnerving. The museum's director, Gabriel E. Miremont, said that she looked so much like a sleeping child that it felt "almost more like a kidnapping than archaeological work."

La Doncella looks perfect. She looks like she is alive. As if she could wake up at any moment. I can assure you, however, that this young woman is quite dead. And has been for 500 years. Appearances can be deceiving.

This poor girl reminds me of a number of Christians I have met. On the outside they seem to be the picture of spiritual health. They have every appearance of life. Under the right light you could easily make the mistake of thinking that they are still warm and breathing. But the awful reality is that they have been spiritually dead for years.

They are frozen solid.

Frozen Christians do not nourish themselves on the Scriptures. They don't walk with the Spirit. They do not talk to their heavenly Father in prayer. They don't embrace holiness. Their hearts don't beat with excitement during worship. They have no passion for their God. And it gets worse.

The atmosphere that surrounds frozen Christians is toxic. If you get too close to frozen people, and begin to breathe their attitudes and values, you will be lulled into spiritual sleep. Their attitude will kill you. Just like it killed them.

You can freeze to death spiritually as well as physically. In Revelation 2, the apostle John gives a stinging rebuke to the Ephesian church because, in spite of their great external appearance, they had lost their first love for God. The ardor had cooled.

Their relationship with God had become rational and disciplined instead of hot and steamy. Their hearts had iced over. Don't let this happen to you.

The God of the universe loves you. His love for you is unreasonable and unfathomable. It is passionate and hot. He has chosen you to be His bride, not His employee. He wants to be the lover of your soul, not just a friendly neighbor to whom you wave as you drive by. He wants to elope with you.

At Woodland Hills Church we want to help you catch fire. To fan your faith until it explodes like a wildfire in the high desert. Our purpose is to introduce people into a passionate relationship with Jesus Christ. That is why we have the worship services we do. And the small groups. Passion for God is the driving force behind all that we do.

Join us in our passionate pursuit of the Son. Together, let's fall desperately in love with the lover of our souls.

Name Index

Subject Index

Scripture Index